Aspects and Issues
in the History of
Children's Literature

Recent Titles in
Contributions to the Study of World Literature

Aspects and Issues in the History of Children's Literature

Edited by *Maria Nikolajeva*

Published under the auspices of
the International Research Society for
Children's Literature

Contributions to the Study of World Literature,
Number 60

GREENWOOD PRESS
Westport, Connecticut • London

Library of Congress Cataloging-in-Publication Data

Aspects and issues in the history of children's literature / edited by
    Maria Nikolajeva ; published under the auspices of the International
    Research Society for Children's Literature.
        p. cm.— (Contributions to the study of world literature,
    ISSN 0738-9345 ; no. 60)
    Selection of papers originally presented at the 9th Congress of
    the International Research Society for Children's Literature which
    was held in Salamanca, Spain in 1989.
        Includes bibliographical references and index.
        ISBN 0-313-29614-6
        1. Children's literature—History and criticism—Congresses.
    I. Nikolajeva, Maria.   II. International Research Society for
    Children's Literature.   III. International Research Society for
    Children's Literature.   Congress (9th : 1989 : Salamanca, Spain).
    IV. Series.
    PN1009.A1A77   1995
    809'.89282—dc20   94-43041

British Library Cataloguing in Publication Data is available.

Copyright © 1995 by the International Research Society for Children's Literature

Library of Congress Catalog Card Number: 94-43041
ISBN: 0-313-29614-6
ISSN: 0738-9345

First published in 1995

Greenwood Press, 88 Post Road West, Westport, CT 06881
An imprint of Greenwood Publishing Group, Inc.

Printed in the United States of America

(∞)™

The paper used in this book complies with the
Permanent Paper Standard issued by the National
Information Standards Organization (Z39.48–1984).

10 9 8 7 6 5 4 3 2

Copyright Acknowledgments

The editor and publisher gratefully acknowledge permission for use of the following material:

Figures reprinted from O'Sullivan, Emer, *Friend and Foe: The Image of Germany and the Germans in British Children's Fiction from 1870 to the Present*. Tubingen: Narr (Studies in English and Comparative Literature, Vol. 6), 1990. Reprinted with permission.

Essay by Karen Nelson Hoyle, "Three Scandinavian Contributions to American Children's Literature" in *Journal of Youth Services in Libraries*, vol. 3 (Spring 1990), pp. 219–225. Reprinted with permission of the American Library Association, from *Journal of Youth Services in Libraries*, Spring 1990. Copyright © 1990.

Contents

Part III. Aspects of National Histories

Part IV. Genres, Modes, Styles

Introduction: Approaches to the History of Children's Literature

This volume comprises a selection of papers from the Ninth Congress of the International Research Society for Children's Literature (IRSCL), held in Salamanca in 1989, and not surprisingly, a variety of approaches to the history of children's literature are represented. Rather than polemicizing with each other, they complement each other, even though these scholars of children's literature come from different traditions and probably have different objectives when they address historical issues. One of the keynote speakers of the Congress, Professor Hans-Heino Ewers from Germany, outlined three principal approaches to the history of children's literature, two of which are radically different from general literary history.

Children's literature, Ewers argued, was from the very beginning related to pedagogics. Children's literature emerged on a larger scale because at some time in the seventeenth century society began to recognize that childhood was a special period in people's lives and that children had their own special needs. Many of the essays in the present volume also make this point. The view of childhood and the educational aspects of reading have been crucial for the evolution of children's literature. It has gone hand in hand with pedagogical views; literature was a means, and a very powerful one, for educating children. Therefore, children's literature has also been studied with this view in mind -- that is, the suitability of books for children's reading.

This pedagogical view has led to a certain bias in the general histories of children's literature. Only books that were considered "suitable" for children have been included in reference sources, according to country, epoch, and the dominating view on childhood. Others have been simply ignored.

As Ewers stated rather provocatively, histories of children's litertature written in this tradition were nothing more than highly manipulated recommendation lists for adults who are to serve as mediators for children. The selection in these publications is always subjective and depends on the editor's pedagogical preferences.

Another type of history of children's literature that Ewers singled out and is quite similar to the first is children's literature in relation to society. The study object of this approach is the triangle Child--Family--School. In this model, works of literature have only a functional, or pragmatic, role in their relation to reality.

Ewers encouraged scholars of children's literature to contemplate yet another viewpoint that children's literature research has quite ignored, that is, children's literature as literature. He stated that this approach had not yet achieved any tangible results. Moreover, in some countries the scholars did not seem to be aware of its existence or necessity.

Although I totally agree with Ewers on the desirability of this innovative look at the history of children's literature, I cannot at the same time deny either the purposes of the first two or the impossibility of a more general look before we have gone through the initial stages. We can never ignore the simple fact that most books for children were in fact produced solely for educational purposes. The present volume presents some radically new models for examining literary history, while it also demonstrates the value and indispensability of more traditional ones.

As I see it, the history of children's literature involves two principal issues. First, is there any difference between children's literature and the general literary history--except for the way of treating it, as Ewers points out? Does the history of children's literature have its own Ancient Age, Middle Ages, Renaissance, Enlightenment, and Modernism? Second, is the history of children's literature national or international? Does it follow the same pattern in different countries, or do national conditions influence the emergence and dominance of themes, genres, and attitudes? I think the present volume gives us at least some answers to these global questions.

When the first books overtly written and published for children appeared, adult literature had already existed as an established literary system for many centuries. Whereas mainstream literature had evolved over several millennia, children's literature developed over only three to four hundred years, and in some countries over a considerably shorter time. The traditional division of literature into epic, lyric, and drama, a tradition dating back to antiquity, was from the beginning irrelevant to children's literature. Even today, poetry and drama for children are, with rare exceptions, marginal phenomena within the system of children's literature. When we speak about children's literature, we most often mean prose stories, that is, the epic form. Thus, the history of children's literature presents mainly the evolution of epic structures.

Children's literature has more or less gone through similar stages in all countries and language areas. First, existing adult literature, as well as folklore (folktales, myths, fables), adapted to what is believed to be the needs and interests of children, according to accepted and dominating views on child upbringing. Next, didactic, educational stories written directly for children appeared. Most often these two periods overlap. Children's literature system began to detach itself from the adult system,sometimes even isolating itself in a kind of ghetto. Usually, books from this period are mentioned only briefly in histories of children's literature. Therefore, I find it satisfying to be able to include some reevaluations of writers from this period in the volume.

Children's literature became established as a literary system with its different genres and modes, and its *canon* came into being. There were clear divisions between books for boys and books for girls, as well as between different genres. The rigid system allowed no deviations, no innovations, or the like. The norms of allowed themes, narrative structures (for instance, "happy ending"), and values were proclaimed.

It is against this established system that contemporary writers for children are revolting, introducing new, daring themes and new narrative devices, bringing children's literature closer to the modern, or if one so wishes, the postmodern novel.

It is illuminating to see the similarities and recurrent phenomena associated with establishing children's literature as a literary system in many different countries. However, before we can come to conclusions, I would like to have examples from countries other than Western Europe and North America. Do the emergence and development of children's literature always and necessarily follow the same pattern? Are we not being ethnocentric in believing that the lines of evolution are predetermined for children's literature and that all deviations are to be perceived as "wrong"? Is there such a thing as national children's literature that reflects national mentality, specific social history, views on education, and so on? Are folktales *always* an indispensable base for children's literature in every country? Are chapbooks an unavoidable companion to the early stages of children's literature? Is humor a universal category?

One impression that we inevitably get from the essays is that in the Western world we indeed share many of the important texts in the history of our literatures for young people. It may be instructive to see in Kari Skjønsberg's essay a reference to the Italian book discussed in detail by Mariella Colin: it seems to have played an important role in Norwegian patriotic education. Children's books in the nineteenth century were much more international than they are today.

While each essay in this volume has a value of its own, together they comprise an interesting unity. Not only do they show the scope of theoretical, methodical, and practical issues, but also they bring us closer to what I personally see as one of the greatest challenges in our scholarship: a comprehensive, universal, and nonbiased History of World Children's Literature.

Aspects and Issues
in the History of
Children's Literature

Literary Ways of Killing a Child: The 19th Century Practice

Judith Plotz

A Trip to Madame Tussaud's

Let me invoke a scene. We are in the dark. The fair-haired boys we contemplate are in the dark too and oppressively close to us, almost touching. They obtrude upon us, invading our safe observer's distance. The space we share is small, crowded, airless; there is barely enough room for the heavy bedstead--carved dark wood, coffin-shaped and shrouded in heavy dark-velvet hangings--where the two black-garbed children huddle together, the 9 year old reading, the 12 year old lost in reverie. The shadows from a chink of light under the heavy closed door fall more darkly in the obscurity of the stuffy bedroom. There is just enough light to make out the English toy spaniel, a fit pet for the delicate children, turning apprehensively, ears cocked, toward the sudden light and the sudden sound. Someone is coming. Something is about to happen.

That's about enough. Let's get out of here. Even describing it makes me uncomfortable, makes me gasp for air. Where are we? Although this may feel like a private nightmare, we are in fact visiting in spirit a place thousands have actually visited before us--and are visiting at this very moment. We are in the heart of London in Madame Tussaud's Wax Museum and we are contemplating two waxwork representations of the doomed princes in the Tower as depicted in Delaroche's famous 1831 painting. The boys are Edward V, boy-king of England, and his younger brother Richard, both murdered--suffocated it is said--sometime during the summer of 1483. First installed in Madame Tussaud's Baker Street premises in 1865, this waxwork effigy of doomed children has been an object of pilgrimage until this very day.

This particular nineteenth-century representation of children on the brink of death is no mere isolated Baker Street irregularity. On the contrary, this particular four hundred-year old child-murder was of general appeal for nineteenth-century artists; art historian Roy Strong lists seventeen different treatments. As Strong remarks, the destruction of innocence, especially innocence personified by a child, was a veritable Victorian "theme and obsession" (199-227). Even the most cursory reader of nineteenth-century European literature can easily compile a long list of childhood deaths in canonical texts--Dickens's Nell and Jo and Paul Dombey, Dostoyevsky's Ilya, Hugo's Gavroche, and Ibsen's Hedvig and Eyolf, to name only the most obvious. Indeed, two of the greatest novelists of the nineteenth century, Dickens and Dostoyevsky, in some sense never really wrote about anything other than insulted and injured children. Such childhood deaths in major texts are not simply poignant but *important*--important in part because they are *obtruded* onto the consciousness and conscience of the reader much as the Tussaud-Delaroche waxworks impinge on the viewer's space and in part because they are central to the major themes in the works.

In his excellent and indispensable *Death, Heaven, and the Victorians*, John Morley reproduces an illustration showing a plaster-of-paris sleeping baby, disturbingly naturalistic, though ghastly white. His caption reads: "Figures of this kind, kept under a glass dome, were used in order to head off tactless questions about the disappearance of a child. 'There's your little brother dear. He's resting'". This is a grotesque instance, but characteristic of an obsessive nineteenth-century drive to contemplate images of a child stilled, "as if embalmed/By nature" (these are Wordsworth's words):

> - through some special privilege
> Stopped at the growth he had--destined to live,
> To be, to have been, come, and go, a child
> And nothing more.
>
> (*The Prelude* 1805, 7:400-404)

Throughout the children's literature as well as the adult literature of the later nineteenth century (1840-1910), we find just such images of "embalmed children," stunning images of children who, like the princes, are arrested. They, too, are dead or doomed and boxed in, contained, fixed, preserved, stilled, revered, and revisited. Thus, in "One Who Lived Long, Long Ago," Frances Hodgson Burnett meditates on "a poor little gray image in a glass case" (*Children*, 86), all that remains of a lively little girl of Pompei. A similar sense of enclosure in equivocal sanctuary is implicit in the titles of such late nineteenth-century works on death as J. Hendrickson M'Carthy's *Inside the Gates*, Burnett's *In the Closed Room*, George MacDonald's *The Golden Key*, and Nehemiah Adams's curious *Agnes and the Little Key* (the last-named work was an American bestseller of the 1860s about a father who carries around with him the key to his dead daughter's coffin). In the same vein, William Canton's *In Memory of W.V.* closes with an evocation of a Danish legend of containment:

[...] when the walls of Copenhagen, as the legend tells, crumbled and fell as fast as they were built, an innocent little girl was set in her chair beside a table, where she played with her toys and ate the rosy apples they gave her while twelve master-masons closed a vault over her; and then the walls were raised, and stood firm for ever after. (225)

As these examples suggest, death in nineteenth-century literature is less a destroyer than a strange preserver. When children die in literature, they are assimilated to fixity, usually perishing in ways that make them clean, quiet, immobile, and permanent. The endless cold bath of Charles Kingsley's *Water Babies* washes little Tom almost as clean as MacDonald's well-bathed Mossy and Tangle or his wind-bleached Diamond who ends up "as white and almost as clear as alabaster" (288). Juliana Horatia Ewing's *The Story of a Short Life* and Florence Montgomery's *Misunderstood* fix boys of quicksilver liveliness into partial paralysis, while *Agnes and the Little Key* explicitly locks a child into security. The troubled lives of Ouida's Nello and Patrasche in *A Dog of Flanders* end in a wintry cathedral among other marmoreal memorial fixities: "They were both dead; the cold of the night had frozen into stillness alike the young life and the old" (55).

What are we to make of all this freezing, bleaching, washing, locking into fixity? Why such insistence on fixing for contemplation the deaths of children? What bearing does it have on the study of children's literature and the literature of childhood? One response, perhaps a human one, is implicit in Oscar Wilde's comment on the protracted death of Little Nell: "Ah Nell! what man of feeling can think of her death without laughing!" Wilde's subtext, as I read it, is that there's altogether too much pleasure, too much gusto in Dickens' depiction of Nell's death. To dwell fixedly on childhood death is a cruelly pornographic delighting in pain and should be avoided. The only humane response is either to laugh with a cheerful bloodymindedness (as Harry Graham so successfully did in his *Ruthless Rhymes for Heartless Homes*, 1899) or to drop (at least to bracket) the subject altogether. Juliet Dusinberre, in fact, has recently argued in her *Alice to the Lighthouse* that the Victorian obsession with death was an obstacle to imaginative creativity that Virginia Woolf and other modernists had to overcome in order to free their art. The death theme, she suggests, inhibited the creative life-enhancing playfulness necessary for the production of major literature. Lewis Carroll, however, taught children's writers (*and* the great modernists) how to bracket death, thus making possible a surge of creativity in children's and adult literature alike. In a word, both Wilde and Dusinberre imply that the privileging of death in the nineteenth century is a morally and aesthetically negative force, one that inhibited imaginative play and does not reward investigation. Futhermore, Dusinberre suggests that the privileging of death is *antithetical* to significant children's literature.

I wish to put a different case. Far from being antithetical to the emergence of children's literature, the death theme seems to be crucial. Not only is the theme pervasive in some of the most important works of the first golden age of children's literature, but also the high tide of cultural concern with death is contemporary with the emergence of children's literature as a recognized genre. Literary representations of childhood death are part of the enabling conditions for creating and recognizing children's literature.

The Superfluous Child and the Essential Child

In nothing more than its preoccupation with childhood death does the nineteenth century seem alien. And so it should. In important ways, especially in some ways germane to our concerns as students of children's literature, the nineteenth century is at once rich and strange and anomalous. In the era roughly between 1800 and 1950, peaking between 1840 and 1910, children achieved a cultural status very different from what it was before and since (a high cultural status does not, of course, guarantee good treatment). It is a matter of the difference between the Superfluous Child and the Essential Child. The child of the early modern period *and* of the late twentieth century (at least of twentieth-century America) is a creature of the cultural margins of society, while the nineteenth-century child was--in a biblical phrase endlessly quoted between 1850 and 1910--"set in the midst," a being of the center.

In speaking of early modern children as "superfluous," I am drawing on John Boswell's new revisionist history of childhood, *The Kindness of Strangers: The Abandonment of Children in Western Europe from Late Antiquity to the Renaissance* (1988). Boswell insists that child abandonment, hitherto regarded as a minor, statistically negligible practice was a powerful social institution in Europe until the late eighteenth century. Rousseau's notoriously cool account of child abandonment--"My third child therefore was taken to the Foundling Hospital like the others, and the next two were disposed of in the same way, for I had five at all" (333)--is not, Boswell argues, the anomalous malignity of philosophers, but just the last gasp of a long-standing pattern of socially sanctioned abandonment. Boswell attempts to substantiate four principal theses. He argues first that abandonment of unwanted infants was a mass phenomenon throughout Europe from late antiquity until the age of asylums, with "from 10 to 40 per cent of urban children [...] abandoned" (48) during the eighteenth century. Second, he holds that abandonment was a nonmurderous, though often inadvertently lethal, institution designed to redistribute redundant children. Third, he holds that abandoned children were quite often successfully fostered as slaves, as apprentices, as prostitutes, as oblates, or even as heirs to the childless. Finally, he insists that no guilt attached to those who abandoned a child, evidence that child abandonment was culturally sanctioned. A reading of Boswell on medieval and early modern Europe suggests that it was once culturally *normal* to regard a large portion of a society's children as superfluous, as unnecessary--indeed as potentially damaging--to its continued well-being.

A reading of the cultural signs in late twentieth-century America suggests that postmodern children are once again being deemed superfluous. Because I come from a city in which the *primary* cause of childhood mortality is *homicide* and where the infant mortality rate is the worst in the industrialized world, I am inclined to concur with the cultural historians who had labeled this the era of "The Disappearance of Childhood" (Postman), and of "Children Without Childhood" (Winn). What can at best be regarded as simple indifference to children's welfare or at worse as sustained hostility emerges in all kinds of postmodern practices. There is the obvious epidemic of child abuse fueled by drug addiction. There is the invasion of psychologically protective domestic space by television. There is the coopting of childhood privilege by therapeutically minded adults so desperate to nurture their own "inner children" (themselves) that they have no time for external actual children. There is even the increasing condemnation of childhood privilege as "politically incorrect."[1] There is also the widespread image in popular culture of the child as a monster eager to destroy Its parents and anything else It touches (you may recall the Child as Lucifer in *Rosemary's Baby,* the Child as Anti-Christ in *The Omen* and *The Exorcist* and the Child as Zombie or perhaps Ghoul in *Pet Cemetary*).[2] Children themselves are increasingly drawn to works that allow them to identify with Aliens and high-tech Super Friends; far better to be E. T. the Alien or a Bionic Being than a poor unaccommodated human child. Both our own condition and Boswell's study of early modern history suggest that it may be normal to regard the mass of children as superfluous, as impediments to social harmony. If we recoil from such a notion,it may be that we are still living off our Romantic legacy, a frequent source of support for specialists in children's literature.

It is clear that the nineteenth-century cultural ideals were different, for nineteenth-century cultural ideals put children smack "in the midst" of the world. In nineteenth-century writing, children are inevitably *centered,* figured in the coming "century of the child" (to cite the title of a book by Ellen Key) as the "one divine majority" (Canton, *A Lost Epic,* 164). The demographic fact that in Britain the number of children had been increasing decade by decade from 1750 is not irrelevant. One demographer has argued that a "flood of children" in the mid-nineteenth century caused a shift "in the social mentality of the decades after 1850" (Hair, 35-37). This shift is implicit in such a work as Wilifred Meynell's anthology *The Child Set in the Midst by Modern Poets* (1892): "Him the Modern Poets have set in the Midst of us even as He was set in the Midst of Men by the Lord of Poets" (ii).

Literal centering is evident in such nineteenth-century paintings as Runge's remarkable "Morning," Orchardson's worshipful "Master Baby," and Drummond's "His Majesty the Baby." In Runge's painting, all nature, especially the sunlight, is worshipfully focused on the sublime golden figure of an infant; in Orchardson's, a Victorian madonna worships her vastly beautiful, delightedly energetic huge infant; in Drummond's painting the traffic on a busy nineteenth-century street grinds to a halt before the progress of "His Majesty the Baby."

One striking manifestation of such centering is idolatry. The admission of idolatry is widespread and largely unapologetic. Even in the explicitly *religious* comfort books intended for those bereaved of children (a genre that flourished vastly between 1840 and 1910), I found regular reference to the tendency "of this era" of "substituting the dead child for God" (Logan, 39). Again and again, writers identify a child as "the *idol* of my heart" (Prime, *Smitten Household*, 1); "She was my *idol*" (Anon., "The Lost Darling," in Smyth); or "I [...] hungered for *my idol's* kiss/Before she went to bed" (Stoddard, "A Household Dirge," in Foxcroft, 29). Meynell's injunction "that the worship of the Child should be fostered" (xxii) (despite the upper case c, he means not Christ but Everychild) emerges from the same literary culture that features Dinah Mulock's adulatory address to a baby, "Philip, My King" (Brownell, 202-205) and Canton's rapturous chant: "Take the idol to her shrine; In her cradle lay her!/Worship her--she is divine;/Offer up your prayer!" (*Invisible Playmate*, 23). Such idolatory derives from the high Wordsworthian tradition manifested in such Romantic tributes to the child as "mighty Prophet! Seer blest!" (Wordsworth), "the perpetual Messiah" (Emerson), "Type of the Divinity" (Alcott), "the world's deliverer" (Chapman, 27), and "His [God's] small interpreter" (Whittier in Meynell, ii); as "director of the parent's education" (Froebel in Dusinberre, 15); as "A lively representation to us of the ideal" (Schiller, 87), a "latter revelation" (A. Snith in Russell, 77); and as "a veritable prophet of silence" (Dubois, 99).

This idolatry is, I believe, the consequence of the Romantic trans-valuation of childhood which imputed to (and newly perceived in) children a set of qualities that designated the Child--the actual domestic home-grown child, the idol of an age from which a transcendent God was disappearing. These Romantically promulgated qualities, which promote childhood even as they demote adulthood, are related to two convictions: childhood is Nature-in-Man, and the child's is the most representative, most creatively unifying human mind.

Children were equated with "nature"--the dynamic, organic universe of both Romanticism and evolution--in three respects. First, if one conceives nature (as Schiller did, for example) as "the subsistence of things on their own, their existence in accordance with their own immutable laws" (84), then childhood is its human embodiment. Romantic writers regularly note the unself-consciousness, self-completeness, physical harmony, "the identity of body and mind" in children (Coleridge, "On Poesy of Art", in Perkins, 496). Second, in their obvious vitality and power of growth, children are indigenes of nature. Third, in the view of one group of American anthropologists, children are the very prophets of the evolutionary process, foreshadowing in their physiology the future of our changing, ever *immaturing* race whose destiny is to become ever more childlike:

The child, the infant in fact, alone possesses in their fulness distinctive characteristics of humanity. The highest human types, as represented in men of genius, present a striking approximation to the child-type. In man, from about the third year onward, further growth is to some extent growth in degeneration and senility. Hence the true tendency of the progressive evolution of the race is to become child-like [...] (Brinton, quoted in Chamberlain, 2)

As Nature's own creature--a being of growth and change in a universe of change, the child is the goal as well as the source of the adult.

The Romantic transvaluation also assigned to children a new set of unitary psychological and cognitive powers, making, in Bronson Alcott's words, "nothing [...] too metaphysical for the mind of a child" (Strickland, 40). The innate powers of childhood consciousness were deemed to be idealism, holism, animism, faith, and psychological self-sufficiency--all modes of putting the world and the self at one. "In the child's mind," Coleridge insisted, "there is nothing fragmentary" (*Coleridge on Logic Learning*, 127). In virtually every comparison, the unitary modes of childhood shame the analytic modes of adulthood as the idiot-questioner of "We Are Seven" is flummoxed by the "simple child."

By associating childhood with the forces, energies, growth, and development of nature, as well as with the mental and spiritual capacities to perceive the world as meaningfully unified, the Romantic transvaluers of childhood created the idolatry we have noted. The Romantic transvaluation made the child available as a powerful transhistorical symbol at a time one was needed. Both "the disappearance of God" (to use Hillis Miller's phrase) and the waning of historical utopianism opened a space for such a symbol, especially after 1848. To invest in the symbol of the Romantic Child--a living embodiment of the future, of Nature's abiding dynamism, and of a possible psychic harmony--was to be able to retain grounds for hope without being obliged to make a leap into transcendental faith or historical engagement. But to invest in the Romantic Child symbolically was to make exorbitant demands on the services of actual children; for Romantic children by definition were the creatures of nature, the creatures of the common day. When such a child died, a child so heavily associated with the indomitable life of nature and with the possibility of unifying faith, it was a terrible disaster that brought on a crisis.

"Traps for Childhood"

The death of so significantly freighted a being demands attention. Because the Romantic Child operates as a representation of the *adequacy of the immanent,* the adequacy of nature without revelation (and history without revolution), the only possible way to respond to a death is to *restore presence.* Only a restored presence can restore meaning. Thus death is characteristically represented in nineteenth-century literature as a presence, not an absence.

In Kipling's brilliant story "They," written after the death of his daughter, the narrator happens on a lovely countryhouse lonely in its woods in the Sussex countryside. Here from afar he catches sight of a number of children at play. Later, he meets the blind proprietress of the estate who is pleased with his love of children and invites him back: "Remember [...] if you are fond of them you will come again." A month later he returns, his car breaks down in the blind woman's woods, and he is half pleased with his mishap:

I made a mighty serious business of my repairs and a glittering shop of my repair kit, spanners, pump, and the like, which I spread out orderly upon a rug. It was a trap to catch all childhood, for on such a day, I argued, the children would not be far off. (*They*, 350)

"It was a trap to catch all childhood". Indeed, as the narrator discovers, the house, the wood, and the blind woman are all part of a loving "trap to catch all childhood." All the children in the woods are ghosts of dead children, drawn back to the skirts of life by the intensity of the blind woman's desire. Present only to those who wish desperately to see them, the ghostly "They"--lovely and playful and *almost there*--exemplify the nineteenth-century way of killing a child, or representing death as presence, or at least as an invocation of presence.

For the rest of this essay I wish to focus on the three modes of invoked presence which dominate nineteenth-century treatments of childhood death from about 1840 to 1910: the mode of transformation, the mode of intensification through pain, and the mode of intensification through vitality.

In the mode of transformation, which is often--though not always--a version of pastoral, a dead child is assimilated to some other being or state. The child may blend into nature as an object or a genius loci; she may go away to become a ghost, or she may merge into or become associated with a living alter ego; or she may survive in art. Wordsworth's "Lucy Gray" is a virtual summary of all the versions of transformation since Lucy, both living and dead, is a natural object: "the sweetest thing that ever grew/Beside a human door!" In addition, she makes a journey from which she never returns except as a spectre who is still seen from afar "to this day [...] Upon the lonesome wild." And finally, her "solitary song/That whistles in the wind" remains too -- both as the wind itself and as the text of "Lucy Gray; or Solitude". More frequently, however, the modes of transformation come singly.

Absorption into the landscape takes several forms. Most common is the pastoral equation of child with plant or flower, often with a flower that fades in one garden but blooms in another. Often the narrative will foreshadow a child's death with the plucking and fading of a bunch of flowers. In Mrs. Molesworth's *A Christmas Child* (1880), 3-year-old Ted brings his mother a bunch of flowers and leaves which she neglects to put in water. They wither. He is crushed, but she picks up the withered bouquet and promises: "I will *always* keep them" (13). After the boy dies at 12, it becomes clear that the long-preserved withered leaves are the very leaves on which the mother-narrator has inscribed this "sketch of boy life." More explicitly in Montgomery's *Misunderstood* (1869), the healthy Humphrey mistakenly uproots some immature corn. Later, his initial words of apology appear as a reprise appropriate to his death:

I will plant them in the sunny bit of our own garden where the soil is much better than here, and where they will grow much finer than if they had been left to ripen with the rest. Perhaps they will thank me someday for having pulled them out of the rough field and planted them in such a much more beautiful place. (257)

The same pattern, though sterner, is found in "Philip's Death; or, The Pains of Children," the finest story in Frederic Faber's disturbing children's comfort book, *Ethel's Book* (1858). Philip, whose worst fault is a penchant for snapping the heads off hyacinths, lies dying in great pain. His sister Edith becomes enraged at God for Philip's suffering: "Surely not everything which God does is right. He can be wrong as well as anybody else. I know he can do what he likes. But sometimes He seems to like very dreadful things [...] I think I am scandalized at God" (34, 36). Edith's indignation is eventually eased not by doctrinal insistence (though there's some of that), but by a series of pastoral visions culminating in Philip's transformation to a hyacinth on the lap of the Virgin: "It was a hyacinth, yet somehow she knew it was Philip, and Our Lord leaned over His Mother, and smelled at the sweetness of the hyacinth" (52). In Burnett's totally secular, totally pastoral "Little Betty's Kitten Tells Her Story" (1894), a kitten-narrator completely assimilates her child-mistress Betty with the natural world as a flower growing under a white rose tree. Betty has a "pink bud of a mouth," "pink soft cheeks," "large eyes, just like the velvet of a pansy-blossom," a "white muslin hat like a frilled daisy," and hair that moves in the breeze with "a vine's sway" (*Piccino*, 134). In death, Betty the flower, covered with roses, goes "where they are always roses" (142).

Sometimes children simply interassimilate with the landscape and become spirits of the place like the children of "They" and "The Comforters" of Dora Sigurson's poem: "The soft little hands of the rain stroked my pale cheek,/ The kind little feet of the rain ran by my side" (de la Mare, 420).

Death is sometimes seen as a withdrawal of the dying child into otherness. Sometimes the withdrawal is merely psychological as into the preternatural goodness of Stowe's Eva, the almost autistic impassivity of Macdonald's Diamond, and the preoccupation of Winifred in Faber's "The Weeping Angel." Such children seem alien in spirit in that they "seem to belong to God only. They die soon, and they like to die" (Faber, 145). The words are Faber's, but wherever there is such a "god's baby" (Stowe), there is such a description.

The most complex and fertile form of transformation is *doubling,* a linking of a dead and a living child which substantiates the identity of the lost child. The habitual pattern is that of a special relationship between two children or occasionally between a child and an adult (often the pattern is, in the words of the epigraph to Cuyler's *The Empty Crib*, that "The one shall be taken and the other left"). A relevant survivor stays behind either to live out or to testify to the possibilities of the other, or even to seek out the other (this is brilliantly the case in Jill Paton Walsh's *A Chance Child*). In Ewing's *Jackanapes*, the protagonist dies to save the life of his childhood friend who in turn becomes a surrogate son to Jackanapes's own surrogate mother. Burnett's Kiplingesque "The Captain's Youngest" depicts a deep friendship between an old soldier, Rabbett, and young Lionel who dies at 14 like a soldier. Echoing Kipling's Barrack-Room Ballad, "Follow Me 'Ome" ("There was no one like 'im, 'Orse or Foot,/Nor any o' the Guns I knew/ An' because it was so, why o' course 'e went 'n died,/Which is just what the best men do"), Rabbett eulogizes Lionel: "There never 'were another like him" (*Piccino,* 81), both by evoking the dream children Lionel would have fathered ("I've even seen little children like him and thought they would have been fond of me as he was", 117) and by elaborately documenting his own emptiness without the boy. Alcott's doubling of Beth and Jo illustrates this pattern, as does Stowe's linking in *Uncle Tom's Cabin* of the earthly advancement of Topsy to the heavenly legacy of Eva.

The most elaborate treatment of such surrogacy is Burnett's *Giovanni and the Other* which involves elaborate doubling and redoubling among four boys: two living, two dead; two present, two absent; two American, two Italian. Convalescing at San Remo from the death of one of her two sons, the American protagonist is touched by the singing of a peasant boy who reminds her of her surviving son back in America. As a gift to the dead Leo, as a way of feeling "that I am not letting him go" (164), the American woman resolves to help Giovanni, to do for Giovanni the good deeds Leo might have done for his friends had he lived (this is more or less what Frances Hodgson Burnett did herself after her son died). In Leo's memory, she pays for the musical education of the commonplace, though talented, Giovanni who thrives and becomes a celebrated singer. But Giovanni is not the only child who sings outside the hotel. There is "another," hiding in the darkness, a child with a cracked and ruined voice who is dying of tuberculosis: "[...] he was never more than a shadow. They always called him 'the Other' and they never saw him; but they spoke of him even more than they spoke of Giovanni whom they saw three times a week." Although "the Other" and Leo are hardly characters in the story, they are actually its heroes who outshine their survivors. "The Other" dies without meeting the protagonist, but she later learns that "the Other" had had an exquisite voice, far better than Giovanni's; that the Other had had a devoted mother, far more loving than the bovine Brigitta, Giovanni's mother; the Other was a boy of generous feelings and intellectual profundity, far nobler than the somewhat grasping, stupid, and philistine Giovanni. There is no doubt that the *living* surrogates are inferior to their dead doubles. Because the drive of the bereaved mother is to make her dead *"more real then anything else"* (163), the two absent dead boys are vividly foregrounded by their talents, by their devoted mothers, and by the inferiority of their living surrogates.

A different pattern of doubling involves an encounter between the living and the dead. William Canton's *The Invisible Playmate* is just such "a Story of the Unseen." A tale of two daughters, *The Invisible Playmate* briefly recalls the six-week life of the author's first daughter, a frail, pallid infant, "so white and frail and old-womanish, with her wasted arms [...] and her thin worn face fading, fading away" (7). He recalls the folly of being comforted for her death: "Job! The author of 'Job' knew more about astronomy than he knew about fatherhood" (95). Principally, however, he exuberantly describes the first three years of his second daughter's life, her stages as "the Heiress of the Ages," the "little quadruped," the "quadrumanous angel," the "bishop," the "animal most gracious and benignant," the "Immortal," the "benign anthropoid," "Pineforifera." She learns to talk and delights her father with her verbal inventiveness; she is courageous with animals, brave in the dark. She acquires an imaginary friend, "an invisible 'iccle gall' (little girl) whom she wheels about in her toy perambulator, puts carefully to bed, and generally makes much of. This is--'Yourn iccle baby, pappa old man!'" (15). She takes this invisible baby to bed withher, putting up her arms to receive the burden from her father: "I not let her fall, pappa."

The girl is taken ill, pines, and dies. Just before the wasted child dies, her father hears her whispering under her breath: "Pappa, I not let her fall." "Who dearie?" "Yourn iccle babbie, I gotten her in her." And her father lifts up the bedclothes:

Close beside her lay that other little one, with its white worn face and its poor arms crossed in that old-womanish fashion in front of her. Its large suffering eyes looked for a moment into mine, and then my head seemed filled with mist and my ears buzzed. I *saw that*. It was not hallucination. It was *there*. (17)

This seeing double means *presence on both sides*.

A similar preternatural doubling is evident in Burnett's revisionist Bluebeard-story. *In the Closed Room* (1904) brings together two little girls, rich Andrea and 7-year-old Judith, the sensitive, fey child of the slums. Judith's parents become summer caretakers of the Fifth Avenue mansion where Andrea has died--instantly, laughing, running to her mother with a flower. Free to go everywhere except into "the closed room" locked at the top of the house, Judith is drawn to the locked room. It opens to her faintest touch, and she enters to meet there and play with the dead Andrea. There at the dead girl's bidding, Judith restores Andrea's toys and furniture to their exact positions at the moment of her death. This scenic duplication (with Judith enacting Andrea's role) is Andrea's message to her mother: "I wanted her to know that I come here. I couldn't do it myself. You could do it for me" (109). The message gets through. Andrea's mother returns and interprets this message from her daughter with"A wild dawning bliss" (126), a "wild happiness" (129) at the recognition that "It is all as she left it [...] She has been here to show me it is not so far" (129). But this message is brought at the expense of the messenger; Judith, Andrea's surrogate, dies Andrea's death in the closed room. In the closed room, there has been a total reversal of life and death which has allowed the dead Andrea to bloom again at the expense of the all-too-willing Judith.

The third type of transformation is that of childhood death into art. In the mode of art, a lost being is retrievable as aesthetic artifact, as Wordsworth's lost Lucy Gray remains inscribed as text or interpretable as song in the wind. The most prominent work of this type is Browning's "The Pied Piper of Hamelin." If we read thematically, shutting our ears to its music, to its rhythms--if, in other words, we read *against* the piper's and the poet's art-- then "The Pied Piper" is a dark poem, a reworking as fantasy of Elizabeth Barrett Browning's jeremiad, "The Cry of the Children." Both poems are laments for the lost laboring children; both treat children sacrificed to the greed of the "Mayor and the Corporation," they are made into etiolated spectres who "cannot run or leap." In "The Pied Piper," the needs of the state lump them with vermin. In "The Cry of the Children," the laboring children are so hard-pressed that they wish for their own death:

> "It is good when it happens", say the children,
> "That we die before our time"
> Alas, Alas, the children! they are seeking
> Death in life as best to have!
> They are binding their hearts away from breaking,
> With a cerement from the grave.

In "The Pied Piper," the vagrant children actually achieve "death in life," becoming the Undead as they emerge in the last lines as vampires in Transylvania. Unlike "The Cry of the Children," however, "The Pied Piper" is overtly a "child's story" with transformations carried out in the mode of art. Just as the piper *seems* at first to resolve all problems of adult Hamelin through music, so the poem transforms its grim subject matter of child destruction into play--the play of meter, of assonance, of consonance, of sustained kinesthesia, of the play of art.

The modes of transformation--into nature, into a surrogate self, into art-- all soften and evade what the next mode, the most characteristic Victorian mode, tends to heighten. The mode of pain intensifies a sense of the child's presence by vividly recreating the pain of a child's death. In works of this kind the life of the child is made precious and actual through the evidence of pain--pain felt by the child, pain experienced by the attendant siblings and parents, pain shared by the reader. Although it is a mode that sometimes courts morbidity since the pleasure of making the lost child present comes at the price of recreating pain, it is principally an activist mode. Works in the mode of pain are sometimes pragmatic, exhorting purposive indignation from their readers. Even more often, they are empowering to the dying child, making his or her last days or hours periods of such intensely willed energy that the value of so brief a life cannot be doubted.

Pragmatic works in the mode of pain give elaborate attention to environment. In such works as Morrison's *A Child of the Jago* (1896), Hocking's *Her Benny* (1879), and "Brenda's" *Froggy's Little Brother* (1875), the great squalid slums of London and Liverpool are the principal characters. Environment is delineated before anything else in these works: Morrison sandwiches the text of his novel between a map of the "Old Jago" at the beginning (actually, the "Old Nichol" in Shoreditch in London's East End) and a "Glossary of Slang and Criminal Terms" at the end. Before little Dicky Perrot is even introduced, there is an elaborate account of the slum in which he lives, "the Jago, for one hundred years the blackest pit in London" and with its "close, mingled stink" (45). Similarly, Froggy and his family are set into Shoreditch squalor, while Benny and his sister Nelly are homeless matchsellers on the streets of Liverpool. Dickens's Jo, the crossing sweeper of *Bleak House,* is initially represented as a human maggot, part of the effluvium of "Tom-all-Alone's," one of "a crowd of foul existence, that crawls in and out of gaps in walls and boards, and coils itself to sleep, in maggot numbers, and comes and goes, fetching and carrying fever..." (167). Even Ouida's gentler *A Dog of Flanders* is only two parts costume drama to eight parts social novel, a child's version of *Main Street* in which a generous protagonist is broken by a mean-spirited provincial environment.

Because Nello, Jo, Benny's Nelly, Froggy's Benny, and Dicky Perrot are all so clearly delineated as the children of a specific dense world--a documented Antwerp or Liverpool or London--deaths don't just happen. They're not nobody's fault. They're everybody's fault, everybody who condones this environment. In a key episode of *Froggy's Little Brother*, the boys' father is lugging his livelihood, a Punch and Judy show, through the crowded city streets when he is knocked down, dragged, and smashed by a careless, drunken driver. This is a characteristically urban death in that it is the family-smashing, childhood-smashing, entirely avoidable result of human action. Such city deaths are often pressed obtrusively against the reader's conscience as in Dickens's confrontational and demanding account of Jo's last moments: "Dead, your Majesty. Dead, my lords and gentlemen, Dead, Right Reverends and Wrong Reverends of every order. Dead, men and women, born with Heavenly compassion in your hearts. And dying thus around us every day" (492).

Froggy's Little Brother also includes direct appeals to Her Majesty and to the child-readers of the book. Within the narrative, Froggy writes a vain letter of appeal directly to Queen Victoria: "Lady Queen--We are two little brothers what live in Shoreditch. We've got no money and no friends" (87). But Her Majesty's messengers do not come riding often, and so Benny dies. In the last lines of the work, the child-readers of the novel are also enjoined to send money to a specific children's charity (this high activist mode is the forerunner of the contemporary problem novel and television docudrama, which are contrived to energize either therapeutic or philanthropic interventions).

Less environmentally specific, less intrusive, but more individually activist are the deathbed poems and death-watch narratives. These forms are everywhere in nineteenth-century literature.[3] I've found hundreds of poems with titles like "The Mother and Her Dying Boy," "The Dying Child to its Mother," "The Dying Boy," "The Dying Infant," "The Dying Child," "The Sick Child's Dream," "I'm Going Away," "The Death of the First Born," "I'm Going Home," "Little Lucy," "Little Bessie," and "Little Johnny." Of these hundreds of poems documenting a vigil at a deathbed, only a few still have general currency--notably, Hood's "The Death Bed" ("We thought her dying when she slept/And sleeping when she died") and Elizabeth Barrett Browning's brilliant "Isobel's Child."

The pattern of the death-watch poems is always the same. The situation is simplified down to a dialogue for two voices--a mother's and a child's--in the dead of night over a narrow bed. In this nineteenth-century dialogue of Self and Soul, this "last battle," an inadequate adult is forced into a remission of her will by the initiative of the child.

In "Isobel's Child," for example, as Lady Isobel watches over her sick baby--"And more and more smiled Isobel/To see the baby sleep so well" (39)[4]--the pair is held isolated, rigid. Isobel is arrested in prayer: "So motionless she sate,/The babe asleep upon her knees,/You might have dreamed their souls had gone/Away to things inanimate" (40). The baby is similarly rigid: "Pale as baby carved in stone /Seen by glimpses of the moon/Up a dark cathedral aisle."Everything throws the solitary couple into relief: the night is dead still with "no wind--no rain--no thunder" save for the single hoot of an old "blind white owl." In this isolation, the dialogue of mother and child is cast as a contest of wills. Isobel exhorts first God for the child's recovery and then--as to an equal power--the baby himself. She holds out to the child a lifetime of play and prayer andlearning: "O baby mine, together,/We turn this hope of ours again." Rather than choosing life, however, the speechless infant preternaturally responds: "O mother, mother loose thy prayer! [...] It bindeth me, it holdeth me/With its most loving cruelty" (44). Like "Isobel's Child," virtually every other deathbed poem also depicts the child defying and resisting a parent's appeal:

> Cease here longer to detain me,
> Fondest mother...
>> ("The Dying Infant")

> Mother, I'm tired, and I would fain be sleeping
>> ("The Dying Child")

> My mother, my mother, O let me depart!
> Your tears and your pleadings are swords to my heart
>> ("The Mother and Her Dying Boy")

> Weep not dear mother, oh! leave off thy wailing
>> ("The Dying Child to its Mother")

As such resistance suggests, the deathbed dialogue may be seen as an enactment in miniature of the fullness of life. Just as Coleridge proclaimed the significance of the life of his son Berkeley, dead in his first year ("My Baby has not lived in vain [...] this life has been to him what it is to all of us, education and development," *Coleridge Letters,* no. 274), so "Isobel's Child" and other deathbed poems recapitulate the process of growing up, the process by which a parent learns to remit her will (on her child's behalf) and a child learns to exercise his own. The fact that in these texts the parents are invariably female (and thus typed for self-abnegation) and the children invariably male (and destined for self-assertion) makes the pattern pronounced.

Death-watch narratives such as Mrs. Ewing's *The Story of a Short Life* and Dinah Mulock's *The Little Lame Prince* are extended versions of the deathbed poem. They involve elaborate treatments of the pattern of simplification, adult witness, and childhood-willed initiative. In each of these works, a potentially active being undergoes a forced constraint--of illness, of lameness, of imprisonment--but through intensity of will substituted for extension of power, he turns these restrictions into an education of how to live. Ewing's Leonard makes an indelible life through translation of his short life into the lasting patterns of art and history: he writes and illustrates the "Book of Poor Things," and he identifies himself historically both with the ancestral past (represented by his "uncle Rupert," the Cavalier boy-soldier) and with the continuing national future (embodied in his cousin's regiment). Mulock's Prince Dolor, faced with similar constraints, constructs a similarly simplified life of vision and supervision.

Works in the mode of pain stress the reality and the use of a truncated life. But works in the mode of vitality stress the joy. The mode of vitality intensifies a child's existence by investing the tiniest remembered details of a child's life with such vitality as to make the child come alive, at least momentarily. Instances and particulars are charged with meaning. This mode courts sentimentality because it depends on disproportion, using small details to exact great effects.

This mode presents a child who is at once vital and static; at once full of the moment and out of time. The vitalistic mode privileges life over death, pleasure over pain, literal concrete particularity over symbolic representation. It centers on the depictions of energies and activities and makes death seem impossible. "I cannot make him dead," begins John Pierpont's often-anthologized poem of perpetual presence ("A Parent's Grief"); "Ye are of the living, not the dead," wrote Mary Howitt to the child who seemed "A privileged being, chartered from decay" ("The Lost One," in Smyth, 232); "I cannot feel that she is dead" is Angier's refrain ("Lines on the Death of an Only Daughter," in Smyth, 248-249) and Hedderwith's: "I never thought of him and death, so far apart they seemed" ("Home Trial").

Embodiments of vitality, the characteristic heroes and heroines in this mode are hellions and busy bees. From his first steps into the duckpond in pursuit of the gosling, Ewing's Jackanapes (the nickname indicates his mischievousness) is perpetually in motion running races and charging up and down on his gypsy pony. Even wilder are Kipling's Jakin and Lew, "the most finished little fiends that ever banged drum of tottled fife in the Band of a Brittish Regiment" ("The Drums of the Fore and Aft," 480). The ill-fated hero of *Misunderstood* is similarly an embodiment of energy:

He thought of the boy's restless activity, his joy in motion and exercise. From dawn to sunset, never still, never weary of rushing about in the open air. There had always been with him a sort of lavish enjoyment of existence for its own sake, as if there were happiness in the mere sense of *being* and *moving.*(227)

Molesworth's Ted, the "Christmas Child," is also noteworthy for his ceaseless busyness--always building treehouses, furnishing a home museum, cataloguing his collection.

Typically, such children are stationed in a setting that heightens their .tality either by contrast or association. The motif of the child in the graveyard appears in a series of works deriving from Wordsworth's "We Are Seven"--Trench's "A Walk in the Churchyard," Aird's "Song of the

Churchyard Children," Dickens's *Old Curiosity Shop* with its graveyard frolics, and Molesworth's cheery account in *Jackanapes* of Tony "lying on a tombstone" sick as a dog from a forbidden cigar. Thus, too, W. V. in the churchyard: "Oh, see, here's a funeral! Which is the bride?" More often a child is placed in a context of natural growth and exuberance. Thus, apple blossoms rain down on laughing Agnes (*Agnes and the Little Key*, 20), and the "Christmas Child" goes charging about his garden lugging huge stones hither and thither.

Sometimes readers are presented with a memoir joined to the literary remains of a dead child. The works of "Pet Marjorie" Fleming (dead at 8), of Thomas Malkin (dead at 6), of Winifred Vida (W. V.) Canton (dead at 10) are all offered in testimony to the lively inventiveness of the children. Both in the truncation of the works--all very much works in progress--and in the idiosyncratic playfulness, these collections create a sense of presence. Marjorie Fleming plays forever in her elegy for the three turkeys consumed at dinner. Of their bereaved mother, she wrote: "But she was more than usual calm,/She did not give a single dam" (Brown, 102). And Tom Malkin, literary prodigy though he was, seems 5 forever in his father's anecdote of the kindly flattery. When that amiable reader suggested that Tom's first poem sounded a little bit like Milton's *Paradise Lost,* the boy was outraged: "His countenance suddenly flashed fire, and heexclaimed with more than ordinary vehemence, 'No! not at all! No such thing! I never set my eyes upon the book!'" (Malkin, 289). And never would.

The vitality of children depicted in this mode is usually an arrested, fixed vitality. An intense attention to small ordinary details of a child's life becomes a mode of preserving that child. According to George MacDonald, intensity of scrutiny is redemptive here and hereafter, for heaven is *nothing but* recapitulation of the intensely seen and loved: "we shall be able to recall anything in nature or in art, we have ever seen with an intensity proportioned to the degree of regard and attention we have given it when it was present to us" (Mifflin, 116). What Canton calls "the beaten way of nature" (60) is therefore good enough for joy, provided that the ordinary has been seen with extraordinary attention.

Because intense particularity is all important, the insistence on concreteness is everywhere. The child-narrator of "Good-Night Winny" hates the pious comforts offered by her relatives for the death of her big sister: "They could not tell me the only things I cared to hear about Winny, what she was doing, what lessons she would have, if she would always wear white frocks [...]" (*Stories*, 352). Thus, this literature is full of frocks. There is a substantial body of writing on clothing, especially shoes and socks, a moderate amount on hair, and a great deal on forsaken toys--Eugene Field's "Little Boy Blue," for example.[5]

Vitalist narratives frequently highlight episodes that are at once trivial and proleptic. Millais's popular painting, "Christ in the House of His Parents (The Carpenter's Shop)" (1849-1850) is a type of this procedure. Here in the midst of the clutter of Joseph's carpenter's shop is the child Christ, a spoiled darling with red hair like his mother's. He has cut himself on a tool and he is pouting; the blood wells up in the center of his left palm while his mother kneels to "kiss him to make it well." Molesworth's Ted, the Christmas child, also blunders into a such a premonitory wound. Early in the narrative, 4-year-old Ted tries to help the gardener trim the flowers. Finding that the huge shears, which remind him of "the great, long, red-legged scissor man" in *Struwwelpeter*, are stuck, he oils them - with cod-liver oil. In a boy's version of the encounter with the Grim Reaper, the shears open too abruptly, and he cuts his leg badly. In Elizabeth Prentiss's memoir of her son Eddy, she illustrates his capacity for nonstop talk at 2, with the anecdote of his address to passersby as, leaning out of his Brooklyn Heights window, he expostulates: "You gemplen! there is a happy land" (40).

Such foregrounding of dynamic moments works to transform dead children into immortal children. By intensity of specific remembrance, the child is arrested in the moment of fullest energy and thus made perpetually present. Even heaven offers nothing better than such presence; thus, according to most Victorian speculation, children in heaven never grow older: "A babe in glory " (Bickersteth, stealing Keats) "is a babe forever" (Bickersteth, 52). Such insistent holding fast to unchangeable childhood made Leigh Hunt's essay, "The Deaths of Little Children" (1820), a leading anthology piece. Hunt argues that there is a connection between early death and perpetual childhood. If there were no childhood deaths, "we should regard every little child as a man or woman secured [...] Girls and boys would be future men and women not present children. They would have attained their full growth in our imaginations, and might as well have been men and women at once." But with a death, "other children grow up to manhood and womanhood, and suffer all the changes of mortality. This one alone is rendered an immortal child" (6).[6]

In one nineteenth-century version after another, the dead children become such immortal children, freed by one tactic or another from the delapidations of time and history. Rather than whisking the dead off the premises to allow the survivors to"deal with" an absence, the nineteenth-century way of killing a child is to restore, indeed increase, presence. The nineteenth-century way of killing a child makes childhood more real than any other period of life.

The literature of childhood death helps legitimize transience by inscribing it as plentitude. Hence, the vivid presence of the short-lived young in all the fixed, frozen, framed constructions we have considered; hence, all the charged luminous moments; and hence, too, the emergence of children's literature as the great post-Romantic genre in the late nineteenth century. Legitimizing childhood transience--both the ordinary transience of growing up and the extraordinary transience of the short life abruptly truncated--was one of the enabling conditions for the confident creation of major children's literature.

NOTES

1. See, for example, David Leavitt. "The Way I Live Now." *New York Times Magazine*, 1989:28-32, pp. 80-83. In an article on AIDS, Leavitt states that calls for special attention to the needs of children with the disease are motivated by homophobia:

I saw what a short ride it was from the inflammatory rhetoric of fundamentalist Christians insisting that AIDS is divine retribution against homosexual sins, to the banal, but equally enraging voice of George Bush declaring his compassion for people with AIDS, "especially the children" (of course, how could he specify compassion for queers and junkies?)

2. On the day I wrote this sentence, *The New York Times* carried a story under the headline "Woman Stabbing Daughter, 9, Is Shot to Death by Policeman", which reads in parts: "[The officer] saw the woman [...] threatening three children with a 14-inch carving knife. Chief Calzerano said the woman was yelling over and over to the children: 'The devil is in you. I have to kill you'" (July 28, 1989).

3. Although there is a rough consensus that *childhood mortality rates, though not mortality rates, fell before 1900*, interpreting the cultural effect of those changed rates is difficult. Some argue that the fall in mortality precipitated the concern about childhood death (i.e., those who are likely to keep their children are likely to invest more concern in them), while others argue just the opposite: that the rapid improvement in mortality late in the nineteenth century led to the disappearance of the theme.

4. There is a clear echo here--"The lovely lady Christabel/Whom her father loves so well"--and elsewhere in the poem of Coleridge's "Christabel." With its motif of child abuse and perverted will, "Christabel" is evidently a text Barrett finds in need of revision. "Isobel's Baby" is that revision.

5. On clothing, see DuBois's eloquent essay on his daughter and her dead brother's sailor suit ("The Unconscious Tribute," *Beckonings*, 119-166). On shoes, see "These little shoes!--How proud she was of those" (Canton, *A Lost Epic,* 178), Bennet's "O, those little, those little blue shoes!" ("Baby's Shoes", in Simmonds, 41), "Little Feet" (Foxcroft, 127-128), "My Darling's Shoes" (Schenck, 263) and "It was only a little sock" (Foxcroft, 109). On hair, see Riley, "When Bessie Died" (Foxcroft, 101-102); Elizabeth Barrett Browning, "Only a Curl."

6. See also:

> I see the seals of childhood fade
> > Slowly from each young living brow;
> Yet still in sunshine and in shade,
> > That infant is an infant now. (Lee, in Prime)

> Oft children living are children lost;
> But our children dead--ah, we keep them all!
> > (Mulock, "A Little Dead Prince," M'carty, 167-168)

How the children leave us, and no traces
Linger of that smiling angel band,
Gone, forever gone, and in their places
Weary men and anxious women stand.

Yet we have some little ones still our;
They have kept the baby smile we know,
Which we kissed one day, and hid with flowers
On their dead white faces long ago.
(Barrett Browning, in Foxcorft, 39)

"The children who die are those who are always ours. It is those who live, who become men and women, who depart to other continents and from other ties, - it is those we lose" (Anon., in Mifflin, 108).

'Twell de li'l angel daughter am de only one Ise kep'
I min' how I faulted Mastuh when de Shadder Vale she cross'
But de ones I tho't I'se keepin' am de only ones I los'
(Long, "Daddy's Pilot" 85)

REFERENCES

Adams, Nehemiah. *Agnes and the Little Key; or, Bereaved Parents Instructed and Comforted.* 8th ed. Boston: Ticknor & Fields, 1863.

Ariès, Philippe. *Western Attitudes Towards Death from the Middle Ages to the Present.* Trans. Patricia Ranun. London: Marion Boyars, 1976.

Avery, Gillian, and Angela Bull. *Nineteenth-Century Children's Heroes and Heroines in English Children's Stories 1780-1900.* London: Hodder & Stoughton, 1965.

Bethune, George Washington. *Early Lost, Early Saved.* Philadelphia: Mentz & Roundt, 1846.

Bickersteth, Edward Henry. *Yesterday, Today and Forever: A Poem in Twelve Books* [1866]. 3rd ed. New York: Robert Carter, 1875

Boswell, John. *The Kindness of Strangers: The Abandonment of Children in Western Europe from Late Antiquity to the Renaissance.* New York: Pantheon, 1988.

"Brenda." *Froggy's Little Brother* [1875]. London: Gollancz, 1968.

Brown, John. "Marjorie Fleming." [1858, 1861]. In *Rab and His Friends and Other Papers.* London-New York: Dent/Dutton, n.d., pp. 83-111.

Brownell, Elizabeth, ed. *Dream Children.* Indianapolis: Bowen-Merril, 1901.

Browning, Elizabeth Barrett. *The Poetical Works.* New York: Hurst ,n.d.

Browning, Robert. *Poems of Robert Browning.* London: Oxford University Press, 1925.

Burnett, Frances Hodgson. *Children I Have Known and Giovanni and the Other.* London: James R. Osgood, McIlvaine & Co., 1892.

---. *In the Closed Room.* New York: McClure, Philips & Co., 1904.

---. *Piccino and Other Child Stories.* New York: Scribner's, 1894.

Burnett, Vivian. *The Romantic Lady (Frances Hodgson Burnett): The Life Story of an Imagination.* New York-London: Scribner's, 1927.

Canton, William. *The Invisible Playmate, W.V. Her Book, and In Memory of W.V..* London-New York: Dent/Dutton, 1912.

---. *A Lost Epic and Other Poems.* Edinburgh-London: Blackwood, 1897.

Chamberlain, Alexander Francis. *The Child and Childhood in Folk Thought (The Child in Primitive Culture).* New York-London, 1896.

Chapman, Elizabeth Rachel. *A Little Child's Wreath.* Flowers of Parnassus XXI. London-New York: John Lane, 1904.

Choron, Jacques. *Death and Western Thought.* New York: Collier, 1963.

Clark, W. B. *Asleep in Jesus; or, Words of Consolation to Bereaved Parents.* Edinburgh: T. Nelson, 1856.

Coleridge, Samuel Taylor. *Coleridge on Logic Learning.* Ed. Alice D. Snyder. Folcroft, Pa.: Folcroft Library, 1973.

---. *Collected Letters of Samuel Taylor Coleridge.* Ed. Earl Leslie Griggs. 6 vols. Oxford: Clarendon, 1956-1971.

Cutler, Samuel. *Our Little Ones in Paradise.* New York: American Tract Society, 1877.

Cuyler, Theodore. *The Empty Crib: A Memorial of Little Georgie.* New York: R. Carter, 1869.

de la Mare, Walter, ed. *Come Hither.* 2 vols. Harmondsworth, Middlesex: Kestrel, 1957.

de la Pasture, Mrs. Henry. *A Toy Tragedy: A Story of Children.* New York: Dutton, 1906.

de la Ramee, Louise [Ouida]. *A Dog of Flanders and Other Stories.*New York: Grosset & Dunlop, 1965.

Dickens, Charles. *Bleak House* [1853]. Cambridge, Mass.: HM, 1956.

---. *The Old Curiosity Shop* [1840-1841]. London: Chapman & Hall, 1871.

Dostoyevsky, Fyodor. *The Brothers Karamazov.* Trans. David Magarshack. 2 vols. [1880]. Harmondsworth: Penguin, 1958.

DuBois, Patterson. *Beckonings from Little Hands. Eight Studies in Child Life.* 4th ed. New York: Dodd, Mead & Co., 1900.

Dusinberre, Juliet. *Alice to the Lighthouse: Children's Books and Radical Experiments in Art.* London: Macmillan, 1987.

"The Dying Child to its Mother". *Songs.* London: H. Printer, 1840.

Ewing, Juliana Horatia. *Jackanapes.* London: SPCK, 1884.

---. *Lob-Lie-By-The-Fire, and The Story of a Short Life.* New York-London: Dent/Dutton, 1964.

Faber, Frederic. *Ethel's Book: or, Tales of the Angels.* London: Thomas Richardson, 1858.

Farrar, Frederic. *Eric, or, Little by Little: A Tale of Roslyn School.* 1858; London: A & C Black, 1899.

Field, Eugene. *The Poems of Eugene Field.* New York: Scribner's, 1922.

Foxcroft, Elizabeth Howard, ed. *Our Glorified: Poems and Passages of Consolation, Especially for Those Bereaved by the Loss of Children.* Boston: Lee & Shepard, 1889.

J.G. *"Why Weepest Thou?" A Book for Mourners.* London, Edinburgh and New York: Thomas Nelson, 1888.

Hair, P. E. H. "Children in Society 1850-1950," in *Population and Society in Britain 1850-1980.*,eds. Theo Barker & Michael Drake. New York & London: New York University Press, 1982, pp. 34-61.

Hocking, Silas. *Her Benny* [1879] Liverpool: Galley, 1976.

Hugo, Victor. *Les Miserables.* Trans. Lee Fahnestock & Norman MacAfee after C. E. Wilbour. New York & Scarborough, Ontario: NAL, 1987.

Hunt, Leigh. "Deaths of Little Children," in *Essays of Leigh Hunt,* ed. Reginald Brimley Johnson. London: Dent, 1891, pp. 1-7.

Jones, John Cooper. *Words of Consolation and Encouragement for the Sorrowing.* Mount Morris, Ill.: Keble Bros., 1908.

Key, Ellen. *The Century of the Child.* London-New York: Putnam, 1909.

Kilvert, Francis. *Kilvert's Diary: Selections from the Diary of the Rev. Francis Kilvert, 1 January 1870--19 August 1871,* ed. William Plomer. London: Jonathan Cape, 1938.

Kingsley, Charles. *The Water Babies and Selected Poems.* Library of Classics. London-Glasgow: Collins, n.d.

Kipling, Rudyard. "The Drums of the Fore and Aft." In *Soldiers Three and Military Tales. The Writings in Prose and Verse of Rudyard Kipling.* Vol. 3, Part. 2. New York: Scribner's, 1917, pp. 474-526.

---."They." In *Traffics and Discoveries. The Writings in Prose and Verse of Rudyard Kipling.* Vol. 22. New York: Scribner's, 1916, pp. 337-375.

Knox, Mrs. John D. *When Sorrow Comes.* Eskridge, Kan., 1931.

Logan, William, ed. *Words of Comfort for Parents Bereaved of Little Children.* 4th ed. London: James Nisbet, 1867.

Long, Solomon. *Child Slaves and Other Poems.* Winfield, Kan: Courier, 1909.

Loraux, Nicole. *Tragic Ways of Killing a Woman.* Trans. Anthony Fraser. Cambridge, Mass--London: Harvard UP, 1987.

MacDonald, George. *At the Back of the North Wind.* New York: Airmont, 1966.

---. "The Gift of the Christ Child," in *The Golden Key and Other Stories.* Grand Rapids, Mich.: William B. Erdman, 1980.

---. *A Light Princess and Other Tales. Being the Complete Fairy Tales.* New York: Watts, 1961.

Malkin, Benjamin Heath. *A Father's Memoirs of his Child (Thomas W. Malkin).* With a design by W. Blake. London: Longman, Hurst, Rees & Orm, 1806.

M'Carthy, J. Hendrickson. *Inside the Gates.* Cincinnati: Hitchcock & Walden, 1876.

Meynell, Wilifred, ed. *The Child Set in the Midst by Modern Poets.* London: Leadenhall, 1892.

Mifflin, Mildred. *Out of Darkness into Light; from the Journal of a Bereaved Mother*. Shelbyville, Ill.: Our Press Words, 1888.

Molesworth, Mrs [Mary Louisa Stewart]. *A Christmas Child: A Sketch of Boy-Life*. London: Macmillan, 1890.

---. *Stories by Mrs. Molesworth*. New York: Duffield, 1922.

Montgomery, Florence. *Misunderstood* [1869]. London: Macmillan, 1913.

Morley, John. *Death, Heaven and the Victorians*. London: University of Pittsburgh Press, 1971.

Mullins, Isla May. *An Upward Look for Mothers*. Philadelphia: Griffith & Rowland, 1900.

Mulock, Miss [Dinah]. *The Little Lame Prince and Other Fairy Tales*. World Juvenile Library. Cleveland & New York: World, n.d.

Perkins, David D., ed. *English Romantic Writers*. New York: HBJ, 1967.

Prentiss, Elizabeth. *How Sorrow Was Changed into Sympathy: Words of Cheer for Mothers Bereft of Little Children*. New York: Anson D.F. Randolph, 1884.

Prime, Samuel Irenaeus et al. *The Smitten Household; or, Thoughts for the Afflicted*. New York: Anson D.F. Randolph, 1856.

---. *Thoughts on the Death of Little Children*. New York: Anson D.F. Randolph, 1852.

Rousseau, Jean-Jacques. *The Confessions of Jean-Jacques Rousseau*. Trans. J. M. Cohen. Harmondsworth: Penguin, 1954.

Russell, Matthew. Little Angels: *A Book of Comfort for Mourning Mothers*. London: Burns & Oates, 1909.

Schenck, William Edward. *Children in Heaven; or, The Infant Dead Redeemed by the Blood of Jesus with Words of consolation to Bereaved Parents*. Philadelphia: Presbyterian Board of Publications, 1965.

Schiller, Frederick von. *Naive and Sentimental Poetry, and On the Sublime*. Trans. Julius Elias. New York: Frederick Ungar, 1966.

Simmonds, William. *Our Little Ones in Heaven*. Boston: Gould & Lincoln, 1858.

Smyth, Thomas. *Solace for Bereaved Parents; or, Infants Die to Live*. New York: Robert Carter, 1846.

Stowe, Harriet Beecher. *Uncle Tom's Cabin* [1852]. New York: Harper & Row, 1965.

Strickland, Charles. "A Transcendentalist Father: The Child-Rearing Practices of Bronson Alcott." *History of Childhood Quaterly*, 1977:1, pp. 4-51.

Strong, Roy. *And When Did You Last See Your Father? The British Painter and British History*. Over Wallop, Hampshire: Thames & Hudson, 1978.

Wordsworth, William. *The Prelude 1799, 1805, 1850*. Norton Critical Edition. Ed. Jonathan Wordsworth, M. H. Abrams, and Stephen Gill. New York-London: Norton, 1979.

Part I

THEORY AND METHOD

The Historical Model of the Development of Children's Literature

Zohar Shavit

Introduction

Is it possible to claim a universal structure for the development of children's literature? (On the question of literary universals and laws, see Even-Zohar, 1978, 45-53; 1990, 53-72.)

Assuming that we understand history as being composed of an endless string of details that may become meaningful only after they are organized under a general structure, this essay argues for the existence of such a universal structure--provided, of course, that we are interested in general patterns and not in minor deviations from them.

Since the issue at stake is historical poetics, it is important to stress that the competence to make generalizations about culture, and to describe its dominant structures is at the heart of the matter. It is one of the most important obligations of historical poetics. That is to say, it is the duty of historiography to explore the structural development of culture, where by "structural" I refer to the material that can be organized as the dominant phenomena in our description of history, and not to the analysis and explanation of all details involved.

Model of Development

On the basis of the rich and highly informative literature on the history of children's literature (see e.g. Avery, 1975; Avery and Bull, 1965; Brockman, 1982; Brüggemann and Ewers, 1982; Grenz, 1981; Ewers, 1980; Ewers, 1989; Macleod, 1975; Muir, 1969; Pickering, 1981; Rose, 1984; Thwaite, 1972; Townsend, 1977; Zipes, 1988) and on the basis of such an understanding of history and historiography, I would like to argue that *a similar historical model is common to all children's literatures both in their inception and later on in their development.* The same stages of development and the same historical patterns recur time and again in all children's literatures, transcending national boundaries and even temporal ones. Regardless of when and where a system of children's literature began to develop, whether its emergence took place a hundred or even two hundred years later, *all systems of children's literature known to us, without exception, pass through the same stages of development. Moreover, the same cultural factors and institutions are involved in their creation.*

The cases of the Puritans first in England and, later, in America, or the Jewish Enlightenment in Germany 150 years later, or the Egyptian Enlightenment at the turn of the twentieth century, all lead to the conclusion that it was always ideology, linked with a strong educational doctrine, which formed the basis of official children's literature. The tenet that children needed books in the course of their education constituted the emergence of a new function in the literary system, that is to say, the emergence of a specific system of books designated for children only.

Once this function was created, the same model of historical development followed: *through a battle between what children were supposed to read and what children actually wanted to read, there gradually emerged a heterogeneous and stratified system of books for children.*

The Link with the Educational System

Arguing for a general model underlying the development of children's literature, I will present its dominant components, focusing on the following two issues:

1. The link between the comprehension of the notions of child and of childhood, particularly within the framework of various educational ideologies, and the writing of texts specifically addressing children.

2. The manner in which two different and, to some extent, contradictory sources in culture were used in order to establish a system of books for children: the new educational system, responsible for the creation of books that suited children according to its understanding of their needs, producing more often than not books children were reluctant to read, and the nonofficial adult system, in most cases chapbooks, which supplied reading material children were eager to read.

Before children's literature could begin to develop, a total reform in the notion of childhood was required, a reform that was described in the pioneering and well-known work of Philippe Ariès and his followers (Ariès, 1962; Arnold, 1980; Badinter, 1980; DeMause, 1975). Before this, before children's needs gained recognition and legitimation as distinct and different from those of adults, children's literature could not have emerged. To repeat John Townsend's formulation: "Before there could be children's books, there had to be children" (Townsend, 1977, 17).

It is not necessary to repeat here Ariès's well-known thesis. For our purposes, it is sufficient to mention that the new notion of the child implied, inter alia, the creation of a new addressee, who was hitherto not recognized as "sui generis," as different from adult addressees, and consequently was not viewed as a subject with distinctive and particular needs.

Once a new understanding of the child and of childhood emerged into societal consciousness (in a long and enigmatic process), a new and previously unknown demand for books exclusively produced for children appeared on the cultural scene. Until then children, who were educated in the framework of the apprenticeship system, did not need books in their educational process. As a new concept of education--the school system-- replaced the apprenticeship system, books became part of the educational system for the first time and an indispensable vehicle for achieving its goals. Thus, the new educational system both legitimized books for children and created a certain corpus of texts and a set of norms according to which official books for children had to be written.

Prior to the seventeenth century, few books were produced specifically for children (on the question of texts addressing children in early times, see Shaner, 1992). Children who knew how to read would have shared adult literature. Most children's exposure to reading was provided in shared reading sessions with adults. Thus, almost three hundred years after the invention of the printing press, children's books, mainly ABCs and "courtesy" books, were few in number and were produced neither systematically nor steadily. The few children's books published prior to the seventeenth century acquired only a limited audience, comprising children who would either hold a suitable place in "good" society or would serve the Church. Children's literature was not yet recognized as a distinct field of culture. Most of the texts that did address children comprised "books of manners" and courtesy books that can be described as part of a larger "culture of etiquette" prevalent at the time and were not at all part of children's literature in its modern sense.

The purpose of those texts was to teach children (obviously of certain social rank) the behavior appropriate to their status in society. The educational system *did not require or leave room for further reading, nor did it encourage further education by means of books*. Moreover, existing books lacked the recognition that became part of the conceptual cultural framework of the eighteenth century--the recognition that children needed books of their own that should differ from adult books and that would suit their needs, at least as understood at the time.

Only toward the end of the seventeenth century, with the emergence of Puritan writing for children, did books for children become a culturally recognized field, as special books were issued in order to fulfill children's educational needs. It must be remembered, however, that the emergence of a new type of books did not imply the total disappearance of texts existing until then. It was typical of this development that "books of manners" and courtesy books continued to exist in the system for a very long period of time. Their demise was not immediate. Their disappearance from the literary scene involved either slow decline or integration into the newly emerging texts for children, implying that they began to carry new and up-to-date functions. Most important of all was their new position in the cultural system: from now on it was the new system of education that determined the nature of texts for children, old and new alike.

Unlike the case of adult literature, the educational system was intrinsically involved in the development of books for children, which later emerged in culture as a system of children's literature. The pattern of development in children's literature indicates that the educational system not only served as a framework for the creation and legitimation of children's literature, but also determined its stages of development. The fact that children's literature relied on the legitimation of the educational establishment, which also served as its contiguous frame of reference, accounts for a recurring pattern typical of all beginnings of official children's literatures: the first official books for children were ABC books, primers, and horn books whose main goal was to teach the child how to read, primarily for religious purposes and in accordance with a certain religious-educational doctrine. Children (first of the nobility, then of the bourgeoisie, and later of the poor as well) were taught how to read, so as to enable them to read the Scriptures by themselves.

Once children mastered reading, however, it became impossible to control their reading material and to determine what they should read, and more significantly, what they should not read. The existing official books for children had little, if any, appeal: they were far too moralistic to be interesting and far too dull.

The process of the emergence of this new system was a tedious one. For rather a long time, the new boundaries between the adult and the children's literary systems were blurred and unclear (see Shavit, 1990). More than one hundred years were needed for cultural consciousness to register the existence of new borders, and more than one hundred and fifty years were needed to make them into a set of *distinct* and *unequivocal* oppositions--that is to say, to make the systemic affiliation definitive. Only toward the middle of the nineteenth century did the systems become *exclusive*: a text could enter either one or the other system. Until then, the pattern of shared elements continued to exist side by side with the new pattern of systems which excluded each other.

The Function of Chapbooks

As a result of the new notion of the child and of childhood, a new reading public came into being in society and a new demand for children's books emerged on the literary scene. This demand could not as yet be supplied in full by the educational establishment, who regarded reading as a gateway to higher religious enlightenment, but absolutely not as a means of entertainment or pleasure. A new function was therefore created in the literary system--the function of supplying reading material to a new reading public, which the existing elements of the official system could not fulfill (Altick, 1975).

The vacuum thus created in the system was filled by an unexpected source: the nonofficial adult literature of the time, that is to say, chapbooks, which children evidently found very appealing (Ashton, 1882; Neuberg,

1968, 1969, 1972, 1977). Quietly creeping into the system, chapbooks largely bore the function of reading material for children. They continued to do so unnoticed for quite a long time, until the notion of children's reading became preponderant in societal consciousness (Darling, 1968).

Officially, the first texts to fill this vacuum were primers and some religious treatises. Unofficially, however, the task was taken over by chapbooks.

I perceived him a very great historian in Aesop's Fables; but he frankly declared to me his mind that he did not delight in that learning, because he did not believe that they were true, for which reason I found that he had very much turned his studies for about a twelve-months past, into the lives and adventures of Don Bellianis of Greece, Guy of Warwick, The Seven Champions and other historians of that age [...] He could tell you the mismanagements of John Hickathroft, find fault with the passionate temper in Bevis of Southampton, and loved Saint George for being champion of England." (cited by Muir, 1969, 23; Darton, 1958, 33)

This is Sir Richard Steele's description, in the *Tatler* of 1709, of his godson's reading material. Sir Richard Steele was not the only one to describe children's reading material in this manner. Similar evidence can be found in almost all European writers of the eighteenth century when they describe their childhood. Be it Boswell or Goethe, all remembered with much nostalgia the chapbooks they used to read in their childhood. In *Dichtung und Wahrheit*, Goethe wrote: "We children therefore had the good fortune to find daily on the little table in front of the second hand bookseller's doorway these precious remnants of the Middle Ages: *Eulenspiegel, The Four Sons of Aymon, Fair Melusine, Kaiser Octavian, Fortunatus*--the whole bunch, right down to *The Wandering Jew*; everything was there for us" (cited by Hürlimann, 1967, xii-xv).

The Struggle over Reading Material for Children

During the eighteenth century, chapbooks became the most important reading material for children. However, neither the religious nor the educational establishments were as delighted as Boswell or Goethe about the reading of chapbooks by children. On the contrary, the more important the child's education (and consequently his reading matter) became, the less the educational establishment was ready to accept children's reading of chapbooks. When the religious establishment began to scrutinize the education of children as well as their reading material, chapbooks had to retreat underground.

"The reading of romance is a most frivolous occupation, and time merely thrown away," wrote Philip Dormer to his son in 1740 (cited by Darton, 1958, 47), and thus joined the war declared on chapbooks. The establishment's fight against chapbooks was not limited to propagandistic articles, however. Major efforts were simultaneously made to overcome the reliance on chapbooks through offering children alternative reading material. These texts, written as the answer to chapbooks, played an important role in enriching the repertoire of official books for children. Thus, out of the competition over children's free time and reading habits emerged a more heterogeneous and diverse system of books for children (Brockman, 1982).

Various Schools of Education and Their Imprint on Children's Literature

Various establishments were involved in the production of official books for children. The new educational system was at first monopolized, as well as institutionalized, by the religious establishment, which was in the best position to supply the newly recognized demands of the schools. The first official books published by various organizations of the Church, mostly by the Puritans, were designed to teach principles of religion. They laid heavy stress on the acquisition of morals and operated on the basis of the assumption that through books (necessarily religious in nature) the child would be disciplined along the path of learning and godliness.

Very soon, however, children's reading matter was constructed on the basis of new models of writing founded on different educational views. These new models emerged from two sources: the commercial and the moralist school of education. The moralist school of education developed during the Age of Reason and was rooted in the writings of either Locke or Rousseau. As an educational doctrine, it gradually acquired a status equal to that of the Puritan approach. Subsequently, it replaced it at the center of official literature for children.

Unlike the Puritans who believed children were sinful by nature, the moralists held the task of education to be the shaping of the child's soul and spirit, and hence the determination of his future role in society. Accordingly, education was allotted a major place in man's life as never before. Moreover, since books were considered the main tools in the process of education, a large demand for them arose, encouraging a change in the existing texts for children.

The most significant change initiated by the moralist school lay in the new raison d'etre of children's books. Unlike the Puritans whose raison d'etre was to teach children how to read in order to improve their comprehension of the Scriptures, the new school of education considered books to be the most appropriate means for accommodating Locke's demand for the fusion of amusement and instruction. Reading was regarded as the best means not for mastering the Scriptures, but rather for achieving several other educational goals.

As a result, two new models were introduced into the system: the fable and the moral tale. The first, the fable, required the accommodation of an existing model to the one legitimized by Locke. The second, that of the moral tale, required the creation of a new model, which was deeply rooted in the Rousseauian doctrine.

As new educational doctrines paid increasing attention to children's reading, children's books began to change. These doctrines allotted to children's reading a much larger space, regarding it as something more than merely a vehicle for achieving religious goals. The homogeneous nature of official books for children was replaced by the variety of texts offered to the child: moral stories, animal stories, instructive stories, primers, and readers were gradually introduced into the system. Their presence in the market attracted commercial publishers, who were catalyzing a whole new field of publishing for children.

Commercial Publishing for Children

Once the establishments involved in the education of the child became aware of the child's reading (Darling, 1968), and once commercial publishing discovered the huge potential of this market, they began to compete with and challenge children's actual reading material. Out of this competition, a heterogeneous and stratified system of books for children emerged in European cultural life.

Commercial publishers became more and more aware of the existence of the field of books for children. The efforts of the educational establishments on the one hand, and the fact that children were reading chapbooks on the other, proved to eighteenth-century commercial publishers that there was a section of the reading public whose needs were hardly being administered to. Once the book trade came to realize the commercial potential of the children's market, it began to produce books for children which could serve as an alternative to the popular chapbooks, but all the same did not violate the values of official books for children.

A typical example of this process is the case of John Newbery, the first commercial publisher who was successful in building a solid publishing business for children. The case of John Newbery is too well known to be repeated here. I would only like to point to his effort to appeal both to the child and to the adult at the same time. Newbery tried to appeal to the child by offering him an alternative to his reading of chapbooks, without losing his advantage over the chapbooks, namely, without violating the values of educators and parents. Newbery was aware of the existing inventory of books for children--chapbooks, lesson books, manuals of good advice, and Aesop's fables--andattempted to use elements of each in order to enhance the competitive capacity of his books as much as possible. In his books, he combined elements of chapbooks which appealed to the child, with morality which appealed to the parent and the teacher (see, e.g., Newbery 1966).

The History of Little Goody Two Shoes, for instance, is a variation on the prohibited tale of Cinderella, which could be found at that time only in the form of chapbooks. It is a story of an unfortunate girl from a good family who suffers many trials and tribulations, but eventually marries the heir of the manor and becomes its noble lady. Furthermore, the heroine, Margery, is involved in strange adventures, including the accusation of witchcraft, typical of chapbooks.

Newbery's use of illustrations is his most noticeable strategy, however. He borrowed from chapbooks in order to compete with them. The use of illustrations attracted much attention and, from that time onward, became an indispensable feature of children's books. Newbery was followed by other publishers who also used illustrations in their children's books and who introduced several additional models of writing for children.

Competition with Chapbooks

As a result of the constant competition with chapbooks, commercial publishing for children had become an established branch of the publishing field by the end of the eighteenth century. Newbery's books had become a model that other commercial publishers sought to imitate. The introduction of both the commercial element and new educational views led to a change in the official system. Gradually, children's literature became stratified and subject to competition between competing elements and competing systems: the official and the nonofficial system of books for children.

Although the various establishments involved in the production of books for children had different motivations and endeavored to achieve different goals, they did share one common denominator: they all tried to compete with chapbooks.

All publishers of books for children attempted to challenge chapbooks, as is clear from the case of Newbery mentioned above. Most interesting, however, is the case of religious publishing for children which, despite its rejection of chapbooks, could not afford to ignore them and actually used them in its writing of books for children. This was, for instance, the case of Hannah More, a philanthropist and great Sunday School supporter. She regarded the spread of chapbooks as a genuine danger to the education of the child and thus to society. Hannah More was the first to understand that there was a need to produce books not on a sporadic basis, but rather to produce a whole literature for children (and the poor). She also believed it imperative to replace what she regarded as crude chapbooks (as well as the current political pamphlets that were then consumed by masses of working-class readers). More urged her evangelical friends at Chapham Common to provide the poor with proper reading material. Aided greatly by their financial support, her efforts proved successful, and in March 1795 the first of the Cheap Repository Tracts was ready.

In the production of these tracts, a steady effort was made to challenge all possible components of chapbooks and to present alternatives to them. In order to compete with chapbooks, thedevice of serialization was used, enhanced by the familiar format of chapbooks, as well as by woodcut illustrations. Some tracts deliberately tried to replace chapbooks by offering attractive titles that resembled well-known chapbooks such as *The Cottage Cook; or Mrs. Jones' Cheap Dishes, Tawny Rachel or, The Fortune Teller,* and *Robert and Richard; or The Ghost of Poor Molly, Who Was Drowned in Richard's Mill Pond.*

Tract writers strove to compete with chapbooks by also adopting familiar chapbooks genres and subordinating them to didactic teaching. Poem-like texts *(The Carpenter; or, The Danger of Evil Company)* were intended to replace bawdy ballads, while Histories *(Tawny Rachel; or, The Fortune Teller)* were to replace frivolous romances and adventures. Even sensational books and manuals were not exempt. Mother Bunch of the chapbooks, who gave recipes for finding the right husband, was replaced by Mrs. James, who taught the art of industry and good management. Criminal stories were also used for moral purposes. Crimes were never, of course, romanticized in religious tracts (as they were, for instance, in Robin Hood), but they were used to teach the right lesson: criminals were always punished. Even ghosts, the slandered heroes of chapbooks, were used for religious purposes. Thus, for instance, in *The Deceitfulness of Pleasure,* the appearance of a ghost, the former sinful lady, brings the heroine Catherine back to religious life.

Most interesting was the manner in which the tracts used fairy tales. Fairy tales posed a more difficult problem than poems or even criminal stories, because they were considered the most dangerous reading material for children. Thus, religious tracts could not openly use them. On the other hand, religious educators wanted to take advantage of their popularity and appeal. A solution to this conflict was found in the following manner: fairy tales themselves were never included in tracts, but their literary model was transferred to an instructive tale. That is, the fairy tale was transformed into a religious power, while giants and wild beasts were replaced by dishonesty, gambling, and alcoholism. In *Madge Blareny, the Gypsy Girl* (1797), for instance, a poor girl has to fight single-handed against the wild beast (the drunken and sinful gypsies). She is eventually saved by religion, which keeps her from falling into sin like her mother. In this manner chapbooks not only set in motion the production of books for children, but also determined to a large extent the nature and character of the texts themselves.

Summary

My discussion of the emergence of the system of children's literature in the eighteenth century describes the scheme of the historical process through which new boundaries between adult and children's readerships were drawn.

When children's literature began to emerge, the new boundaries were at first partial and ad hoc. The new function of children's reading was fulfilled by systemically undefined elements such as shared reading material and traditional reading material which was regarded as part of the entire literary system. In order for the new boundaries to stabilize, there evolved a need to find elements for the new functions, in order to distinguish between the two systems.

These elements were generated through the transplantation of new functions onto existing (sometimes even reluctant) elements; through the translation of old functions into new ones; through the creation of new elements; and through the adaptation of existing elements. The first three procedures characterized the operations of the official system, while the last one was typical of the nonofficial system, which formed the basis of the stratification of the new system of books for children.

Even after the new boundaries had been culturally recognized, and even after they became distinct (the discrepancy between these two stages was rather extensive), they never remained the same. The relations between the boundaries have always been dynamic; the systemic opposition between children's literature and adult literature continues to be one of the most prominent oppositions in the literary polysystem, but its concrete manifestations change from one period to another, thus reshuffling the boundaries. The function of distinguishing between adult and children's literature has changed historically as well, although this change was much slower and required many decades before it was accepted and recognized by culture.

REFERENCES

Altick, R. D. *The English Common Reader*. Chicago: The University of Chicago Press, 1975.

Ariès, Philippe. *Centuries of Childhood*. New York: Vintage, 1962.

Arnold, Klaus. *Kind und Gesellschaft in Mittelalter und Renaissance*. Wurzburg: Ferdinand Schoningh, 1980.

Ashton, John. *Chapbooks of the Eighteenth Century*. London, 1882.

Avery, Gillian. *Childhood's Pattern*. London: Hodder and Stoughton, 1975.

Avery, Gillian, and Angela Bull. *Nineteenth-Century Children: Heroes and Heroines in English Children's Stories, 1780-1900*. London: Hodder and Stoughton, 1965.

Badinter, Elisabeth. *L'amour en plus: Histoire de l'amour maternel (XVIIe-XXe siècles)*. Paris: Flammarion, 1980.

Brockman, Bennett H. "Robin Hood and the Invention of Children's Literature," *Children's Literature*, 10 (1982), pp. 1-17.

Brüggemann, Theodor, and Hans-Heino Ewers. *Handbuch zur Kinder- und Jugendliteratur von 1750 bis 1800.* Stuttgart, 1982.

Darling, R. *The Rise of Children's Book Reviewing in America, 1865-1881.* New York: Bowker, 1968.

Darton, H. F. J. *Children's Books in England.* Cambridge: Cambridge University Press, 1958

DeMause, L., ed. *The History of Childhood.* New York: Harper & Row, 1975.

Even-Zohar, Itamar. *Papers in Historical Poetics.* Tel Aviv: Porter Institute, 1978.

---. "Polysystem Studies." *Poetics Today,* 11:1 (1990).

Ewers, Hans-Heino. *Kindheit als poetische Daseinsform.* München: Wilhelm Fink, 1989.

Ewers, Hans-Heino, ed. *Kinder- und Jugendliteratur der Aufklärung.* Stuttgart, 1980.

Grenz, Dagmar. *Mädchenliteratur. Von den morlichbelehrenden Schriften im 18. Jahrhundert bis zur Herausbildung der Backfischliteratur im 19. Jahrhundert.* Stuttgart, 1981.

Hürlimann, Bettina. *Three Centuries of Children's Books in Europe.* London: Oxford University Press, 1967.

Macleod, Anne Scott. *A Moral Tale.* Hamden, Conn.: Archon Books, 1975.

Muir, Percy H. *English Children's Books.* New York: Fredrick A. Praeger, 1969.

Neuberg, Victor, E. *The Penny Histories.* London, 1968.

---. "The Diceys and the Chapbook Trade." *Library* 24 (1969), pp. 219-231.

---. *Chapbooks: A Guide to Reference Material.* London, 1972.

---. *Popular Literature.* London, 1977.

Newbery, John. *A Little Pretty Pocket-Book.* A facsimile, with an introductory essay and bibliography by M. F. Thwaite. Oxford, 1966.

Pickering, Samuel, F. *John Locke and Children's Books in Eighteenth-Century England.* Knoxville: University of Tennessee Press, 1981.

Rose, Jacqueline. *The Case of Peter Pan.* London: Macmillan, 1984.

Shaner, Mary E. "Instruction and Delight: Medieval Romances as Children's Literature." *Poetics Today* 13:1 (1992), pp. 5-15.

Shavit, Zohar. *Poetics of Children's Literature*. Athens: University of Georgia Press, 1986.

---. "Cultural Notions and Literary Boundaries: On the Creation of the Systemic Opposition between Children's Literature and Adult Literature in the 18th Century." *Proceedings of the XII Congress of ICLA*. München: Iudicum Verlag, 1990, pp. 414-429.

Thwaite, Mary F. *From Primer to Pleasure*. London, 1972.

Townsend, John Rowe. *Written for Children*. Harmondsworth: Penguin, 1977.

Zipes, Jack. *The Brothers Grimm--From Enchanted Forests to the Modern World*. New York, 1988.

Children's Literature as a Cultural Code: A Semiotic Approach to History

Maria Nikolajeva

The historical approach to literature inevitably tends to be descriptive. Since children's literature research on the whole lags behind the general literary criticism, the descriptive tendency is all the more evident in the field. It is very difficult to construct acceptable models of the historical development of children's literature, whether it be a national literature or a general outline or a study of a concrete period. We must therefore try to search for adequate methods in other fields of research. One that I have found quite fruitful is the modern semiotics of culture, as understood by the Russian semiotic school and presented in the works of Yury Lotman.[1]

Thus interpreted, the history of children's literature can be seen as a succession of changing cultural codes. The notion of the cultural code implies in this case that children's literature presents a code, or a system of codes (a "semiosphere"), different from those in adult or mainstream literature. The unique feature of children's texts, as compared to mainstream literature, is the presence of *double* code systems, which may be called the children's code and the adult code.

The most important aspect of semiosphere is its dynamic character. In other words, the children's code and the adult code change throughout history, converging, diverging, and overlapping at various points. For instance, some books regarded as "adult" become part of children's literature and the other way round. In addition, the attitude toward children's literature as opposed to mainstream literature varies.

The code shift *within* children's literature implies that central phenomena become at length supplanted by borderline phenomena. When *The Catcher in the Rye* by J. D. Salinger appeared in 1951, it was unique, but today it has become the central archetypal text for a whole tradition, sometimes called "jeans prose."[2] That is, the book has generated what may be termed "jeans code. "Many taboos that existed in children's literature during its early periods are today being withdrawn. This change has not,however, happened overnight. Texts that discuss some earlier forbidden theme, like violence or sex, appear first on the borderline. Since it is the borderline that is active in any semiosphere, while its center is passive, the borderline texts move successively toward the center. Today we can discover open descriptions of sexual relations in children's books on a scale unheard of twenty years ago. We can also see the appearance of a further breakthrough in the periphery. For instance, *Dance on my Grave* (1982) by Aidan Chambers was among the first junior novels to take up homosexuality, but this subject was soon covered in more novels. The process may be schematically depicted as

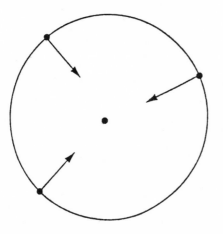

This model, which, of course, pertains to any semiotic system, becomes more complicated in the case of children's books owing to the double code system. The centripetal movement of the peripheral phenomena is disturbed by the duplicated semiosphere centers:

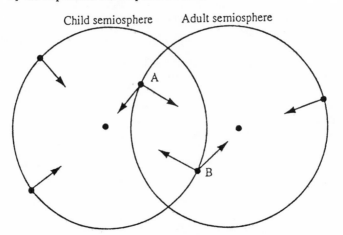

Another important idea developed by Yury Lotman is that the evolution of cultural semiotic systems is predictable only to a very limited extent. This idea, like so much in Lotman's theories, comes from the natural sciences, more particularly from Ilya Prigogine.[3] In Lotman's model, constructed after Prigogine's description of some chemical, physical, and biological processes, cultural evolution is predictable only to a certain point, a critical moment when something crucial happens.[4] Prigogine calls these moments *bifurcation points*. After these events, there maybe an indefinite amount of possible, unpedictable ways of evolution. Only one of them is, however, followed in reality and thus becomes predictable, up to the next bifurcation point:

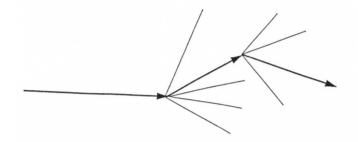

Going back to *The Catcher in the Rye*, we may say that the appearance of this text was the crucial moment in the history of children's and youth literature. After that, the ways of children's literature change in a manner that no one could possibly have predicted. On the other hand, it is easy to predict the appearance and evolution of jeans prose, up to a certain point, which most probably has not taken place yet. *Pippi Longstocking* (1945) by Astrid Lindgren is doubtlessly a bifurcation point in Swedish children's literature.

Thus, it is the task of a semiotically minded historian of children's literature to discover these bifurcation points--that is, literary or sometimes extraliterary phenomena that dramatically change the historical evolution. At the same time, it is essential to study the predictable evolutionary lines--that is, the slow movement of the new, innovative literary phenomena from the periphery of the semiosphere, where they first occur, toward the center. This model helps us to see the history of children's literature in an essentially new light, although it naturally puts higher demands on the researcher.

This semiotic model for historical literary studies can be applied to various types of investigations. For instance, it can be used to examine the development of the poetics of children's literature at various periods; to interpret more accurately the history of any particular genre or kind of children's literature; to explain the evolution of some patterns generally believed to be essential for children's books (like journey, homecoming, and happy ending); or, as has just been shown, to account for the appearance of earlier taboos (like death, sex, or violence) in modern books for young people.

Next, I will give a few examples to illustrate how the model works; I do not intend to produce a comprehensive historical analysis. These examples do not have any apparent relation with each other, but they are purposefully chosen from different genres and text types in order to show that the model is indeed universal and applicable for historical studies on a larger scale.

From Visual to Verbal Code

Before 1917, children's literature in Russia was dominated by sentimental and moralistic stories and verses, often written bywomen authors with limited talent. The world of children's literature was restricted to the nursery. Maxim Gorky and Korney Chukovsky took the very first steps in creating a new children's literature based on totally new principles and ideas. Chukovsky's first children's story in verse, *The Crocodile,* was written in 1916, but was not published intil the summer of 1917 after quite a few publishers had rejected it on the grounds that it was "a book for guttersnipes." And it certainly was! In this book, the hurly-burly of street life intrudes into the safe nursery world of earlier children's literature. The burlesque, witty verse breaks all the rules for the old children's poetry: its protagonist was not a pretty kitten or bunny, but an abominable reptile, and it appeared in the very streets of Petrograd.

Indeed, this first postrevolutionary children's book in Russia was a peripheral phenomenon, but it took no more than several years before this new kind of literature superseded the early trash. Children's literature came out of the nursery into the open--into the streets, the workplace, real life. The prevailing code of the old children's literature (which may be compared to Victorian literature in Britain) included the closed, limited space, lack of freedom, and good manners. The new code is based on open, free space, free imagination, and wild, creative play. Of course, this change does not happen over the night, the process is dynamic, and the old code, banished from the central position, nevertheless remains on the periphery even today. It is hoped that it will never be permitted to come to the center again.

Another important aspect of the clash between the old and the new children's literature, which its promoters were well aware of, was that the prerevolutionary children's books were addressed primarily to children from well-off families who could read and whose parents could afford books. Since eliminating illiteracy was one of the most acute problems of the new regime, the result was the dominant visual code of the new children's literature.

When we compare early Soviet picturebooks with contemporary political posters, we see a striking similarity. This similarily is not exclusively explained by the fact that many poster artists also produced picturebooks for children. The aestethics of the 1920s in Russia appealed to thousands and millions of illiterate and half-literate citizens, children as well as adults. The typical propaganda posters from that period present vivid colors and simple, concrete contours, that are easy to memorize and easy to recognize. The principle for the first picturebooks was exactly the same. It was during the 1920s that the only true picturebooks were ever produced in Russia--that is, books where the verbal and the visual aspects are the inseparable whole and cannot exist without each other.

When in the 1950s and later Chukovsky's verses were published again after years of oblivion, they were illustrated byartists other than those in the original picturebooks. While the matter of the artistic merits of both is arguable, the very idea of a picturebook as an organic whole apparently became alien to Soviet publishers from the 1930s onward.

This seemingly incomprehensible phenomenon is quite easy to account for with the help of our model. By the beginning of the 1930s, illiteracy in the Soviet Union had been defeated; and from then on the verbal aspect began to dominate literature for the young. Now there appeared stories, fairy tales, and juvenile novels, all of which were often richly illustrated, yet always with an emphasis on the text. These predominantly verbal children's books, in consistency with our model, appeared on the periphery, but very soon, by the middle of the 1930s, they took the place of earlier picturebooks and took firm hold of the central position in children's literature which they still have today. The first ventures with modern picturebooks in the 1980s have completely different prerequisites. Their origins should be sought in the Western picturebook, comic strip, animated cartoon, and the like--that is, in the context of totally different cultural codes.

In one of his articles on the typology of culture, Yury Lotman shows the essential difference between the written and the prewritten type of culture. In developing his model, we may say that the difference between Soviet children's literature of the 1920s and the 1930s is typological. While the culture of the 1920s is primarily visual, that of the 1930s is predominantly verbal. The disappearance of the early picturebooks is but one link in the general shift of the typology of culture.

From Certainty to Hesitation

In his famous study of fantastic literature, the French scholar Tzvetan Todorov makes a clear distinction between the fantastic, the marvelous, and the uncanny. His material is eighteenth and nineteenth century literature, and he is not concerned at all with children's fantasy. If he were, however, it would most probably fall under the category of the marvelous. For Todorov, the foremost criterion of the fantastic is the hesitation of the protagonist (and the reader) as confronted with the supernatural.[5] In early fantasy for children the matter of belief is most commonly taken care of by explaining the wonderful adventure as a dream, as does Lewis Carroll in *Alice in Wonderland.* Another device is introducing a visible instrument of supernatural events, for instance, a magician or a magic object. This pattern is wellknown from the fantasy novels written by Edith Nesbit and many of her followers.

As early as the 1950s, however, the fantasy code became subject to a change. In the books by Lucy M. Boston or Philippa Pearce, the mechanism of the marvelous events is not revealed, and both readers and characters are confronted with mystery and hesitation as to reality of the magic--that is, exactly what Todorov's definition of the fantastic prescribes.

Upon contemplating the reasons, we must agree that modern fantasy is created within a different cultural context. The evolution of science and technology has radically changed our attitude toward a rich variety of phenomena dealt with in fantasy novels: parallel worlds, nonlinear time, extrasensory perception, and other supernatural events that modern science cannot explain but accepts as possible. Because modern science tolerates alternative explanations, in their texts writers can also give room to ambivalence, allow young readers to draw their own conclusions, and accept the notion that there can be more than one truth. The bifurcation itself may thus be said to have extraliterary sources, but it is quite easy to discover texts that mark the bifurcation point.

The later the progression in the evolution of the genre, the more hesitation we discover in fantasy texts. The boundaries between reality and the magic world are dissolved; the passage becomes less pronounced. Thus, the marvelous code--the "children's code"--gives way to the fantastic code in Todorov's meaning--the "adult code." The narrative patterns of fantasy for children become more sophisticated, which allows each pattern to contain more significant meaning. This is quite obvious in the fantasy novels of Alan Garner, Ruth Park, and Diana Wynne Jones.

From Social Engagement to Imaginative Writing

The 1960s and 1970s in Sweden were years of social engagement in children's literature. The authors began to take up a vast variety of issues that can affect children in society: parents' divorce, alcohol addiction or criminal behavior; the nightmares of school start when teachers fail to understand the child's psychology; the trauma of moving from countryside to large city, with subsequent mobbing by cruel classmates; sibling rivalry; unmarried teenage mothers; and so on.

This was a necessary and understandable reaction to the earlier idyllic children's literature which has sought to protect the young reader from the less attractive aspects of society.

But once the socially engaged code dominated children's literature, all other codes were banished to the periphery, among them the imaginative code of fairy tale and fantasy. Fairy tales were considered outdated and simply harmful to young readers because they were believed to take the child away from real problems, from everyday life with its misery, loneliness, and anguish--the key words of the Swedish children's books of the 1960s.

In 1973, Astrid Lindgren published *The Brothers Lionheart*, which burst all boundaries in the tight ghetto of children's literature. The book is imaginative, romantic, and full of adventure. It describes an alternative world, and it deals with death as an event that is, if not positive, at least nothing to be anxious about. All these aspects and many others gave rise to a storm of criticism against the book. Today the immediate reviews accusing Astrid Lindgren of escapism, of giving the young reader a wrong orientation in existential problems, and of using the fantasy form strike us as ridiculous. But the book did have its subversive effect, and it initiated a total shift in the main trends in Swedish juvenile prose.

Thus, *The Brothers Lionheart* can be regarded as a bifurcation point. Before it was published, the evolution of children's literature in Sweden was more or less predictable, in consistency with the dominating code. After *The Brothers Lionheart*, children's literature returned to imaginative writing. Today Swedish children's literature is following the path paved by Astrid Lindgren's novel. We cannot predict when the next bifurcation will occur.

True, imaginative literature remained in the borderline zone for quite a long time, and during the whole of the 1970s the social-realistic juvenile novels continued to appear. But already in 1980-1981 *two* basic studies were published in Sweden on fantasy for the young,[6] and the genre was generally accepted as appropriate and even welcome for children. In the early 1980s, a storm of fantasy enveloped Sweden, mostly in the form of translations, which both filled in previous gaps (such as *A Traveller in Time* by Alison Uttley from 1939, and some of Edith Nesbit's fantasy novels not published in Sweden before) and caught up with the development of the genre around the world, with names like Susan Cooper, Lloyd Alexander, and Patricia Wrightson.

The code shift did not directly affect Swedish children's literature in itself. Swedish fantasy is still practically nonexistent as a tradition, in spite of a few bright examples. Some attempts in the early 1990s were mostly derivative. But the indirect impact of the shift was all the more remarkable. The socially engaged juvenile novel did not, of course, vanish completely. It still exists, on the periphery, and it has elisited very little attention from either critics or readers. What has developed instead is historical and retrospective literature, often romanticized as the so-called *Shadow*-series by

Maria Gripe, which at first sight has all the earmarks of a traditional Gothic novel. Mystery, adventure, and the supernatural have become keywords in today's Swedish literature for the young; but this new code is by no means identical with the traditional adventure code known from Robert Louis Stevenson or Sir Walter Scott. It is not adventure or mystery for its own sake; it is the people that are brought into highlights. The supernatural is used to investigate how it can affect the young.

In this way, this new kind of literature (I do not venture to call it a genre since it involves many different genres and also to a great extent a convergence of genres) often manages to discuss the same issues and to convey the same ideas as the purely realistic literature of the 1960s and 1970s, without being as didactic as it often tended to be. Today's historical and retrospective literature plays the same role as fantasy does in some other countries. As Susan Cooper has put it: "Fantasy is the metaphor through which we discover ourselves."[7]

Moreover, when we reread some of the best Swedish children's books from the 1960s and 1970s, for instance, Maria Gripe's *Elvis and His Friends* (1972) and sequels, we discover that they, too, are not thoroughly realistic, rather, they also have tiny elements of the supernatural and the fantastic, which, of course, were completely ignored by the critics whose attention was focused exclusively on the social, mimetic codes of the texts.

From Circular to Linear Journey

The basic pattern in children's literature is the circular journey, that is, the plot development home--departure from home--adventure--return home. This pattern, which has its origin in the European Romantic philosophy, can be traced in practically any children's text, and not necessarily only to what is traditionally labeled as adventure genre. It can be found on different levels and in different shapes in all formats, ranging from picturebooks (Maurice Sendak's *Where the Wild Things Are* to take one example) to psychological novels like Cynthia Voigt's *Homecoming* (1981). Note the title of Voigt's work. The purpose of the journey is the maturation of the child (protagonist as well as the reader). But the return home is a matter of security: whatever hardships and trials are endured, safe home is the final goal.

A splendid example of this pattern is Edith Nesbit's short tale "The Town in the Library," written in 1898. The two children in her story get into the toy town they have built, and, escaping from hostile toy soldiers, they find their own house there. In that house, there is one more town which they in turn enter. Nesbit plays with the idea that this could go on forever, the children getting "deeper and deeper into a nest of towns in libraries in houses in towns in libraries in houses in towns in... and so on for always--

something like Chinese boxes multiplied by millions and millions for ever and ever." But this way, Nesbit continues, they would be getting further and further from home every time, and she hurries to take the children back to their own world and bring the story to a safe and happy ending.

The circular journey code has dominated children's literature since its very beginning, but very early we can discover sprouts of the opposite code on the periphery. One of the first authors to break the circular pattern, if only tentatively, was George MacDonald in *At the Back of the North Wind* (1871). At the end of the book it is understood that the boy Diamond will leave this world and enter the beautiful country at the back of the north wind which he previously was only allowed to watch. His death becomes the passkey to the other world, and death, at least in the Western tradition, can only be conceived as a linear journey.

A similar example is to be found in the last book of the C. S. Lewis's Narnia series. In the previous volumes, the children are brought into Narnia to perform a task, whereupon they are transported safely back into their own world. But in *The Last Battle* they die in a railway accident and are thus allowed to proceed into a world beyond this, beyond the point of no return. Here I will not discuss the possible interpretations of this passage, for I am interested in the pattern: the subversive linear code within the dominating circular code of traditional children's literature. Astrid Lindgren was, as in many other things, well before her time when she describes a linear journey in *Mio, My Son* (1954); she repeated the pattern twenty years later in *The Brothers Lionheart*.

The linear code is, of course, much more daring, and it presupposes the author's total confidence in the reader. It demands a good deal of courage for a child to accept the absence of security that brings the protagonist back home. The reader's own belief in the security of the world is shattered. But at least some modern authors take the challenge. The so-called open ending which is gradually becoming more frequent in juvenile novels should be seen as a modification of the linear code. Children's books with ready solutions bind the child's imagination and free thought. It is treacherous to give a modern sophisticated child-reader a "rational" explanation at the end: "And then he woke up, and it has only been a dream." This is by no means satisfying for a critical and creative author, who sees the open ending as the only possible way of appeal to modern young readers. I see the open ending as the utmost transformation of the "telling gap" of the reception theory. The presence of telling gaps in the narrative can be regarded as a criterion of literary quality: the more contemplative questions the reader is presented with, the better the writer has performed his task. The open ending is a way to stimulate questions. Therefore, the code shift toward the dominating open ending may be perceived as the most interesting feature of modern children's literature.

Peter Pohl, one of the best contemporary Swedish juvenile novelists, has renounced the old code. His characters are never brought back into the safety of home and family; instead, they leave security for whatever fate they may meet. If one ventures to summarize the experience of the 1980s, Pohl's highly appraised first novel *Johnny My Friend* (1985) is undoubtedly one of the central events in Swedish juvenile literature of the past decade, the bifurcation point that will set up a new code for future authors.

I have deliberately chosen examples from different kinds of literature as well as different periods and countries. I believethat my proposed model can be used in many types of research whenever a diachronical character of the studied phenomenon is to be underlined.

NOTES

1. Lotman's theory of cultural semiotics is best summarized in his *Universe of the Mind. A Semiotic Theory of Culture* (London: Tauris, 1990).

2. The term *jeans prose* was coined by Aleksander Flaker in his study *Modelle der Jeans Prosa* (Kronberg: Scriptor, 1975). The term is widely used in European research. See also Dagmar Grenz's essay in this volume.

3. Ilya Prigogine and Isabelle Stengers, *Order out of Chaos. Man's New Dialogue with Nature* (London, 1984).

4. Lotman, *Universe of the Mind*, pp. 230ff.

5. Tsvetan Todorov, *The Fantastic: A Structural Approach to a Literary Genre* (Cleveland--London: Press of Case Western Reserve University, 1973), p. 25.

6. Göte Klingberg, *De främmande världarna i barn- och ungdomslitteraturen* (Stockholm: Rabén & Sjögren, 1980) [The Strange Worlds in Children's Fiction]; Ying Toijer-Nilsson, *Fantasins underland. Myt och idé i den fantastiska berättelsen* (Stockholm: EFS-förlag, 1981) [The Wonderland of Fantasy. Myth and Ideology in Fantasy Literature].

7. Susan Cooper, "Escaping into Ourselves," in *Fantasists on Fantasy*, eds. Robert H. Boyer and Kenneth J. Zahorski (New York:Avon, 1984), p. 282.

Writers Writing a Short History of Children's Literature within Their Texts

Isabelle Nières

Who is best able to perceive the production destined for children as a history made up of inventions, traditions, and splits, and not simply as a juxtaposition of books one happens to come across in a bookshop or library? The answer is straightforward: it is the adult and not the child, for the effort demanded relies heavily on the ability to capitalize on cultural knowledge and to build explanatory models. And who is trying to write this history? The answer in this instance is all of us, whose field of research rests on pictures, texts, pedagogical models, or the sociocultural conditions of production. In this essay I wish to draw attention to another adult who, *before the researcher,* also writes in his own way something resembling a short history of children's literature: here I mean the children's writer. And what he writes about the history of this literature, no one could get closer to children than he, because he places it within the very fabric of the texts that he writes for them.

Traditionally, children's literature has occupied only a marginal place in our culture as compared to adult reading; it is denied recognition by institutions, it is not accorded any literary esteem, and it is readily labeled "subliterature." Literature and subliterature are opposite inasmuch as literature writes within its texts the history of its practices and subliterature often seems to be written in a sort of naive ignorance of its own history. Bearing this perspective in mind, we can consider the presence of different intertextual games in children's literature--in particular, quotations, parodies, and references to a text, an author, or a genre--as so many attempts on the part of the writer to place his work in children's culture, and to define his aesthetic and ideological vision by affinity or opposition with other works. Thus, he establishes within his own text a small fragment of the history of children's literature that researchers can later build on and write.

The presence of a text within another text is of interest to the historian of children's literature from two standpoints. On the one hand, a quotation, in whatever shape or form, gives us a clue, among others, as to how famous or how esteemed an author or work is in a given culture during a particular epoch. On the other hand, references--whether they be mocking or respectful-- that an author or an illustrator may make with regard to a predecessor seem to be the authors' means frequently used most to define their aesthetic vision and their conception of books for children. These are the two points I want to discuss in more detail in this essay.

References and quotations are always good indicators as to the fame or esteem an author or a text enjoyed at a given moment in time within a particular milieu or a given national culture. Not everything is quotable. To be able to be used as a quote, a text must have a certain standing. In other words, it must be deemed worth quoting, and it must also be known widely enough for the reference not to be lost on the readers it is aimed at. Thus, although the quotation is less frequently used in children's literature than in literary adult culture, it is far from being a rare phenomenon. Here a further distinction must be made between the quotation that appeals directly to children and one that goes well over their heads and is meant uniquely for the benefit of adults. For the time being, I am going to put the second one aside and concentrate on the first. By compiling a list of quotations, references, and allusions, we can build up an impressionistic picture of a fictional body of readings and knowledge common to children of the same cultural background at a given moment in time, and, into the bargain, assess how long an author or work survived in collective memory. When does one give up quoting Arnaud Berquin and Miss Edgeworth? The most frequent references are based on the widest possible cultural background. Since the eighteenth century, Robinson Crusoe on his island has occupied such a place. Throughout the nineteenth century, many novels were redolent of Robinson Crusoe who still remains with us today in those dreams of islands common to both the writer andreader. Children play at Robinson Crusoe in Enid Blyton's *Secret Island* and Astrid Lingdren's *Pippi Longstocking*. Since the nineteenth century, ten or so fairy tales have established themselves in the realm of children's books: Little Red Riding Hood, Cinderella, Hansel and Gretel, Snow-White, the Ugly Duckling, Goldilocks and the three Bears, and so on. I will cite some examples of references or allusions to these fairy tales later in this essay.

References to readings, whether they be those the author makes through the hero or those he expects from his young readers, also give us an idea of the age group that such and such a text targets. Thus, to go into the detail of just how tiny the cross stitches of Charlotte and Emily's great grandmother were, the narrator of Rumer Godden's *The Doll's House* invites his young readers to think back to their reading of *The Tailor of Gloucester*, and she quotes the last sentence of Beatrix Potter's book: "so small, so small they looked as if they had been made by little mice."

Here the pleasure for the reader is doubly felt. The first pleasure is that of recognizing the quote, and the second, that of sharing the same cultural background as the adult. But the quotation of the first text by the second makes the child aware of the long path that must be trodden on between the moment when he read the little books by Beatrix Potter and that when he discovers Rumer Godden's novel. The anteriority of the quoted text over quoting text underlines the fact that the child has grown up and that each age group has its own readings. These stages, which come one after another in the readings of childhood, are sometimes presented as battles won in theprogression to new fields. Thus, in the most famous schoolbook, issued in France during the Third Republic, *Le Tour de la France par deux enfants* (The tour of France by two children) by Madame Bruno, the owner of a ship questions the 7-year-old hero whom he has just discovered reading: "What are we reading here? The story of Tom Thumb or is it Little Red Riding Hood?"

The child raises his head in protest because he is actually reading a history book that presents a treasury of biographies of all the great men of France. "Tales, [...] oh certainly not sir; these are beautiful stories, I assure you. And even the pictures in the book are real. Look, take this one; that is a portrait of La Pérouse, a great navigator, who was born in Albi."

It is as if each age group should shrug off the precedent, and it is very significant that it is in a schoolbook that we find this suppression of pleasure in fiction and, on the contrary, the value placed on moving on to the readings of "true happenings."

In a way that is not quite so common, we can discover a text that is cited not as reading already done by the child-hero or the child-reader, but as suggested further readings. In Suzanne Prou's *Caroline et les grandes personnes* (Caroline and the grownups), there is an old clock which, at night, explains to the heroine, a young girl of about 8:

Sometimes [...] in exceptional circumstances children can actually pass through mirrors. One day this happened to a young girl whose name I'm sure you know, she was called Alice, you must have read her story that Mr Lewis Carroll told so well.--I haven't read it, said Caroline.--Well, you should have, it is a most beautiful story. You will read it.

Suzanne Prou's work dates back to 1978, and the reference to *Through the Looking-Glass* is a good indication of Lewis Carroll's standing at that particular time in the French cultural climate. Less well-known and recognized much later than *Alice's Adventures in Wonderland,* the sequel is regarded as more difficult than the former and therefore is reserved for cultivated adults and an élite of children who are good little readers.

Two remarks are brought to mind concerning the capacity of one book referring to another. One concerns translation, and the other the presence of pictures in children's books.

Children's literature has always been translated and cross-translated. hence, translation has strongly contributed to create an international children's culture, as the above example from Suzanne Prou's book testifies. It is perhaps through these literary references that the translator has not chosen, but that are imposed on him by the text he is translating, that we can measure the opposite fact, that is, a resistance to the internationalization of culture. When a text for children is translated, and thus when it finds itself displaced from its own culture into quite another culture, it is most interesting to examine what part of the intertext has remained, what part is explained by a footnote, and what part is merely dropped or replaced in the translated text by new references, borrowed this time from the culture of the children, for whom it is translated. Here, I will take only one example. *Little Women*, Part I, by Louisa May Alcott, has been translated time and time again intoFrench since its first translation in Lausanne in 1872. The filigree presence of Cinderella "en les pantoufles jolies" to suggest Meg's joy at the ball does not create any trouble for the translator because the allusion is readily spotted by the young French reader. More awkward are Jo's readings when crying over *The Heir of Redcliffe*, quoting *Uncle Tom's Cabin*, devouring *The Vicar of Wakefield,* or founding the Pickwick Club with her sisters. The temptation is great (and even greater today when *Uncle Tom's Cabin* is the only title that still means something for a French reader) to cut everything out or simply to write, as a recent translation offers, that Jo bit into her apple "crying all the while over a book she was reading."

As far as "playing Pilgrims" is concerned and the references which Louisa Alcott makes throughout her novel to John Bunyan's *Pilgrim's Progress*, all translators know that they are looking at a canonical text of English Protestantism which is practically unknown in France and completely alien to the dominant Catholic culture. Most of these references are cut, and a few are translated and explained in extensive footnotes.

Thus, the treatment of references and allusions allows us to distinguish, for each particular country and period, the part of that culture that is felt as international and accessible to the young reader and that which the translator thinks is out of reach because they are out-of-date or indomitably too national. Translation reveals the unknown: it gives an insight into the secret frontiers of cultures.

My second remark concerns the presence of pictures in children's books. Quotations, references, and allusions are not necessarily textual; they can be in pictorial form. Pictures can either make allusions to a text or cite another picture. In a double page of *Rouge, bien rouge* (Red, truly red) by Nicole Claveloux, children "recognize" Little Red Riding Hood without hesitation, which leads them to look for and identify the wolf in the shadow of the curtain. It's Little Red Riding Hood yet again and a variation of her adventures with the bad big wolf which they can follow all through Claude Ponti's picture book *Adéle s'en mêle* (Adéle moves in). But it's a picture that Agnès Rosenstiehl cites in *Mon premier alphabet* (My first alphabet) by choosing the famous laughing cow, drawn before World War I by Benjamin Rabier for a brand of cheese, to stand for the letter V. Etienne Delessert cites one of the Wild Things drawn by Maurice Sendak in the illustrations he made for Eugène Ionesco's *Conte numéro 1* (Story number 1), as one of my children points out to me. Finally, Mitsumasa Anno combines the twofold power of the picture to refer to both texts and pictures in *Ce jour-là* (That day) and *Le jour suivant* (The day after). One can recognize pictures by Van Gogh, Seurat, Courbet, Millet, Cezanne, and Renoir. The eye scours the picture over and over again and takes in Tom Sawyer, the Pied Piper of Hamelin, Romeo and Juliet, Don Quixote, Little Red Riding Hood, Alice in Wonderland, the Three Little Pigs, the Ugly Duckling, Cinderella, Pinocchio, Ali Baba and the Forty Thieves--the list never ends. As for the second volume, one must add the life of Christ which is omnipresent throughout. Purposely dropping the barriers betweeen adult culture and children's culture in these picturebooks, Mitsumasa Anno offers us a shortened version of European culture as seen through the eyes of a twentieth-century Japanese. In his way, he gives living proof of the internationalization of several classics of Western children's culture.

I should like to make three additional points concerning the capacity of the picture for quotations. First of all, it is clear that to make a reference to a text effectively, the illustrator not only has to call upon a famous narrative, but also to give pride of place either to a character whose physique or clothing is in a way his claim to fame (e.g., Little Red Riding Hood or Pinocchio), or scenes that remain in collective memory like emblems of the whole narrative: Cinderella losing her slipper, or Don Quixote charging at windmills. However, it can be noticed that Mitsumasa Anno indirectly cites Lewis Carroll in reusing the same profile that John Tenniel gave to the rabbit in *Alice's Adventures in Wonderland*. Here can be seen how, through a daisy-chain pattern of borrowings by an illustrator from another, a body of interpictorial references is born within children's literature itself. It must also be pointed out that, however famous a text cited by a picture, this fame may be limited to that very culture. Such is the case with the oral repertoire of songs and games which, unlike those fairy tales, do not cross borders freely. Where the text is translated, the picture is not. The picture does not succumb to the curse of Babel. This is the reason why in *The Jolly Postman* by Janet and Allen Ahlberg, the young French reader has no problems with Goldilocks and the Three Bears or Little Red Riding Hood and the wolf, but he cannot get the picture quotation on the last page because he has no knowledge of the nursery rhyme, "The cow jumped over the moon."

Finally, let us return to Etienne Delessert's quotation from *Where the Wild Things Are*. The point is not just to emphasize that the child should be acquainted with Maurice Sendak's picturebook to understand that there is an allusion from the one book to the other, but to wonder why Delessert chooses to refer to Sendak's book. And this leads to one last point I want to raise: Why does an illustrator cite another? Why does a writer refer to another writer or to a genre other than his own?

Allusions or references to writers or works commonly found in a children's repertoire are the means by which the author places himself with regard to his predecessors or his contemporaries, by which he can outline, by opposition or affinity, his own ideological and aesthetic vision.

This opposition can be stated and written down. This is how Arnaud Berquin, one of the founders of French children's literature, opens his foreword to *L'ami des enfants* (The children's friend):

This work has the double role of entertaining children and bringing them naturally to virtue by portraying it only in the best possible light. Instead of nonsensical fiction and of the fairy tale world in which their imagination has been led astray, children will find here only adventures they could actually come across in their everyday family lives.

This "nonsensical fiction" and "world of fairy tales" which have led children astray for so long are obviously the tales against which Berquin sets up his pedagogical project through short realistic narratives that take place in the child's day-to-day life. What is announced here in a foreword meant for adults can actually be put in the narrative itself, thus being aimed more precisely at child-readers. This is what we find in *Moineau la petite libraire* (Moineau the little bookseller), a novel by Trilby which dates back to 1936 and which clearly opposes two models of young girls. We read the following:

Each evening, since Mama's illness, she promised the one who listens to all prayers, to be a model little girl, not like those in Madame de Ségur's but a little girl who would be both model and modern, a little girl who wants to help Mama in her work because work spells independance, and one has the right to be proud of that independance.

A more complex and richer way for the writer to define himself by opposition consists in ridiculing the bygone models. Irony and parody become favorite tools. While making both adults and children alike laugh, the author forces them all to cast a critical eye on a children's culture which, for the adult was once their lot, or, for the children is still theirs. From the very first chapter of *Alice's Adventures in Wonderland*, Lewis Carroll denounces the pedagogues' use of fiction to dictate to children. Alice has just read "Drink me" on the label of the bottle and she hesitates, "for she had read several nice little stories about children who had got burnt, and eaten up by wild beasts and other unpleasant things, all because they would not remember the simple rules their friends had taught them."

Far from stopping at narrative literature duly illustrated by Mrs. Sherwood's *Fairchild Family*, Lewis Carroll will go on and scatter, as we well know, his story with parodies of certain poems and songs for children. He condemns with gusto their pathetic affectation, aesthetic poverty, and moral hypocrisy. Only the nursery rhyme in next to last chapter escapes hislashing tongue. Jumping the gun, we could say that Carroll defines the project of his first long narrative for children in opposition to a tradition of conventional edifying children's literature and with a strong affinity for the apparent gratuity of nonsensical nursery rhymes. Carroll makes general references to genres, whereas Edith Nesbit chooses to refer precisely to two great names to situate her own work. Nesbit's book *The Story of the Treasure Seekers* stretches between two pillars of English literature for children--the writing of Maria Edgeworth which dates back to the beginning of the nineteenth century and that of Kipling, a contemporary of Edith Nesbit. Nesbit writes *against* Maria Edgeworth and *for* Rudyard Kipling.

There is a chapter in Nesbit's novel in which the children, always wishing to restore the lost fortune of the Bastable family, imagine they can, as in Miss Edgeworth's novels, get protection from a "generous benefactor." They would only have to lie in wait on the moor for Lord Tottenham to pass that way, to get the dog from the house to attack him and then go to his rescue. The whole business falls through. The times of Miss Edgeworth and the "generous benefactors" have obviously gone.

But more important perhaps than discrediting the bygone models is the pleasure of introducing the new models, kinships, and admirations. Authors and illustrators seem to be bent on creating their imaginary family. I will just give a few examples here. In *La tarte volante* (The flying cake) by Gianni Rodari, the two heroes, Paolo and Rita, discover that the mysterious flying saucer is a gigantic cake. They dig out a tunnel, and from chocolate to crystallized fruit they get to the heart of the cake. And then what do they see?

In the middle of the grotto, sitting on the ground, a man was scribbling notes in the light of an electric lamp embedded in a plump crystallysed fruit.
--But it's Gepetto! murmured Rita.

Paolo and Rita follow in Pinocchio's footsteps and rediscover in the middle of the cake the very heart of Italian children's literature. Through Gepetto's double, Gianni Rodari joins up again with Collodi as if it was necessary for his writing to claim his roots and rediscover the founding father too.

A child is well able to recognize Gianni Rodari's reference to *Pinocchio's Adventures*, even if he is unable to grasp some of the reasons why. But we must point out that these references from one creator to another are not usually aimed at children. It is as if they were for private use. The artist is telling himself or other artists of his admiration, his friendships and his models. Claude Roy is speaking more of Claude Roy vis-à-vis Lewis Carroll, than he is speaking of Lewis Carroll to the children when, in *Le chat qui parlait malgré lui* (The cat who spoke despite himself), he slips in the following philosophical essay: "The question for that year was for the candidates to comment on a sentence by the famous thinker Ludwig Karol: 'Cats are philosophers without knowing it, just like philosophers are cats who know it.'" In the same way an illustrator can express his admiration for a painter or another illustrator. We know of the wealth of contemporary references to René Magritte. Philippe Dumas pays homage to André François in *Odette*, and it should not be difficult to compose a collective homage to Maurice Sendak from the picturebooks written and illustrated by Etienne Delessert (*Story number 1*), Tomi Ungerer (*The Beast of Monsieur Racine*), Mitsumasa Anno (*U.S.A.*), Susan Varley (*The Monster Bed*), Claude Ponti (*Adéle et la Pelle*), Mem Fox and Vivienne Goodman (*Guess What?*), Beatrice Poncelet (*T'aurais tombé*), and Gwen Strauss and Anthony Browne (*The Night Shimmy*).

The use of a picture to point to a literary model is rarer and more sophisticated. One example is in a picturebook by Christian Bruel and Anne Bosellec, published in 1986 under the title *Venice n'est pas trop loin* (Venice is not far off). The reader happens upon a photograph that has been touched up, accompanied by a hand-written comment: "That photo rings a bell!" It is a famous group photo of the authors published by Jérome Lindon of Les Editions de Minuit. Keeping adults in mind, we observe that the illustration here points to what the picturebook attemps to do, that is, to incorporate something of the narrative structures of the "nouveau roman" in literature for young people.

The author or the illustrator's ability to situate his own work with regard to his predecessors or his contemporaries is of great interest to the researcher. It actually shows that the artist consciously takes an active part in the changes in aesthetic and ideological norms. This intertextual or interpictorial presence constitutes material for any reflection on literary periodization within the production for children.

I should like to make two final points. The first is that authors and illustrators are not necessarily creators about whom we may have lots of information and documentation. Their books are one of the places, sometimes the only place, where they talk indirectly about their work and about their consciousness of it. The second point is that the presence of intertextual and interpictorial references undoubtedly shows an aspiration to cultural legitimacy and social recognition. Their presence or their absence therefore indicates the stature of the author or the work within a given children's literature. By their very presence, quotations, allusions, and the various forms of references possible are already a significant piece of information for the historian.

Equal But Different? The Incorporation of Children's Books in National Histories of Literature

Sonja Svensson

How should historical accounts of children's literature be related to the history of adult literature? An answer to that question is suggested here through a discussion of three basic patterns as well as my personal experiences with applying one of them.

Let us start with the obvious. In the beginning, books for children were an offspring of adult literature and were regarded as a means of education and upbringing rather than as works of art. From our point of view, such labels on the results were not totally unjustified. With the aesthetic development and growing quantities of this literary kind, however, came the need for documentation and evaluation. Our early colleagues were often pedagogues, educating future intermediaries, that is, librarians and teachers. Like the times they lived in, their minds were set on providing standards and ideals rather than literary surveys. Nevertheless, they took the first steps toward a goal we have not yet been able to reach: the recognition of children's books as part of any nation's total literary achievement.

History--But How?

The three patterns for relating children's books to the history of adult literature may be named *separation*, *incorporation*, and *integration*. Before concentrating on two of them, I will briefly define and discuss them all. Had I "but world enough and time" I would of course draw parallels with other types of literature often neglected by literary historians: chapbooks, women's literature, best-sellers, and so on, but here it must suffice to mention that such comparisons could easily be made.

Separation

Although the start was reluctant, and occurrence must be seen in relation to the total output and general status of children's books, the separate national history of children's literature is by now a flourishing and even, in prestigious publishing houses, a well-recognized professional genre. However, there are gaps to fill in, and it is probably safe to say that in most countries, early periods, classics, and other literary highlights are more thoroughly investigated than, for example, the last decades and all kinds of trivial reading matter. Very obvious, too, is a general tendency to make amends for old sins by including more illustrators and picturebooks in recent surveys.

Incorporation

The good idea of inserting special sections on books for children in national literary histories was implemented by the German Wolfgang Menzel as early as 1827 (*Die Deutsche Literatur*). Well-known examples from our century are Harvey Darton's and Algernon Tassin's contributions in the Cambridge histories of English and American literature, respectively (published in 1914 and 1919). The Nordic countries have been more reluctant to recognize such a basic equality. In the last decades, however, Denmark, Finland, and Norway have all published extensive historical surveys carrying sections on children's books. In Sweden this was not done until 1989. Since I have been involved in that process myself, I will presently return to the subject.

Integration

By the term *integration* I understand the principle of dealing with authors for children alongside their "adult" colleagues instead of gathering them in special sections, not forgetting children's books when double authorships are examined.

My readers may be better informed, but personally I have never come across such an all-embracing history of literature. And despite the attraction of the project it also implies some problems. First of all, where are the polyhistorians to master such masses of literature? If both kinds are to be seen simultaneously against relevant background (and as we all know children's literature needs thorough interdisciplinary treatment) won't the representation of, for example, each literary epoch be unwieldy and make literature itself a secondary matter? And finally, provided that such obstacles could be eliminated, does anyone actually need this total integration all along the line? My answer to that slightly rhetorical question is the negative.

Separation--A Happy Divorce?

Some advantages of the separate history of children's books are so obvious that in mentioning them I must ask the reader not to take offense. Everyone realizes that, given a certain space, by concentrating on one kind of literature, you can expand its background, exhaustively discuss genres and subgenres, and include more names and titles. Thus, a separate history of children's books may afford the luxury of an interdisciplinary approach as well as accounts of special literary media such as the widespread readers, periodicals, and, of course, picturebooks--to name just a few.

But there are other benefits. A specialized writer can count on a more homogeneous audience and therefore presuppose some knowledge of the basic writings as well as the definitions andterminology of the field. This, of course, saves space for more intriguing arguments. It also facilitates insider references and even jokes that may enliven both reader and author.

Finally, the author of a separate study of children's books should be able to desert the defensive positions that are so often taken in the presence of adult literature. The aim of well-informed, committed but not unduly apologetic writers in this genre should be less persuasive description and backbone praise and more intelligent, critical analysis.

But much as I believe that we need the concentration *and* expansion of the separate history, I can see dangers in that method too.

The primary risk, and one that breeds others, is, of course, that of isolation. A "ghettoization" of children's literature should also be avoided in theoretical applications of our subject. And surely there are studies of children's books that seem to ignore even highly useful achievements in other parts of literary research and historiography. For example, the definition and naming of certain literary epochs and genres according to special conditions in children's literature must not be an end in itself, so that obvious parallels and connections are overlooked. Neither should we reverse the common mistake made in studies on adult literature that seldom mention children's books even by very prominent authors. And perhaps most important of all, if the two literatures are kept apart, many professional and otherwise interested individuals might never get to know the history and development of children's literature and therefore not realize the essential unity of any nation's literary heritage.

By now, you may believe that the totally integrated history is not such a bad idea after all. However, in my opinion, the best complement to separate studies--which we can never do without--is the incorporation of sections on children's literature in all national histories of literature. Let me finally share some personal experiences of such a project with you.

Sweden Incorporating--At Last

In 1984, plans were made for a seven-volume history of Swedish literature which would include popular reading matter and children's books. Sweden's most prestigious publishing house, the Bonnier Company, had engaged Professor Lars Lönnroth of Gothenburg and the famous author and literary historian Sven Delblanc, as writing editors, so to speak. When asked to cover children's literature, I was inclined to accept the challenge, although one basic condition was far from favorable. The space allotted equaled only sixty pages, distributed on two of the planned volumes. That was a rather tight order, even though bibliographical references were to be published separately. But there were redeeming factors too. Space had been reserved in the right volumes, allowing me to investigate our two golden eras: the turn of the last century and the postwar period. Condensed accounts of the beginnings and later development of children's literature in Sweden were also requested. The plans for interspersed articles on literary media, genres, and authorships, together with promises of ample space for illustrations, indicated some extra possibilities.

As I see it, a historical survey of this kind should try to cover all the important phases and tendencies in children's literature. How can we otherwise assert the basic oneness of literature that I have referred to before? I firmly believe that rather than picking the plums, that is, a few authors already known to each and everyone, out of the cake, one should leave children's literature for the specialized study.

Since I could agree with the general layout of this project, I accepted the offer and set to work in the summer of 1987. By then I had also participated in workshops with other authors involved, where problems of both general and specific interest were discussed and important demarcations made.

As pointed out before, ample space and a homogeneous audience are advantages of the separate study. Consequently, the opposites are likely to complicate the incorporation of special material into a more comprehensive account. Not surprisingly, the restricted space proved to be my biggest problem, at times nearly heart-rending. The mixed public called for some rather basic discussions, and there were heaps of books and authors that had waited too long for this kind of recognition. An institution like Astrid Lindgren should have had at least ten pages, but could be assigned only three. Moreover, backgrounds had to be reduced to sketches, the individuality of each period defined without much ado and authorships and books singled out for closer scrutiny with the utmost care. The danger of mere enumerating was imminent in covering the postwar period, when the number of well-established authors and illustrators has grown immensely. Here I had to disregard personal attachments and the awareness that every entrance--or lack of such--would be noticed in the end. Thus, authors sure to be included in a specialized study are left out or mentioned very briefly, either because they do not reach a certain artistic level or because they appear more typical of a genre or a trend than genuinely original.

Condensation in subject and style has its benefits too, of course, and most of the problems caused by limitation of space were solved tolerably well in the end. But one consequence I have not been able to avoid. Sorely aware of the fact that by criticizing I would have to disregard objects worthy of praise, my presentation is on the whole more apologetic than it ought to be. So it appears that the sound and intelligent criticism recommended earlier must await ampler space.

No doubt it was easier to cope with the other main problem, that is, deciding whom to address. The general aim of this work was to create a truly modern history of Swedish literature: easy and stimulating to read, lavishly illustrated, and free of old academic prejudices against popular taste and new media. The intended users were university students as well as high school students and anyone with an interest in literature. Although doubtful about the interest in schools, I could go along with the purpose--all those people certainly need more information about children's books. Still I soon found myself addressing a more specific individual: a fictitious colleague in adult literature, skeptical at first but in the end readily exclaiming: "Well, I never knew--this is indeed very interesting!" Whether this conception would help others in the same situation I do not know, but for me it worked. Even writers of nonfiction need their implied readers at times.

Different But Equal--Concluding Remarks

With few exceptions, children's books differ in one way or another from adult literature, and therefore experts should make penetrating investigations of their history and characteristics. For reasons already given, this is best done in separate studies. But children's literature is nevertheless equal to literature for adults in the sense that they are both parts of the literary assets of a nation. This, of course, is the best reason for incorporating children's literature in any extensive account of literary history.

A final remark on the work I have been involved in: On the whole, the volumes have been very favorably received and have sold well. For my own part, I think the result has been--almost--worth the toil. Still it is clear that some extra pages would have made my work easier and the picture of Swedish literature more accurate. My advice to anyone with a similar task is therefore to fight for space! In that way we can eliminate the idea that any author for adults merits more literary attention than even the most distinguished creators of children's books.

Part II

INFLUENCE AND INTERACTION

Germany and the Germans As Depicted in British Children's Literature from 1870 to the Present

Emer O'Sullivan

How are Germany and the Germans portrayed in British fiction for young readers? This question was at the center of a research project carried out at the Freie Universität Berlin[1] in which texts published by British authors since 1870, the time of the Franco-Prussian War and the foundation of the German Empire, were traced and analyzed. Naturally, no limit was specified for the times in which the stories could be set, and the interrelations between dates of publication and times in which the texts were set provided some of the most interesting results of the study. All in all, 245 titles were found which were well distributed over both of these time spans, allowing quantitative statements as well as comparisons to be made about and across them.

The original question developed into a triple task for the study. The first was to establish how Germany and the Germans were portrayed in the texts. The second was to ascertain to what extent these images of Germany and the Germans were affected by the times during which the texts were actually written and what influence was exercised by the periods in which they were set. The final task was to analyze in detail how elements of the image of Germany were used in different texts and to see what functions were allocated to them.[2]

The results of this study, in which a variety of facets of the image of Germany were explored, revealed, and discussed, may be found in O'Sullivan (1990). Here only part of one particular aspect of the study can be discussed in detail: the interrelations between the time in which a story is written and the period in which it is set. This will be done by looking at some points in the distributions of the texts within the time spans of the first dates of publication and of time settings; going on to address the question of the attitude toward Germany revealed in the texts in relation to these distributions; and concluding with a comparative analysis of two books, written at the same time but set during different periods, to illustrate the influence of the relationship between these two time axes on the treatment of the image of Germany in the texts.

Dates of Publication and Time Settings: The World Wars

It is a truism to say that works of fiction are influenced by the period in which they are produced and that periods of time bring forth fiction that at least partially reflects their preoccupations. If we take the corpus of almost 250 texts written for young readers by British authors which have something to do with Germany and examine their dates of publication, it is immediately apparent that the times of the two world wars, years of open hostility between those two nations, were periods[3] of substantial production in Britain of such fiction with a "German" connection. 20% of all the books in the corpus were published between 1914 and 1920, and 15% during the Second World War. In a period of just 14 years, that is, in just under 10% of the total amount of time covered by the corpus, 35% of all the texts found which were relevant to this study was published. The leanest period is also interesting: that of the Weimar Republic and Hitler's *Machtergreifung*, a time during which much about Germany (and especially Berlin) was written by British authors for an adult readership. During this period, at least initially, when it had suddenly become fashionable among the literati to "praise everything German,"[4] only 3% of the corpus was published.

If we look at the distribution of the periods of time in which the texts of the corpus are set, we see that, here too, the time settings of the world wars clearly dominate: each accounts for about 27% of all time settings in the corpus. Thus, over half of all the texts are set in the two world wars.[5]

How do these time settings relate to the dates of publication? We have seen a dominance of two time settings--that of the two world wars. We have also seen a glut of books produced during those periods. Does this mean that the dates of publication and the time settings concur, or are these time settings also to be found in texts published at later dates? If so, at which later dates?

Distribution of World War Settings over Periods of Dates of Publication

Not surprisingly, we find the First World War to be the dominant time setting in the books published between 1914 and 1919 and in the interwar period. Immediately after that, however, in books published during the

Second World War, this time setting vanishes completely. Not one single book of all those published between 1939 and 1946 is set between 1914 and 1919. The First World War, therefore, which could have been used as a mode of writing about the enemy of the time in fiction without ostensibly dealing with the present, does not feature as a historical foil in the books written during the years of the Second World War. All the texts about Germans at war published during that time are topical, referring only to the current war. In the books published between 1950 and 1967, only two feature the time of the First World War as a setting, but since the end of the 1960s we find a sudden surge of interest in that period (15 out of 67 texts being set then).[6] This result is not a coincidence: it is almost exactly repeated in books published during the same period and set in the Second World War. Not many of the books published between 1950 and 1967 have the Second World War as their time setting (5 out of 24 texts), but after 1967, after the 25 years have passed which, according to Mary Cadogan and Patricia Craig is the length of time a period takes "to progress from dullness or desolation to absorbing interest,"[7] the number is 26 out of 67 texts.[8]

If these figures applied to war in West German children's literature, an explanation for the rise and fall of frequency would not be too difficult to find: the 1950s and early 1960s with the *Wirtschaftswunder* and integration of the Federal Republic of Germany into the Western bloc suppressed the topic of war. Not until the events of 1968 rekindled the discussion of the past did it become a focus of attention. But it is not German children's books which are the issue at hand, but British ones, and so this explanation cannot apply. Britain's relationship to the war is a totally different one: the victories and heroic deeds, the "doing without" of the population at large and their brave endurance are celebrated in British culture. Why, then, was there a restraint in writing about that time and about Germany's part in it during the 1950s and 1960s? Could it be that the cognitive dissonance between Germany on the one hand as the enemy during the Second World War, and on the other hand the newly founded Federal Republic as one of Britain's NATO and trade partners led to the topic of war being pushed into the background in the 1950s and early 1960s, and that it wasn't until after 1967 that the *Zeitgeist* and temporal distance permitted it to be brought up again? Or was it simply a case of having had to wait until a generation of writers came of age whose formative years had been during the war and who now wanted to write about that time?[9]

The popularity of wartime settings among British children's books that feature Germans is not to be seen simply as a result of the periods of hostility between Britain and Germany. War settings have always proven popular in children's books, providing a context of conflict in which, for example, bravery, cunning, and loyalty in the face of an enemy can be shown.[10] However, the dominance of this theme and setting does seem to point toward a prevailing association of Germans with war in British children's fiction, which says as much about Britain's preoccupation with the war (the reason for which must also be sought in the importance of the perception of those periods for Britain's positive self-image) as it does about the image of Germany in Britain.

"Attitude" Toward Germany in the Texts

As we have seen, the time settings of war, especially those of the world wars, dominate in the corpus. The results of quantifying the times in which the texts were published and the periods in which they are set are interesting, but these figures alone do not indicate how the subject of Germany was (and is) treated in the various texts written and set in all the different times. For example, does each portrayal of Germans in a book set during the war times discussed here necessarily mean that they are portrayed as the Enemy, that they are depicted in an exclusively negative light? In order to try to answer such questions, to ascertain the general attitude toward Germany which prevailed in the texts, and to try to quantify it (knowing fully that this undertaking is a very risky one)[11] one of three evaluations, "positive," "negative," or "neutral," was allocated to each of the texts in the corpus.[12]

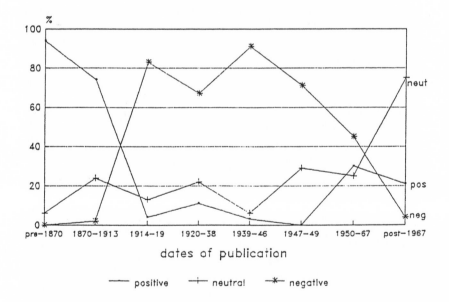

Figure 1. Attitude toward Germany in the texts of the corpus according to periods of dates of publication, from O'Sullivan, 1990, 78.

Attitude and Date of Publication

The results show that the negative evaluation, attributed to 40% of the texts of the corpus, is the most common one. However, the texts that are not negative are in the majority at 60% (31% neutral, 29% positive). When these evaluations of attitude are split up according to the periods of dates of publication, the immense differences between the periods is apparent. Figure 1 shows the attitudes of the books according to the periods of time in which they were published. The changes in attitudes can be seen to correspond to historical events. A positive attitude dominates in texts published before 1914, the outbreak of the First World War, after which the proportion of that attitude apparent in the texts drops drastically. Four out of five books written during the First World War are evaluated "negative." This attitude only lessens slightly during the interwar years to rise again, reaching a peak of 91% during the Second World War. After that, the proportion of "negative" texts diminishes, but even in books published during the 1950-1967 period, in which the share of neutral books reaches its second highest figure up to that point (25%), almost half the books (45%) are negative, with 30% positive. Not until after 1967 does anything that would seem to resemble the pattern observed before the First World War recur, with just 4% of texts negative (1870-1913: 0%) and 96% not negative (1870-1913: 100%).[13]

Attitude, Time Setting and Dates of Publication

Returning now to the periods of time in which the texts are set--again taking the times of the two world wars as our examples--relating them to their dates of publication and looking at theattitudes evident according to those dates, we obtain a concretization of the general results discussed above.

Figures 2 and 3 show the attitudes to be found in books set during the two world wars according to their dates of publication. The parallels are striking. Stories set in both periods and written before 1968 reveal an almost exclusively negative attitude toward Germany. The picture changes drastically after 1967 in both cases, mirroring the general result already obtained. Not a single book in either setting published after that date could be rated negative in attitude. Although the neutral books dominate (13 out of 15 books) among those published after 1967 which have a First World War setting, those rated positive are in the majority for the books published after that date with a Second World War setting, accounting for 19 out of 26 texts.What this result does not mean is that the First World War is seen in a neutral light and that the deeds of the Germans during the Second World War are praised in books written after 1967. According to the criteria for evaluating the texts, it means that in the case of the neutral books, the author--on balance--neither comes down on the side of the Germans nor attacks them. The positive books set in the Second World War do not support the Nazi cause. They are largely books in which one main German character (often a prisoner of war in England) is presented with almost exclusively agreeable characteristics and in such a way that the readers are likely to respond to him affirmatively. The negative, brutal side of Germany during this time also features in most of these books, but the positive power of the individual German character dominates.

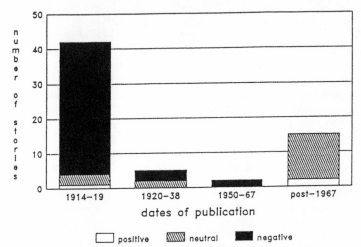

Figure 2: Attitude toward Germany in stories set in time between 1914 and 1918 according to the dates of publication, from O'Sullivan, 1990, 84.

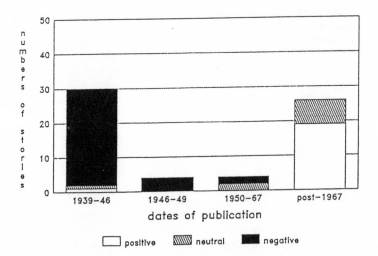

Figure 3: Attitude toward Germany in stories set in time between 1939 and 1945 according to the dates of publication, from O'Sullivan, 1990, 85.

The interrelations between dates of publication and time settings are at their most apparent when dealing with the treatment of the time setting of the Second World War in books published during that time and in those published over twenty years later. The authors publishing during the war felt they had to keep their young readers' spirits up to help them to believe that the British cause was just and that the Germans were evil, and that Britain would conquer in the end. Examples of the titles produced at that time are Charles Gilson's *Through the German Hordes* (1941) or W. E. Jones's *Biggles Defies the Swastika* (1941). The writers of retrospective books about the Second World War could, on the other hand, describe it from the tranquility of peacetime and could allow themselves to present a more complex and differentiated picture of events. The readers, too, more than twenty years later, were growing up secure in the knowledge that the war had been fought and won. They could be presented with a more equivocal approach and should be in a position to question motives and to accept the notion that good and evil could be found on both sides. This differentiation was not--could not have been--asked of their young readers by authors publishing during the war years. The radical change in attitude toward Germany and the Germans of the war years in books published after 1967 shows that the time had come for a more discriminating treatment of the world wars in British children's literature. In the case of books set in the Second World War, it was thought that they would help counteract the all too frequent equation German = Nazi.

Those differences in attitude relate to the treatment of the same time settings in texts that were published in different periods. In order to show the ways in which Germans can be portrayed in texts published at the same time but with different time settings, I would now like to briefly discuss two texts written in the 1970s, one set during the Second World War and the other set contemporaneously in the late 1970s.

Retrospective Germans: *The Machine Gunners*

The first book, *The Machine Gunners*, earned the Carnegie Medal for its author, Robert Westall, in 1975. It is set in the time of the Second World War, and in it a group of English children who are determined to "have a go" at the Germans encounter Rudi, a German rear gunner, who falls from the skies into their lives. Rudi is presented as a totally positive figure. The contrast to "the Germans," who are talked about a great deal but who do not appear as persons in the book, begs to be made. While they are presented as faceless hordes, Rudi is an individual; while they are described as destroying everything around the children in war, he treats his young friends with the utmost consideration; while they are dedicated to fighting for their Fatherland and for Hitler, he rejects both of these. When the children first set eyes on him, they realize that he does not conform to their ideals about what a Nazi was supposed to look like:

And indeed the tattered wretch before them was not much like those black shiny-booted storm troopers who goose-stepped nightly through their dreams. "He ain't got no swastikas!"--"He's not a blond beast!" [...] His hair was long, black and greasy, and going a bit grey at the sides, like Mr. McGill's. He really looked like somebody's dad; a bit fed-up and tired. (p. 117f)

Rudi is a German, but at the same time he is not a "German." As a character, he is presented as the ideal type of a non-German,where "German" is taken to be synonymous with "evil" and "Nazi"as it undoubtedly is in the imaginations of the English characters in the book. The author develops his positive figure against this background of negative Germanness. Rudi does not think and behave the way Germans are expected to. *But he exists only in contrast to them.*

If "not being evil" is subtracted from the characterization of Rudi, not much remains. He never speaks about his country orhimself to the children. The only German things about him are his uniform and his language. To the same degree to which "the Germans" are dehumanized in the imaginations of the English in the book, the humane German is de-Germanized.

Knowing Rudi does not change the children's hatred of and determination to fight against "the Germans." The reason for this is to be found in the time setting. The work is set in the Second World War, and the children's fear and loathing of the Germans and their desire to fight against them is presented as being historically valid. Those facts cannot be changed. So although they become very attached to an individual German, it does not affect the way the children feel about "the Germans." The nice individual German in the story is a concession to the time in which the story was written. Modern-day readers should be shown that there are "nice Germans," too. That is the function of Rudi, the nice German in *The Machine Gunners;* a lesson in international understanding. The time setting is that of the Second World War, the logic of the children's actions tallies with that period, but the exclusively positive German owes everything to the time in which the book was written, the 1970s.

Contemporary Germans: *Albeson and the Germans*

I would like to contrast *The Machine Gunners* with a book that was written around the same time but has a contemporary time setting. Jan Needle's *Albeson and the Germans* was published in 1977.

At the outset of the story, Jimmy Albeson is playing truant. He hears from his little sister that two German children are coming to their school. If there is one thing Albeson is certain of, having heard it often enough from his grandfather, it is that Germans are cruel monsters who eat people. He decides that every effort must be made to prevent the Germans from coming.

He and his friend Smithie seek the help of a supposed witch who says that the boys have to break into the school on the weekend. The prospect terrifies Albeson, but he is prepared to do anything to stop the Germans. Smithie goes berserk when in the school, and he wreaks terrible damage.

They both have to run away, and Albeson ends up as a stowaway on a ship which he believes to be English. As it happens, however, it is a German ship. When Albeson realizes this--he thinks he hears someone saying "Donner und Blitzen"--he panics, climbs up the mast, falls, injuring himself badly, and has to be confined to a sick-bay until the ship returns to his hometown. During this time, he becomes friendly with some of the crew, and when he leaves theship for hospital he has decided to learn the German language.

Albeson "knows" about the Germans from the stories his grandfather told him, from the films he has seen, and from war comics. One of his dreams is populated by

the countless hordes from off the pages of his favourite comics, all shouting "Achtung," "English pigdog," "Donner and Blitzen" and other peculiar oaths. Albeson had found himself time after time stuck on the barbed wire at the top of a prison camp fence as the machine guns opened up from the guard towers and the searchlights lit up the fangs of the dogs at the bottom waiting to tear him from limb to limb. (p. 25)

This image of Germany motivates the actions that get him deeper into trouble until, as a stowaway, his final stereotype-induced deed takes place and he almost manages to kill himself as a result of his panic.

On the ship he meets his first real Germans. All the crew are exceptionally kind to Albeson, and they have a good time laughing and joking together. Albeson's attitude toward Germans undergoes a sea-change after which he even finds the German language attractive. He listens to the sailors as they sometimes "spoke in German to each other, which seemed to relax them. Albeson decided he'd learn German when he got back to England. It sounded good" (p. 121).

The daydreams Albeson has about Germans at the end of the book are very different from those he had at the beginning. He sits in the hospital garden imagining that Hans and Erica Grundmann--the German children he was so afraid of at the beginning--come to visit him there, and he says to them: "Guten Tag. You can call me Albeson" (p. 121). But if this had happened it would have been laying on the happy German end a bit thick, so the author wisely decides to conclude the daydream and indeed the whole story with the words "But of course, they never came" (Ibid).

The Interrelations Between the Dates of Publication and Time Setting of *The Machine Gunners* and *Albeson and the Germans*

The comparison of *The Machine Gunners* and *Albeson and the Germans* illustrates some aspects of the interrelations between the dates of publication and time settings. The portrayal of the Germans in the two books displays a certain similarity; in both, images of brutal, ruthless Germans are pitted against those of kind, caring ones. The difference in time setting, however, with the first book set during the Second World War, means that, although the negative images in *The Machine Gunners* are granted a certain historical validity, justifying the actions of the youngsters against the Germans, they are shown to have none at all in the late 1970s, the time in which *Albeson and the Germans* is set.

The validity of negative images of the Germans and the response to those images is therefore seen to be influenced, if not determined, by the choice of time setting in books written at the same time. The use of positive images is also interrelated to the dates of publication and the time setting. The presence of a Rudi, a good, nice German deserter, would have been unthinkable in a book set in the Second World War and published at that time. That both authors under discussion here are keen to show that "there are nice Germans" is evident, but the consequences for the narrative are not the same because of the difference in time settings. In *The Machine Gunners,* the "good" German who is born out of the spirit of the 1970s competes with the images of the "evil" Germans. The two time axes determine elements of the story which, on the level of the narrative, run on parallel lines and fail to interfere with or influence one another. The contrast, the point of connection between the two, has to happen in the head of the reader. The "good" German never represents more than a positive cliché characterized by the absence of the negative clichés of the Germans dominant in the time setting of the story. This is a well-intentioned attempt to show a good person in the midst of a barbaric war, but, because of the time setting in the Second World War and because of the undifferentiated characterization, it does not and cannot lead to any examination of or discussion about the different images of the Germans in the text.

In *Albeson and the Germans,* we find images of the Germans which are rooted in the time of the Second World War and are used in the narrative to illustrate that they are no longer relevant in the 1970s. These images drive Albeson to do his utmost to prevent the German children from coming to his school. They not only provide a theme or an illustration of an idea, but they also form an intrinsic part of the narrative. Without them there would be no story. The concurrence here of time setting and date of publication means that, while using images from the 1940s, Needle can functionalize them to illustrate that they have no justification thirty years later without having to contend, as Westall did, with questions of past validity. The interrelationship between the different time settings with the same dates of publication in the case of these two books written in the 1970s can, therefore, be seen as a determining element in the treatment of the German theme in British children's fiction.

NOTES

1. The project was funded by the Berlin-Forschung section at the Freie Universität Berlin.

2. A theory of the different functions and uses of national stereotypes in fictional texts is developed in Emer O'Sullivan, *Das Ästhetische Potential nationaler Stereotypen in literarischen Texten. Auf der Grundlage einer Untersuchung des Englandbildes in der deutschsprachigen Kinder- und Jugendliteratur nach 1960.* (Tübingen, 1989).

3. I must ask the reader to accept, without a detailed explanation on my part, the periodization decided upon in the analysis. A discussion of it can be found in Emer O'Sullivan, *Friend and Foe. The image of Germany and the Germans in British Children's Fiction from 1870 to the Present.*(Tübingen, 1990), pp. 59ff.

4. Cf.John White, "Sexual Mecca, Nazi Metropolis, City of Doom. The Pattern of English, Irish and American Reactions to the Berlin of the Inter-War Years". In: Derek Glass, Dietmar Rösler and John J. White, eds. *Berlin. Literary Images of a City. Eine Grosstadt in der Literatur* (Berlin, 1989) p. 125.

5. If those set in the Thirty Years' War and the Franco-Prussian War are added to these, the total sum of books with wartime settings is 60%.

6. Even though, as Cadogan and Craig wrote in 1978, "the first world war has not yet begun to exercise the fascination of the second. Its appeal is perhaps less nostalgic than historical" (Mary Cadogan and Particia Craig, *Women and Children First. The Fiction of Two World Wars.*London, 1978, p. 111).

7. Ibid., p. 365.

8. Cf. O'Sullivan, 1990, p. 73.

9. This explanation is suggested in Carmel Egan, "Children's Second World War Novels". M.A. Thesis in Librarianship (University of London), 1985, p.23.

10. Margaret Marshall writes about the general attractiveness of war as a historical setting in children's literature in her *An Introduction to the World of Children's Books* (Aldershot: Hants, 1982) p. 74.

11. A discussion of the pros and cons of such a procedure can be found in O'Sullivan, 1990, pp. 75ff.

12. The three evaluations were used as follows: "Positive" denotes texts in which authors write about Germany or Germans in such a way that the readers are likely to respond in a positive manner. It can happen by an author choosing a German setting for a pleasant tale, for example, or by presenting Germans with almost exclusively favorable characteristics. "Negative" denotes texts in which Germany and the Germans are presented in an almost entirely unfavorable light, having few redeeming features, as in propagandistic texts, for example. "Neutral" books--usually the most differentiated ones--are those in which the author neither comes down on the side of the Germans nor rails against them. In many of the "neutral" texts, both "negative" and "positive" Germans are to be found.

13. The difference here is that the distribution of positive and neutral is almost reversed. Between 1870 and 1913 the positive count was 94% with 6% neutral; after 1967, the positive count was 21% with 75% neutral.

Children's Literature in France and Italy in the Nineteenth Century: Influences and Exchanges

Mariella Colin

All those who are interested in children's and young people's literature know that this is one of the most international of all literary branches, and since its rise to fame, it has been the object of endless translations and exchanges throughout European countries.[1] Even if they have sometimes been far from perfect these translations have become a special means of international communication, by stimulating exchanges and giving free vent to foreign influences.

A historical study of the interactions in this domain between France and Italy during the nineteenth century will give us an idea of the importance of exchanges between these two countries whose geographical proximity and linguistic similarities have been the source of intensive and lasting political and cultural relations. This study required first an elaboration of a *corpus* of French and Italian works of which Italian and French versions, respectively, were found. Next these texts were analyzed by situating them in the context of both their country of origin and the country for which they were translated. Thus, in the case of each country the ideological, cultural, and literary currents are considered, together with the state of international relations between the two nations.

The method used in this analysis has enabled an estimate of the part played abroad by both these national productions in the light of a precise historical perspective. It has also made it possible to go beyond a simple statement of the gross figures concerning the published translations. In order to establish the results of this study in comparative literature, I concentrate on the most fertile epochs of exchanges and borrowings: first of all, the period between the end of the eighteenth century and the end of the First Empire (1770-1815); then the twenty years of the Monarchy of July and the Italian Risorgimento (1830-1850); and finally, the years of the establishment of the Third Republic and the Kingdom of Italy (1870-1900).

The Birth of Children's Literature in France and Italy, 1770-1815

The origins of children's literature go back to the Enlightenment when the beginnings of a new pedagogy placed childhood at the center of philosophical thinking and led to the creation of works specially conceived for children's emotional needs and intellectual capacities. The development of this new genre occurred under the impetus of cultural and ideological currents that influenced the whole of Europe and caused writers in every country to write works with pedagogical aims in view. The rise of literature for children and young people took place simultaneously in the various European nations, thus corresponding to the realization of a vast movement of ideas that had begun in the seventeenth century. Among the early French authors, Mme. Leprince de Beaumont and Mme. de Genlis wrote works of didactic and moralistic inspiration--*Le magasin des enfants* (The children's magazine, 1757), and *Le magasin des adolescents* (The adolescents' magazine, 1760), in the case of Mme. de Beaumont, and *Adéle et Théodore* (1782) and *Les veillees du chateau* (Winter evenings in the castle, 1784), for Mme. de Genlis. At the same time, in Italian Lombardy, which was then governed by Austria, where the pedagogical revival instituted primary schools, Father Francesco Soave, one of the innovators in this revival, wrote his *Novelle morali* (Moral tales, 1782), for Italian youth.

The first translations into Italian of the principal French books for children, in particular of Mme. Leprince de Beaumont and Mme. de Genlis, date from the last decades of the century. In the same period, Father Soave's *Novelle morali* were printed in France, first in Italian and then in a French version.[2] In the cosmopolitan context of the European Age of Enlightment, there were continual crosscurrents and exchanges, while English and German educational writers also had great influence.

Thus, the works of French and Italian pedagogues belong to the Age of Enlightenment and conform to the philosophical ideals of that time. Above all, they were inspired by the theory of sensism, which taught that the senses were the inevitable source of all intellectual knowledge, and also by a taste for encyclopaedic knowledge. The authors made little allowance for child psychology, and wrote moral tales for children where the protagonists were adult, young, but almost always married men or women.

On the other hand, a new trend occurred in France with Arnaud Berquin. His well-known anthologies, the *Ami des enfants* (The children's friend,

1782-1783), and the *Ami de l'adolescence* (The adolescents' friend, 1784-1785), were much more accessible to children, and they featured child characters within the family circle. Their themes were continuously taken up by children's literature of the nineteenth century; among these themes were charity and good deeds, the beauties of nature, the education of the capricious and imperfect child, and a humanitarian attitude toward domestic pets. The publication of this French writer's works was favored throughout the country by the reverberations first of all of the French Revolution, and then of the Empire. Rapidly translated into Italian, *L'amico de' fanciulli* (The children's friend)[3] was published again several times and inspired a certain number of imitations, such as the homonymous *L'amico dei fanciulli* (a combination of the *Ami des enfants* and the *Ami de l'adolescence*), published in Milan in 1812. The *Novelle morali* and *Racconti storici* (Historical tales, 1800) by the priest Giuseppe Taverna were among the various imitations of Berquin's works. In his preface, the author openly admitted this borrowing, saying he had been inspired by the French author's accuracy of style and soundness of thought. "I too have thought," he remarked, "that one should show children's activities to children, and that they should be entertained by stories featuring children of the same age."[4]

Throughout the period of Napoleonic domination, Italian books and publications for children remained under French influence. French books arrived in the original text, or else they were printed on the spot in their Italian version. Along with those French authors already mentioned, there was Jean-Nicolas Bouilly, whose anthologies of tales translated into Italian[5] were to be continually republished and have a lasting influence. They circulated narrative themes and clichés similar to Berquin's (the improvement of children's behavior and the eulogy of social virtues). These writers' well-known works were accompanied by countless tales and stories by minor or even anonymous French authors, such as the innumerable *Etrennes á la jeunesse* (Gifts for youth) which combined moral tales in verse and in prose with biographies of famous historical characters and elements of natural history.

Following on this period, the fall of the Emperor Napoleon signaled the end of French political and cultural hegemony in Italy and the return of Austrian domination, which produced few new cultural trends because of the extremely reactionary nature of its political regime. In addition, the literary production for children during the Restoration, which had arisen between the end of the eighteenth century and the beginning of the nineteenth century went into decline and came to an end throughout Europe, until 1830. The return to former models led to the translation of didactic, moral, and religious works in France and in Italy.

Religion and Education, 1830-1850

The end of the Restoration epoch in France came with the Revolution of July, and, with the liberal Orleans monarchy, Bourbon absolutism became a thing of the past. However, these political changes did not affect society throughout and did not have a radical effect on culture. On the whole, children's and young people's literature remained much the same. The selling of young people's literature remained in the hands of Catholic publishers established in the provinces, and among these were Alfred Mame at Tours, Martial Ardent at Limoges, and Louis Lefort at Lille. Specialized in prayer books and prize books, these "bookshops for good books" put literature for children into a new category of pious and edifying literature.

These publishers, who wished above all to protect religion and Catholic morality, had many associates recruited among the provincial nobility who had been ousted from power after the *ultras* of Charles X had been replaced by the liberals of Philippe of Orleans. Without losing hope, the French Catholic legitimists devoted themselves to the education of future generations. Accordingly, they doubled their efforts to spread their faith by means of innumerable gifts and prize books given as presents to well-behaved children and to the best pupils. In their search for texts corresponding to their intention, they came across works by the Catholic writers Silvio Pellico and Alessandro Manzoni, and they adapted them to the youth of their country because of their edifying contents. Thus, these foreign authors for adults were translated into French in impressive quantities and published in expurgated and abridged versions. The fact that they were now part of literature for children and youth had been desired by the Catholic conservatives who made these Italian writers into ideal instructors for young readers from 1830 to the close of the Second Empire.

In the first half of the nineteenth century, public opinion expressed sympathy with the oppressed nations such as Italy and supported the cause of Italian patriots, victims of Austrian absolutism. Silvio Pellico was undoubtedly the most famous of these patriots. His autobiographical work, *Le mie prigioni* (My prisons, 1833), which related his memories of ten years' suffering in the Austrian dungeons, was to sell better than any work ever before in Europe. It was said at the time that it was to do "more harm than a lost battle" to the Austro-Hungarian Empire. Nevertheless, the reasons that caused this book to figure among the French best-sellers of the Monarchy of July[6] do not seem to be as closely linked to politics as has been believed. If we study the various translations and editions, it becomes obvious that it was the Catholic publishers who achieved the exceptionally widespread distribution of this work in France. Intheir prefaces and introductions, the translators proved that the interest of Pellico's prison memories lay in his religious faith, which was composed of both humility and resignation, and not in his condemnation of Austria's imperial oppression. The "martyr of Spielberg" was replaced by the "Spielberg convert" who, during his captivity, was an example of how the infinite consolations of the Catholic religion helped those who put their trust in it.

The Catholic writer, now steeped in piety and spurned by Italian patriots, exhorted the young to be pious, resigned, and socially conservative. Without the chapters relating his platonic idyll with the daughter of one of his jailers, the book was available in all the collections "destined for Christian youth," published by the publishers mentioned above.[7]

The manner in which the Catholic and moralistic school exploited Silvio Pellico's autobiography, as well as the manual of morality by the same author, entitled *Dei doveri degli uomini* (Of the duties of man), opened the way to a similar use of the great Italian writer Alessandro Manzoni. His famous historical novel, *I promessi sposi* (The betrothed, 1827), was especially appreciated by the clerical party, who made this illustrious romantic writer the other champion of Catholic literature and recommended his masterpiece for schools and as an edifying book for families. The success of *My Prisons* meant that publishers and translators adapted the work for a young and conventional public by falsifying and suppressing the parts that could seem either improper or critical as regards the Church.[8] They also published it in their "good books" collections in which Alessandro Manzoni's name figured beside Silvio Pellico's: "Instructive and entertaining library," "Young ladies' library," "Religious, moral, and literary library for children and young people."[9]

At the same time in Italy, Tuscany was the only regional state that experienced a revival of interest in childhood and books for children. The Austrian hegemony had been less rigorous there than elsewhere, and the relative freedom of expression made it possible for fresh pedagogical and literary iniatives to take place. Among the Catholic liberals gathered around the Vieusseux Cabinet, there was the writer and journalist Pietro Thouar who wrote *Il giornalino dei fanciulli* (The children's newspaper, 1834), *Letture dei fanciulli* (Reading for children, 1836-1846), and *Letture di famiglia e scritti per fanciulli* (Family reading and writings for children, 1849-1860), in collaboration with the priest Lambruschini. His publications for children not only preached faith in Providence and resignation to poverty, but also the patriotic sentiment that inspired the Risorgimento patriots. As his knowledge of French was good, he translated several little didactic and moralistic works from beyond the Alps into Italian. The Catholic tone of these texts was in keeping with the thought of the group of moderates he belonged to.[10]

Thus, for twenty years religion and education were shared by a community of writers and publishers of works for young people in France and in Italy. However, this common understanding masked a basic difference in political attitudes between the legitimist French Catholics and the liberal Italian Catholics, because the French were situated in their country among the reactionaries, whereas the Italian were among the progressives. In 1848, history dissolved this misunderstanding: the Catholics in France were horrified when the Roman Republic got rid of the Pope in 1849, and they applauded Louis Bonaparte for having made the troops intervene to reestablish Pius IX's temporal power. They were then the best allies of the Second Empire until the day that Napoleon III, wishing to exercise a foreign policy imbued with personal prestige, helped establish the Kingdom of Italy and provoked the lasting hostility of the French clerical party. Thus, the publication of Italian Catholic works by French publishing houses went into decline, just when the new Paris publishers were interested in publications for children, and Pierre-Jules Hetzel and Louis Hachette gave new impetus to children's and young people's literature.

Children's Literature in France and Italy: The Age of Widespread Publication, 1870-1900

In France, it was during the Second Empire that the production of children's and young people's literature became really widespread. While Catholic editors continued to prosper in the provinces, Paris editors in their turn started to attack a market which the development of schooling made most promising. Louis Hachette, who until then had concentrated on schoolbooks, now launched the children's collection that was to have such lasting success, the "Bibliothèque Rose." The books in this collection were sold in railway stations by the "Bibliothèque des chemins de fer" (railway station book-shops). Hachette enlisted the services of a team of women writers whose moderate Catholic ideas resembled those of the authors published by Alfred Mame: the Countess of Ségur, Zulma Carraud, Zenaide Fleuriot, and Julie Gouraud. A few years later, Pierre-Jules Hetzel, on his return from voluntary political exile in Brussels, founded the *Magasin d'education et de recréation* (Educational and Recreational Magazine), and gathered aroung him a group of writers who were to prove representative of French nonreligious, positivist ideas--Jean Macé, Jules Verne, and André Laurie (pen-name of Paschal Grousset). Hetzel himself also wrote for his collection under the pen-name of Pierre-Jules Stahl.

Hachette and Hetzel renewed children's literature both in form and content, and organized the widespread distribution of French children's literature in what was its Golden Age. Hachette's and Hetzel's books, which were chiefly bought for middle-class children but also reached the lower classes in the form of school prizes and through school lending-libraries, radically changed young readers' tastes and sensibilities.

In Italy, however, this change was much slower in coming. In 1860 the Kingdom of Italy was a backward agricultural country without industrial development. Schools did not exist except in Piedmont and Lombardy, and no market for books could develop thanks to the widespread illiteracy and general poverty. A cursory examination of the books written for children and young people between 1860 and 1880 shows that these are didactic moralizing works in no way different from those destined for primary schools, with the emphasis on religion, morality, and the exaltation of patriotism. In Italy at that time, the only works that can be considered what we call "children's literature" were translations of foreign books, chiefly French.

It was the Milan editor-booksellers, especially Emilio Treves, the first modern editor in nineteenth-century Italy, who started Italian versions of the books published in Hachette's and Hetzel's children's collections. Treves had lived in France and was in touch with Paris editors, which facilitated his importation of French works, so that he brought out Italian editions of books that had known considerable success in France, such as Jean Macé's *Historie d'une bouchée de pain* (Story of a mouthful of bread) and *Les serviteurs de l'estomac* (The servants of the stomach).[11] Soon other Milan editors followed suit and published the first translations of the works of the Countess of Ségur[12] and Zulma Carraud.[13] During the following years, Emilio Treves continued to translate the Countess of Ségur[14] and Jean Macé[15] and then Jules Verne. Jules Verne's works were brilliantly successful in Italy. They were first published by different Milan editor-booksellers (Treves, Tipografia Lombarda, Sonzogno, and Carrara), and then distributed throughout the peninsula.[16] In fact, Jules Verne's books found such favor among Italian readers of all ages that they were translated and published in Italy as fast as they came out in France, so that they were far more widely known in Italy than the works even of Italian writers.

The enthusiasm for Jules Verne brought in its wake a considerable increase in the number of Italian translations of French children's and adolescents' books during the 1880s. There were, for instance, translations of Hector Malot's *Sans famille* (Tale of an orphan),[17] P. J. Stahl's works,[18] and Louis Boussenard's series *Aventures d'un gamin de Paris* (Tales of a Paris lad).[19] These and the previously mentioned translated books, of a far higher quality than the works written by Italian pedagogues, encouraged the development of a native literature that was still searching for models to follow in this domain. Thus, translated works both preceded the growth of Italian children's literature and continued even when it flourished and produced those two masterpieces of the last century, Collodi's *Le avventure di Pinocchio* (The adventures of Pinocchio, 1883) and Edmondo de Amicis's *Cuore* (Heart, 1886).

Italian children's literature was therefore indebted to French influence from its very origins, and in addition, several Italian writers openly imitated French models. Before writing Pinocchio, for instance, Collodi was influenced by the fairy tales of Mme. d'Aulnoy, Mme. Leprince de Beaumont and Charles Perrault, and he produced a free adaptation of these in *I racconti delle fate*. He later imitated *Le tour de la France par deux enfants* (Journey through the French provinces) by G. Bruno (alias Madame Feuillée) in a work entitled *Il viaggio per l'Italia di giannettino*.[20] Zulma Carraud influenced the moralizing Catholic writer Giulio Tarra, while Jules Verne provided Emilio Salgari with outstanding models for his adventure stories. In addition, the *Magasin d'education et de récréation* (Jean Macé edited the educational pages of this magazine) gave rise to a whole series of positivist-inspired works that provided middle-class Italian children with scientific information in a lively and well-illustrated form.[21]

At the same time that original Italian works were appearing, increasing numbers of readers acclaimed French books. At the end of the century, new editors in Rome and Florence joined theolder, established Milan publishers. Among them, Adriano Salani of Florence was to play an important part in the twentieth century children's literature field. He specialized in the publication of fairy tales for children, publishing, for instance, in the 1890s the volumes edited by P. J. Hetzel in his first *Nouveau magasin des enfants* (New children's magazine).[22]

In France during the Third Republic, Italy and Italian literature did not at first interest the French intelligentsia. Those Italian works that were translated were only re-editions--and even these were rare--of the works of Catholic writers of the first half of the century, together with a few small religious works of the "intrasigent" priest, Dom Jean Bosco.[23]

At the time of the "Roman problem," the French had a very poor opinion of Italy, which was not corrected by any counterreaction on the part of the nonreligious forces in France. National antagonisms made for open enmity between French republicans and the Italian liberal monarchy. This antagonism was strengthened by the French occupation of Tunisia that pushed Italy into the Triple Alliance with Germany and Austro-Hungary. This treaty, which made Rome the ally of the worst enemies of France, led the French to reject both the politics and the literature of their "Latin cousin," so that they stayed proudly ignorant of the literature that was being produced there.

It was only in the 1890s that, despite continuing bad international relations, French intellectuals suddenly became enthusiastic about the work of D'Annunzio. Then they became intensely curious about Italian literature, for adults first and then about Italian children's literature. The translations of D'Annunzio's novels opened the way for the translation of other Italian works, including De Amicis's *Cuore*, which was the first modern work of Italian children's literature to be translated into French. This book, published in 1886, had known an unparalleled success in Italy, and it was immediately translated into several languages. The French version, translated in 1887, had to wait for signs of a lull in the political tension between the two countries before it was published, only in 1892, by the Paris editor Delagrave.[24] This book that purports to be the diary of a primary schoolchild of the Kingdom of Italy, was to become one of the most popular children's books of the Third Republic because of the family and social values it preached. Its humanitarian and patriotic ideology accorded perfectly with the ideals of the republicans that then governed France, who saw in state education a path to national unity.

Cuore, together with other works of De Amicis translated into French,[25] helped introduce other Italian writers into France at the end of the nineteenth and beginning of the twentieth centuries. There were, first, the works of Emilio Salgari,[26] who thus paid France back the debt he owed Jules Verne, and then *Les aventures de Pinocchio,* translated for the first time in 1902.[27] This breakthrough of Italian children's and young people's literature into the French market was to be triumphantly confirmed by the attention it received from one of the most illustrious of literary critics. On the eve of the First World War, Paul Hazard published in the *Revue des Deux Mondes* the first of his great articles on children's literature, entitled "La litérature enfantine en Italie" ("Children's literature in Italy").

This, then, is a brief historical summary of the influences and exchanges between French and Italian children's literature in the last century, when this type of literature was just developing. The first point is the obvious one that French influence predominates and indeed had the most important impact on Italian children's literature. Under centuries of foreign domination (Spanish and then Austrian), Italy had lagged behind the more nothern European countries, such as France, in the general evolution of society and culture. Geographical and linguistic proximity meant that this powerful "Latin cousin" had a lasting influence on Italy. Indeed, it was often the means by which currents of thought and literary developments reached the Mediterranean.

On the other hand, Italian influence on French children's literature was also important and twice played a particular part in French society. First, it encouraged a certain conservatism that upheld the religious convictions of the legitimist Catholics, turned as they were toward the past during the July Monarchy. Second, Italian influence helped spread the educational and philosophical ideas of the Third Republic. In the following century, *Les aventures de Pinocchio* was to be recognized as a world classic. In short, the exchanges between the two countries were unbalanced--French influence was continuous, whereas Italian influence came and went. But this discontinuity was made up for by its strength, for no French book knew in Italy such widespread success as *Cuore* and *Pinocchio* in France.

The history of foreign influences is far from straightforward. I hope that this short study has brought out some unexpected points and shed some new light on children's literature, while at the same time adding something to our knowledge of cultural exchanges between two neighboring nations.

NOTES

1. Concerning the translation of children's and young people's literature, see the Third Congress of the IRSCL in 1976, *Cahiers du Cerulej* 1 (1985), "Traduction et adaptation en litterature d'enfance et de jeunesse."

2. Mme. Leprince de Beaumont, *Il giornalino delle fanciulle, ovvero Dialoghi tra una savia Direttrice e perecchie sue allieve di grado illustre*, Vicenza, by Francesco Vendramini Mosca, 1774, 4 vols., and *La Biblioteca dei fanciuili, ossia raccolta d'opuscoli instruttivi e dilettevoli adattati alla capacità dei medesimi* (Florence: Stamperia Banducciana, 1771). The French publications in Italian of the *Novelle morali* by F. Soave are very numerous. Other translations followed (cf. *Nouvelles morales exemplaires et amusantes à l'usage de la jeunesse*, translated from the Italian by F. Soave, 2nd ed., Paris: H. Agasse, 1802).

3. *L'amico de' fanciulli, o sia il morale istruttore della gioventu'*, accresciuto dal francese di Berquin, London: S. Hooper, 1788-1789, 4 vols.

4. G. Taverna, *Letture morali* (Parma, 1800), "Prefazione."

5. G. N. Bouilly, *Racconti a mia figlia* (Milan: Batelli e Fanfani, 1820); *Consigli a mia figlia* (Milan: Fanfani, 1824); and *Racconti alle mie piccole amiche* (Milan: Truffa, 1830).

6. From 1831 to 1835, *Mes prisons* by Silvio Pellico was in ninth place among French best-sellers, then seventh place.

7. The editor who published most was Alfred Mame, who successively published in his "Bibliothèque de la jeunesse chrètienne approuvée par Mgr. l'Archévèque de Tours" the translation by Father Bourassé (1838) and the one by Mme. Woillez (1846). Next came editions "à l'usage de la jeunesse" by F. Guyot of Lyons, L. Lefort of Lille, Barbou Frères, and Martial Ardant of Limoges.

8. Thus, the character Monaca di Monza was either modified or excluded, condemned to monachal seclusion by her family, and guilty of sacrilegious crimes. Her role was essential for the rest of the story, and so her disappearance or disguise made the plot incomprehensible.

9. The publisher who ensured the most widespread distribution of the *Promessi sposi,* abridged and adapted for young people, was E. Ardent of Limoges in his "Bibliothèque religieuse, morale, littéraire pour l'enfance et la jeunesse."

10. See the following works: Mme. Chapman, *Conseils aux jeunes filles* (Paris: Baudoin Frères, 1825); Mme. Montgolfier, *Jeux et leçons en images* (Paris: Martinon, 1854); B. Delessert, *La mormale en action ou les Bons exemples* (Paris: Kugelmann, 1842); F. Mignet, *Vie de Franklin* (Paris: Pagnerre, 1848); J. J. Porchat-Bressenel, *Trois mois sous la neige, journal d'un jeune habitant du Jura* (Paris: Dezobry et Magdaleine, 1848); Th. Lebrun, *Livre de lecture courante à l'usage des écoles primaires* (Paris: Hachette, 1836-1838, 4 vols).

11. By 1885, this book had already run into ten editions.

12. S. de Ségur, *Nuovi racconti delle fate per i fanciulli* (Milan: Sonzogno, 1869).

13. Z. Carraud, *Lezioni in famiglia* (Milan: Agnelli, 1872); *Racconti e novelle* (Milan: Agnelli, 1873); *Racconti e storielle* (Milan: Agnelli, 1880).

14. S. de Ségur, *L'albergo dell'angelo custode* (Milan: Treves,1878); *Il cattivo genio* (Milan: Treves, 1878); *Il generale Durakine* (Milan: Treves, 1881).

15. G. Macé, *I comandamenti del nonno* (Milan: Treves, 1874); *La botanica di mia figlia* (Milan: Treves, 1876).

16. I cannot possibly list all the Italian translations of Jules Verne's works, for they take up several pages in the *Catalogo generale della libreria italiana.*

17. H. Malot, *Senza famiglia* (Milan: Sonzogno, 1881).

18. Stahl, *Marussia* (Milan: Menozzi, 1879); *La prima causa dell'avvocato Giulietta* (Milan: Assinoni, 1888); *Le imprese della signorina Ladretta* (Milan: Treves, 1885); *Storia di un asino e di due fanciulle* (Milan: Carrara, 1884).

19. L. Boussenard, *Il giro del mondo di un Parigi: attraverso l'Oceania; nel paese dei leoni; nel paese delle tigri; nei paese dei bisonti*, 1884; *I Robinson della Guiana*, 1885; *I cacciatori di cautciu'*, 1889; *Il tesoro dei Re Cafri*, 1886; *I drammi dell'Africa Australe*, 1886; *Le gola d'inferno*, 1892. All these works were published by Sonzogno, Milan.

20. C. Collodi, I racconti delle fate (Florence: Paggi, 1875); *Il viaggio in Italia di giannettino* (Florence: Paggi, 1880-1886, 3 vols).

21. See, for instance, Cordelia (V. Treves Tedeschi), *Il castello di Barbanera* (Milan: Treves, 1883); G. Milani, *L'abbicci' della Fisica* (Turin: Paravia, 1885); Vamba (L. Bertelli), *Ciondolino* (Florence: Bemporad, 1896).

22. See, for example, E. de la Bedolliere, *Storia di un gatto* (Florence: Salani, 1897); A. Dumas, *La pappa della contessa Berta* (Florence: Salani, 1898); O. Feuillet, *Vita di Pulcinella e sue numerose avventure* (Florence: Salani, 1897).

23. Dom J. Bosco, *Conseilsà un jeune homme pour acquérir l'habitude de la vertu, et indications des principales choses qu'il doit surtout éviter*, 1882; *Historie sainte à l'usage des classes et particulièrement du cours élémentaire*, 1889; *Le petit patre des Alpes, ou Vie du jeune François Besuco d'Argentera*, 1883; *Vie du S.François Besucco d'Argentera*, 1883; *Vie de Saint Joseph*, 1883; *Vie du jeune Dominique Savio, élève de l'Oratoire de S.François de Sales*, 1884. All these works were published by the Patronage St. Pierre at Nice.

24. Cf. M. Rigotti Colin, "Da *Cuore* a *Grands Coeurs* fine '800," *Belfagor* 3 (1986), pp. 297-310.

25. These were the French versions of the short stories in the collection entitled *La vita militare: scènes de la vie militaire* (Paris: Librairie illustrée, 1886) and *Sous les Drapeaux* (Chaux-de-Fonds: F. Zahn, 1892).

26. In 1899, the Paris editor, Montgredier, published *Les Mystères de la jungle noire*. After this, Delagrave published *Les Naufragés de la Djumma*, 1902; *A la côte d'ivoire*, 1903; *Au pôle nord*, 1901; *Au pôle sud à bicyclette*, 1906; *Le capitaine du Yucatan*, 1902; *Chez les anthropophages*, 1904; *Le Corsaire noir*, 1902; *Le Ko-hi-noor*, 1905.

27. C. Collodi, *Les aventures de Pinocchio* (Paris: Tramelan, L. A. Vaussard, 1902).

Scandinavian Writer/Illustrator: Bicultural Contribution to American Children's Literature

Karen Nelson Hoyle

Scandinavia's fascination with the New World, including the Native American Indian, began early. The Vikings, under the leadership of Norwegian Leif Eriksson, journeyed by long boat to "Vinland," now Nova Scotia, as early as A.D. 1000. According to Norse saga, they were rebuffed by the fierce North American Indians.

It was from Nordic seamen that Columbus learned that the world is spherical like an orange, not flat and round like a plate. He implemented their expertise and sailed to the New World in 1492. A century and a half later, in 1638, Swedes founded a colony in what is now the state of Delaware, absorbed later by the Dutch-Americans who purchased Manhattan from the Indians.

Two more centuries of intermittent conflict with the American Indian passed before the European public had available popular books about the indigenous people. Ralph Waldo Emerson's lecture at Harvard College in 1837 challenged Americans with an "Intellectual Declaration of Independence," which would make them artistically free of England and Europe and create American stories, paintings, and sculpture, using American ideas and American scenes. One series book novelist, using New World material had already made an impact in America, and its reverberations reached Scandinavia. James Fenimore Cooper (1789-1851) was born in the eighteenth century and wrote during the nineteenth century when European Romanticism flourished. Cooper attended Yale, and then joined the navy and merchant marine before settling down to write. His books, though part of the American Romantic movement, did not sentimentalize the characters. Cooper's best known novels are those in the "Leatherstocking Series," which is replete with American Indian characters. Although he did not write in the chronological order of the events, they can be rearranged to form a whole. Beginning with *The Pioneers* (1823), the series includes *The Deerslayer* (1841), *The Pathfinder* (1840) and *The Last of the Mohicans* (1826). His familiar character Natty Bumppo has alternative names in his works--Deerslayer, Pathfinder, Hawkeye, and La Longue Carabine. Cooper's works--entire novels or excerpts--were assigned reading in American schools for decades. By the 1850s, his popular books were translated into the Scandinavian languages, along with German, French, and Italian.[1] His stories, intended for adults, were read by children in countries where available. As Elva Smith points out,"Ironically, although Cooper has lost his appeal to the adult 'general reader' in his own country, he has an enormous following through foreign language editions abroad."[2] Cooper attracted many imitators. A German author, Karl May (1842-1912), for example, and others wrote about the American Indian without ever visiting the New World. The American Indian continued to fascinate Europeans, and Scandinavians were no exception.

One hundred years following the publication of the first of the Leatherstocking Series, three individuals immigrated from Sweden, Denmark, and Norway respectively, who would create for the American children's book scene. They were Swedish Gustaf Tenggren (1896-1970), Danish Robert Hofsinde (1902-1973) and a Norwegian woman who collaborated with her husband, Ingri Maartenson d'Aulaire (1904-1980). The oldest of the three and the first to immigrate to the United.States was Tenggren, born in Magra Parish in Västergötland. His grandfather carved in wood for his community churches had and other commissions, work that Gustaf carefully observed. The family sacrificed so that the young Gustaf could attend the then famous Våland School of Art in Gothenburg. In 1916, he had his first one-man exhibition in Gothenburg, and later, as a student, he exhibited in Stockholm and Copenhagen. For five years, he painted portraits in both Sweden and Denmark. In addition, he illustrated children's books for the Asbjornson Publishers in Copenhagen. His public learned to know and recognize his work in the Swedish folklore annual, *Bland Tomtar och Troll*, which he illustrated for nine years.[3]

At the age of 24, Tenggren emigrated to Cleveland, Ohio, where his sister had settled. He stayed there for two years, working as a commercial artist. Then he moved to Greenwich Village in New York City to acquire work in illustrating magazines, newspapers, and children's books. Among his early magazine assignments were the popular *Collier's, Cosmopolitan, Good Housekeeping, Ladies Home Journal, Life, Redbook*, and *Woman's Home Companion*.

During this first phase of his work in America, he also illustrated children's books of European origin. His illustrations for a two-volume set of the Brothers Grimm *Fairy Tales* (*Udvalgte Eventyr*) were published simultaneously in Copenhagen and Berlin in 1923.

Most of his children's book assignments were non-American texts, such as the Swiss Johanna Spyri's *Heidi* (1923), the French d'Aulnoy's *Fairy Tales* (1923), and Scottish Andrew Lang's *The Red Fairy Book* (1924). His drawings for the German *The Ring of the Niebelung,* written by Gertrude Henderson for the opera made famous by Richard Wagner (1932), reveal his skill in depicting the fantasy and realism of the stories. Not surprisingly, he illustrated an American Hans Christian Andersen edition of *Fairy Tales* (1935).

He also drew for American books such as Nathaniel Hawthorne's *Wonder Books and Tanglewood Tales* (1923). Evidence of visits to Mexico and Canada can be seen in his illustrations for Frances Courtenay Baylor's *Juan and Juanita* (1926).

The short-lived second American period was the Disney stint, when Tenggren shifted his focus and concentrated on the work of the Disney studio animated films. Walt Disney hired Tenggren and other artists trained in the Old World to provide background material for the selected European folktale themes for his forthcoming full-length feature animated films. Tenggren contributed to scenes and characters for *Snow White and the Seven Dwarfs, Pinocchio, Bambi,* and *Fantasia.* He left the Disney studios in bitterness, at the end of a three-year contract, because Disney did not reward him financially or give him sufficient credit for his contribution to the success of the film venture. His widow, Mallie Tenggren, stated that the Disney experience helped him to acquire a proficiency in style and high productivity, which he later put to good use when the next venture presented itself.[4]

The third and final American phase of Tenggren's working career was spent with the Little Golden Books and the aftermath of that continuing endeavor. Lucille Ogle and others at Golden Press/Western Publishers conceived of a publishing scheme that would print thousands of books in the same format, market them differently, and sell them cheaply. Golden Press hired good artists, including Gustaf Tenggren. Even though the United States was then at war, the press was able to print thousands of copies, using an inexpensive cardboard cover and staple binding.[5] *The Poky Little Puppy* by Jeanette Lowrey and *Bedtime Stories* were among the first to be published in 1942. The one billionth Little Golden Book was printed in 1988, and Tenggren's *The Poky Little Puppy* continues to be the best-seller on the list.

Tenggren never resisted bringing his Swedish heritage into his children's books. Even *Farm Stories* (1946) includes the predictably blond mother with a circle of braids at the back of her head, serving soup in large bowls. In the early 1940s, Tenggren and his wife purchased a large collection of Swedish folk art objects and antiques.[6] Some of these artifacts were used as models for his illustrations in folktale books and surprisingly in books with American subjects. In 1944 he interpreted Hans Christian Andersen's *The Little Match Girl.* First, he changed the text to conclude with the child sleeping in a luxurious bed rather than freezing to death. Tenggren incorporated ornaments from his Swedish childhood memories on the

Christmas tree, such as the marzipan pig, food, and real candles. The Swedish pewter candelabra and a dessert dish are further evidence of his re-creating Swedish folk life objects.

Among the more than fifty books Tenggren illustrated were some that were especially patriotic. During World War II, he illustrated a book, written by Helen Dike, about Italian and German opera, entitled *Stories from the Great Metropolitan Opera* (1943); the work downplayed the enemy countries by enhancing the role of the New York company. In 1944, Tenggren illustrated Opal Wheeler's *Sing for America*, a book whose negative ethnic stereotypes make it ineligible for reprinting today.

American Indians particularly delighted Tenggren. *Tenggren's Cowboys and Indians* (1948) with stories by Kathryn and Byron Jackson reflects no interest, however, in unique tribal characteristics. The end papers depict a scene in which cattle, bucking broncos, and buffaloes intermingle. Indians with both buffalo horns and eagle feather headdresses dance, drum, and ride horseback, while white cowboys participate in rodeo-like activities. For the story about the first buffalo, Tenggren drew a nondescript Indian boy with drawn bow. For the chapter entitled "Indian Housecleaning," a dozing brave is depicted with a porcupine quill vest of a woodland tribe, while the woman carries pottery reminiscent of a southwest tribe--a gross stereotype at best. In the Little Golden Book, *The Little Trapper* (1950), Tenggren drew a fawning Indian girl with unspecific garb. Swedish mushrooms, with characteristic red caps dotted with white, appear underfoot; while an entertaining touch it is inaccurate because they do not grow in the United States.

An Indian doll with a feather headband is one of the presents left by Santa in another book. The quintessential American book is Clement Clarke Moore's *The Night Before Christmas*, originally published in a 1823 newspaper and illustrated by innumerable artists. Swedish artifacts abound in the book. For example, the fireplace scene includes a wooden tankard, pottery plate, candelabra, three-legged coffee pot, and bellows of folk art tradition. Similarly, the children dream of gingerbread cookies and wrapped sweets. Tenggren illustrated at least sixty-four American children's books, occasionally re-doing illustrations for new editions. Many of them provide hints as to his country of origin.

A second significant author/illustrator who enhanced the children's book scene was Robert Hofsinde, who emigrated from Odense, also the hometown of Hans Christian Andersen. Hofsinde attended the Royal Academy of Art in Copenhagen from 1916 to 1922 and settled in Minneapolis. There he worked with Waldemar Kjelgaard at the Minnesota Academy of Science and attended the Minneapolis School of Art and Design night school in 1922 and 1923.[7]

While drawing Minnesota flora near MacGregor, Minnesota, Hofsinde happened on an Ojibway boy who had fallen into an animal pit trap and broken his leg. Recalling his Danish Boy Scout training, Hofsinde set the compound fracture and then pulled the boy on a sled to the winter encampment. In an appreciation ceremony, the tribe made him a blood brother and named him Grey-Wolf. Hofsinde claimed that this experience was different from the ceremony described in James Fenimore Cooper's novels. He remained with the Ojibway and spentsixteen years conducting research among them and the more westerly Blackfoot tribe. He lived among other tribes as he rode horseback from Montana to Arizona.

Hofsinde married Geraldine in 1939, the year they founded a daily Chicago radio program, "Grey-Wolf's Tipi." Three years later, the couple performed at school assemblies throughout the country, commenting on Indian lore. During this period he also wrote articles about aspects of native Indian life for *Popular Mechanics, Popular Science*, and children's magazines such as *Ranger Rick*. In addition, he painted murals and scenes for New York City clubs.

Unlike the other two immigrants cited in this essay, Hofsinde illustrated no books with Scandinavian themes. After illustrating Allan A. Macfarlan's book, *Indian Adventure Trails* (1953), Hofsinde debuted with what would become a sixteen-book series concerning Indians. Each book concentrated on a specific subject, such as homelife, costumes, and sign language. Examples of titles are *Indian Beadwork* (1958), *The Indian and the Buffalo* (1961), and *Indian Hunting* (1962). Hofsinde was responsible for both the text and full-page ink drawings. Only one, the first he both wrote and illustrated, *The Indian's Secret World* (1955), had color illustrations. Hofsinde consistently pointed out specific characteristics of Indian tribes in his verbal and visual descriptions. For example, an illustration of the painting of a tipi includes a description of Blackfeet people named Spotted Eagle and his wife, Singing Moon, in the text. Accompanying text about the Cheyenne warriors' exploits was an accurate illustration of a tipi interior and tribal dress, including the eagle headdress.

The third in the triad of Scandinavian immigrant author/illustrators, Ingri Maartenson, was born in Kongsberg and studied art in her native Norway, as well as Germany and France. She met her husband, Edgar Parin d'Aulaire (1898-1986), at an art school in Munich. He illustrated seventeen books in Germany between 1922 and 1926. They married in the summer of 1925. They journeyed to the United States in 1929, where the New York Public Library children's librarian, Anne Carroll Moore, encouraged them to collaborate.[8]

Their creations included the following arduous process. Edgar would draw lines on the lithographic stone for the black lines, while Ingri did an overlay for each of the primary colors. Many of the portraits in their books were based on their sons Per Ola and Nils Maarten as models. *Nils* (1948), for example, is based on their son's experiences.

The d'Aulaires interwove contemporary, historical, folktale, and realistic books about Norway with other assignments. As a couple, they illustrated John Matheson's *The Needle in the Haystack* (1930) and Florence and Howard Everson's *Coming of the Dragon Ships* (1931), a work about the Vikings. After creating *Ola* (1932) and *Ola and Blakken* (1933) with Norwegian settings, the d'Aulaires worked on *The Conquest of the Atlantic* (1933), which was preceded by research in the New York Public Library, the University of Norway, Oslo Library, and the Louvre in Paris. As did Tenggren, they selected a Hans Christian Andersen tale to retell and illustrate, *Don't Count Your Chicks* (1943). A trip to Lapland materialized in the book, *Children of the Northlights* (1935), dedicated to Princess

Ragnhild and Princess Astrid of Norway. In *Leif the Lucky* (1941), they wrote about the Viking leader who discovered the New World. As with other biographies, they devoted a considerable portion of the text to the leader's childhood.

During the next period, they interspersed American subjects with Scandinavian. Ingri and Edgar Parin d'Aulaire produced two books about American presidents--*George Washington* (1936) and *Abraham Lincoln* (1939). Their American book about the Revolutionary War hero and first president of the United States uses a curvilinear device on the title page, similar to the Norwegian folk art, rosemaling. Colors are close to the primary palette, and flowers are usually flat and forward, similar to folk art. The d'Aulaires frequently reminisced about their research ventures. They not only used library and museum material, but they also walked George Washington's territory in Virginia, camped out on Buffalo Bill's prairie, and pitched tents along Lincoln's trail. Even though their book *Abraham Lincoln* won the coveted Caldecott Award as the most distinguished picture book of the preceding year, critics Bertha Mahony Miller and Elinor Whitney Field complained, "Perhaps the American scene and material needed a longer period of assimilation."[9] Later, they would write and illustrate books about other American historical figures, such as the inventor-statesman *Benjamin Franklin* (1950), the folk hero *Buffalo Bill* (1952), and the Italian discoverer of the New World, *Columbus* (1955).

New World Indians were incorporated into the books about Leif Eriksson, Columbus, and George Washington, who had historic encounters with them. One title, *Pocohontas* (1946), centered on the famous girl who saved Captain John Smith's life and later married and journeyed to England, where she died. The creators discreetly selected the information they considered appropriate to the child audience at the time. In the book, Buffalo Bill and accompanying Indians toured Europe with a show that claimed to portray the American West. Even the d'Aulaires considered him an extraordinary showman.[10]

During World War II, they illustrated the American national anthem, *The Star Spangled Banner* (1942). The d'Aulaire book reviewed the country's history, such as the landing of the Pilgrims, with nostalgia. Flags and symbols such as the Liberty Bell abound, but the book lacks evidence of cultural pluralism. It shows no American Indians or Asians, and only a token black is featured in the contemporary scenes. In all, Ingri Maartenson d'Aulaire illustrated more than thirty books with her husband, many of which have some relevance to her Scandinavian background.

In summary, all three artists--Tenggren, Hofsinde, and Maartenson d'Aulaire--dealt with American themes, including at least some aspects of American Indian life. D'Aulaire's *Pocahontas* is in the form of historical fiction, while Tenggren's *Cowboys and Indians* is light and entertaining. Sixteen of Hofsinde's books, solely about American Indians, are descriptive nonfiction. Only two of the three Scandinavian immigrants created children's books using the subject matter and motifs from their familiar homeland. Today, only one of the Tenggren, three of the Hofsinde, and three of the d'Aulaire books remain in print and are available for purchase in the United

States, though their other books can be found in public and school libraries. These literary and artistic creations remain part of the heritage of the Scandinavian immigrants of the 1920s who made a lasting impact on the children's book scene in the United States.

NOTES

1. Russel B. Nye. "James Fenimore Cooper." In Jane Bingham, ed. *Writers for Children* (New York: Scribner's, 1988), pp. 147-153.

2. Elva S. Smith. *The History of Children's Literature*, rev. Margaret Hodges and Susan Steinfirst (Chicago: American Library Association, 1988), p. 139.

3. The biographical information given here and below is drawn from the Gustaf Tenggren Papers, Children's Literature Research Collections, University of Minnesota Libraries, Minneapolis.

4. Author's interview with Mallie Tenggren, Dogfish Head, Me., September 21, 1971.

5. Barbara Bader. *American Picturebooks from Noah's Ark to the Beast Within* (New York: Macmillan, 1976), pp. 42-46, 281-283.

6. Florence Maxwell. "Gustaf Tenggren, Artist". *Christian Science Monitor*, 1948:7, p. 23.

7. Author's interview with Robert Hofsinde, Monroe, N.J., September 12, 1971.

8. Margaret Lesser. *Ingri and Edgar Parin d'Aulaire* (New York: Doubleday, 1940).

9. Bertha Mahony Miller and Elinor Whitney Field. *Caldecott Medal Books: 1938-1957* (Boston: Horn Book, 1957), p. 59.

10. Art Buchwald. "P.S. from Paris," *New York Herald Tribune*, October 30, 1956.

International Influence on the Nineteenth Century Finnish Children's Literature

Riitta Kuivasmäki

A Finnish publisher once asked me to write a ten- to fifteen-page article on the history of books for children and young people. The article was to present the development of both Finnish and international books for children and young people up to the present day, and it was to appear in a publication under way, an encyclopedia of literature. How would you have responded to a request like this?

Since the publisher had asked for articles of the same length on some other topics, too, such as Japanese literature, the length of the article was not the main problem. The problem was rather how to synthesize all the information I had collected from various sources and how to find connections, influences, tendencies, and so on. I needed a relevant history of books for children and young people, a history of different genres within children's literature, a history of different influences, a history of literary conventions and departures from them. In short, I needed a comparative world history of children's literature.

Some attempts have been made to compile a general history of children's literature. In the Nordic countries, as early as the 1960s, the Danish scholar Vibeke Stybe undertook this difficult task, and her book *Fra Askepot till Anders And* (From Cinderella to Donald Duck, Copenhagen, 1962) is still being used as a general history in this field. The Spanish researcher Carmen Bravo-Villasante's work *Literatura Infantil Universal I-III* from the year 1971 (translated into German under the title *Weltgeschichte der Kinder- und Jugendliteratur*) consists of presentations of children's literatures of various countries and nationalities, but even this work lacks a general overview of the whole of children's literature. However, Bettina Hürlimann's *Europäische Kinderbücher in drei Jahrhunderten* (1959) is perhaps the best synthesis of European children's literature. The second, expanded edition from 1963 was translated and edited into English by Brian Alderson in 1967. As the title of the book, *Three Centuries of Children's Books in Europe,* shows, Hürlimann mainly concentrates on European children's literature. The Nordic countries are not totally passed by, but almost; six Swedish authors are mentioned, while Denmark is represented--naturally--by Hans Christian Andersen and Norway by Per Christian Asbjørnsen and Jørgen Moe, and Torbjørn Egner. As to Finland, only one name is included, Tove Jansson. Of course, we know that, even in the Nordic conutries, Finnish works are often neglected because of the unique, Finno-ugric language.

Where could we find such a polyglot who is able to write a broad-based comparative history of books for children and young people? Hürlimann says: "It has become quite impossible today for one person, however conscientious, to survey the whole field in just one country, let alone a continent or the world itself" (p. viii). Naturally, what we need first of all is high-quality national histories, but even here it is not possible for a single person to perform the task. For each language or group of languages, we need to gather a work team of experts.

Next, I am going to deal with the history of Finnish literature for children and young people, which, even internationally, is on a very high level but which is often neglected in reference works and encyclopedias.The following presentation about Finnish children's literature in the nineteenth century may also be seen as one example of comparative research.

One of the central ideas and problems concerning a comparative study of literature is intertextuality or defining the special quality of a work of literature by relating it to works written before and afterward. Important concepts in this study are tradition, evolution, revision, adaptation, convention, period, epoch, and influence.

Background

The nineteenth century was especially remarkable for its literary traditions. In Finland, as in many countries, Romanticism brought with it so-called national movements. The leading figures in this movement in Finland, Elias Lönnrot, Johan Ludvig Runeberg, and Johan Vilhelm Snellman, were active in various branches of culture and had a profound influence on the rise of Finnish nationalism and, in fact, on the development of Finnish society as a whole. A leading figure of Finnish nationalism in the nineteenth century, Zacharias Topelius (1818-1889), is highly regarded as the creator of Finnish literature for children and young people.

Although Finland became an autonomous part of the Russian Empire in 1809, its cultural ties with Sweden after five hundred years of Swedish rule were still strong. The stubborn Finnish-speaking population with the tradition from the national epic *Kalevala* stood between two cultures, the East and the West. But the Finns wanted to keep their own language and culture alive. Some Swedish-speaking Finns, especially Snellman, realized that making Finland a civilized nation among other civilized nations was possible only by using the language of the people. And as we have seen in many small nations both in the past and today, the real strength of a nation depends on its level of civilization. Many fennophiles thought that the first priority was to educate the young. In those days, there was not much of a Finnish literary tradition; there were very few authors, so all those who were able, mainly teachers, priests, and editors, took on the task. Zohar Shavit has claimed that literature for children and young people cannot created without the existence of an institutionalized literature for adults (Shavit, 1986, 3). This was not the case in Finland. The literature for grown-ups and that for children were developed side by side in the nineteenth century.

Translations were the first step toward the development of an original Finnish literature. It was considered very important that Finnish-speaking children become good readers of Finnish literature. Thus, the high number of adaptations of world literature. Classics, such as *Gulliver's Travels* (*Gulliverin matkustukset tuntemattomissa maissa*, 1876) and *Don Quixote* (1877), appeared for the first time as adaptations. These translations greatly influenced Finnish literature and provided a model for young authors.

The German Influence

Children's literature from Germany had a far-reaching effect on Finnish children's literature. The bulk of the children's books that were published in the Nordic countries in the nineteenth century were originally from Germany, the cradle of Romanticism. Fairy tales by the Grimm Brothers appeared in Finnish as early as 1848, which inspired the publication of a great number of Finnish folktales in the 1850s (*Suomen kansan satuja ja tarinoita*, 1852-1866). Because folklore was seen to strengthen patriotic feelings in children, folktales were, under certain conditions, allowed in children's books, too. As was true of every other area in Europe, fantasy, however, had been neglected for a long time. Grown-ups did not want fairy tales to lead their children into the realm of imaginary fantasies and away from reality.

As in many other countries in the nineteenth century, short prose and stories were typical of the genre of children's literature. Because real children's books did not yet exist, these mainly translated and religious stories and novels were published in anthologies and the many magazines appearing at that time. German, strictly Lutheran ideals were well matched with Finnish attitudes. One of the most popular works was *Genoveva* by a German priest, G. von Schmid. This book, which appeared for the first time in 1847 in

Finnish (first in German in 1810), is a story of a virtuous child who grew up to be Genoveva, a chaste wife with high moral standards. The book appeared in ten editions. The mode of the story was still being used in the first Finnish novels for girls published at the end of the century, such as Immi Hellén's *Aune* (1896).

Even Finland's first picturebook came from Germany. *Struwwelpeter* appeared in Swedish in 1849 and in Finnish in 1869. Although the book appeared in three new editions in the nineteenth century, it did not inspire the publishers to support this type of book written originally in Finnish. *Struwwelpeter* was a radical work in Germany, while Oscar Pletsch was a representative of the mainstream. Approximately fifty of his idyllic child portraits appeared in Germany, and about five of them appeared in books written in Finnish. In addition, Finnish artists imitated this European model. Such artists as R. W. Åkerblom and R. Herzberg depicted round-cheeked children on a background of idealistic Finnish landscapes in Finland's first picturebook *Ur Lifvets vår* or *Lapsien elämästä* in 1875. Oscar Pletsch was also plagiarized by many artists, such as Hilkka Finne in 1918 and Venny Soldan-Brofeldt in 1898 (*Pienokaiset: Pienokaiset & Kylän lapset*). A well-known fennophile Julius Krohn, alias Suonio, wrote small poems based on the illustrations. Later, when Oscar Pletsch's name was forgotten, the following editions appeared under the name of Suonio.

The English Influence

In the Finland of the 1870s, when more books were written in Finnish than in Swedish, literature coming from the Anglo-Saxon countries began to gain popularity. WIth regard to the contents of the books, there were no big differences between the German and the Anglo-Saxon literatures; Anglo-Saxon literature, too, was very religious and included all kinds of Sunday School and mission literature material. These books were published in long series. Charlotte Tucker, alias A.L.O.E. (a Lady of England) and Sara Smith, alias Hesba Stretton, were among the most popular English-speaking authors. Their production included novels and stories with strict Christian didactic ideals and urging to pray and resist the evils of sin. It is apparent that Finnish publishers encouraged the Finnish children's authors of that time to produce the same kind of literature.

Harriet Beecher Stowe's *Setä Tuomon tupa* (1856, *Uncle Tom's Cabin*, 1852) was one of Finland's first translations from English; it was adapted into a booklet of twenty three pages. It was a real wonder that this book resisting slavery appeared in the Finland of the 1850s, because publishing literature in Finnish dealing with other than religious and economic issues was then forbidden by the czar. Children's literature was not so strictly limited, which may explain why a book with such revolutionary ideas could be published. J. V. Snellman presented the translation with cautionary remarks in his literary journal *Litteraturbladet* (1856, no. 11). He said that this booklet was a well-chosen collection of stories from *Uncle Tom's Cabin* and that it would therefore be very suitable reading for children. He did not mention the content of the book.

Times change, and in a shortened version from the 1890s the translator, Maikki Friberg, who was a well-known and active force in Finland's cultural life, hoped that this book would open readers' eyes to all the injustices in the world and lead them to fight for the truth and the good. One critic in the journal *Valvoja* also pointed out the social issues of the book, saying: "We also believe that this book has helped us to realize the human value of negro slaves and everybody's right to live free. For it is not unfairness but a brave fight for fairness that arouses in a child faith in justice and thereby the power and the will to fight the wrong." This spirit was greatly needed during the difficult years under the Russian regime until 1917 when Finland finally gained its independence.

Although there was no book like *Uncle Tom's Cabin* in Finnish children's literature, the shortened versions of the book influenced people and their ways of thinking. Even historic novels, which were designed to give high ideals to children, were recommended for young people, and these books were included in the book series for the young. Sir Walter Scott was being translated as early as in the 1870s, and his work was a model for Zacharias Topelius. Although Topelius's historic novel series *Välskärin kertomuksia* (Field's Surgeon's Tales, 1853-1867) was not aimed at child readers, it became very popular among young people.

Daniel Defoe's *Robinson Crusoe* appeared for the first time in Finnish in 1847; it was only in a shortened version, however, as were many later editions of the book. In 1911, Siviä Heinämaa, a teacher, created one of the most interesting adaptations of Defoe's work. The book, entitled *Risto Roopenpoika*, was being used in schools in some parts of Finland as late as the 1960s. This teacher with her strict morals found Friday unnecessary and totally eliminated him from the book.

Mark Twain's *Tom Sawyer* was translated into Finnish in 1879, three years after the book came out in the United States. Louisa May Alcott's *An Old-fashioned Girl* (1870, *Tytöistä parhain*) was published in Finland in 1889, and Francis Hodgson Burnett's *Little Lord Fauntleroy*, (1886, *Pikku Lordi*) in 1892. In this way, Finland's children's literature obtained models for books for boys and girls from the Anglo-Saxon literature at the end of the nineteenth century. However, in the twentieth century new winds began to blow in Finland's original children's literature. The new era started with Anni Swan, whose production of fairy tales can be characterized by symbolism and, especially in her novels for young people, by Alcottian influences and conventions.

The French Influence

In Finland realism was at its peak in the 1880s, when a new kind of realistic adult literature of a very high quality appeared (Minna Canth, Juhani Aho).

France, the cradle of realism, offered science fiction, and since the 1870s, Jules Verne had become extremely popular. The first Verne translation was *Matkustuus maa ympäri 80 päivässä* (in French, *Le tour du monde en quatre-vingt jours*, 1872). By the end of the century, eight novels by Verne had been translated. Finnish authors, too, chose Verne-like themes: Tyko Hagmann depicted traveling to the moon, and Reitto Aalto wrote adventures featuring a main character who greatly resembled Phileas Fogg. In his book *Kolmen fennomaanin matkassa* (1874), Aalto proved that it was possible to travel all over the world using only the Finnish language. Like Münchhausen he conjured up exaggerated stories: for example, he created a glorious history of the Finnish people, and he even went so far as to claim that Finland had created the Roman empire.

Original Finnish Texts

The first Finnish writings for young people were weak and of poor quality-- "watery gruel" as the famous Finnish author Eino Leino called them in 1898. In other words, these works were bloodless and spiritless, and so was most of the other literature published in Finnish in those days, including translations. The chief purpose of children's books was to educate young people and to make them hard-working and humble before state and God. Children were taught to respect honesty and Christian values. If books written in some other language than Finnish met these requirements, publishers took the risk and had the book translated.

This is a very familiar situation to anyone who knows anything about the history of children's literature. The same adult values prevail in children's literature all over the world, be it the United States, Germany, or the Nordic countries. The Topelian, post-Romantic spirit was prevalent until the end of the century in Finland. The biggest changes in Finnish children's literature.took place after World War II. Fantasy and lyricism appeared in works by Tove Jansson and Kirsi Kunnas, and, in the 1960s, books began to deal with everyday realism, side by side with fantasy. Today translations comprise more than half of children's literature in Finland, which means that influences from other countries remain strong.

Part III

ASPECTS OF NATIONAL HISTORIES

Nationalism as an Aspect of the History of Norwegian Children's Literature, 1814–1905

Kari Skjønsberg

In the nineteenth century, children's books were to a large degree used to convey religious, moral and informative matters, but even other kinds of lofty sentiments could be presented without actually turning the books into vehicles of open propaganda. This essay takes a closer look at the idea of nationalism as expressed in Norwegian children's literature in the nineteenth century, also glancing briefly at material from other Nordic countries.

One of the most powerful and influential ideas in the nineteenth-century Europe was the doctrine of nationalism which was most explicitly declared in Germany by J. G. Fichte's *Reden an die deutsche Nation* (Speeches to the German Nation, 1807-1808). About the same time, German folksongs were collected in *Des Knabes Wunderhorn*, while the Brothers Grimm were bringing to light what they regarded as the heritage of the orginal German spirit, "der urdeutsche Mythos," the German folktales, which would first be published in 1812. This interest in the past of the *folk* soon spread to the Scandinavian countries where the best known followers of the Brothers Grimm were Per Christian Asbjørnsen and Jørgen Moe who in 1841 published the first volume of Norwegian folktales.

Fichte's rationalism was a product of the Napoleonic Wars, which not only changed the map of continental Europe, but also affected even the Scandinavian countries; In order to understand nationalism in reference to children's literature, we have to know something about the political situation in the Nordic countries. Finland, which had been colonized by Sweden for almost six hundred years, was lost to Russia in 1809, and when at a peace settlement in January 1814 Norway was given to Sweden as compensation for the loss of Finland, four hundred years of union between Denmark and Norway were ended. Nobody asked the Norwegians, but as soon as the news reached Norway that it was ceded by Denmark, the Norwegians called a national convention, and on May 17 the deputies signed the constitution.

Although Sweden had been the traditional enemy of Denmark-Norway, large parts of Norway having been lost and incorporated in Sweden, the Norwegians, after being defeated in a short war, had to accept the new union which gave them greater domestic independence. Norway had to share the king with Sweden, and the foreign policy was conducted from Stockholm, but Norway got its own State Council.

As a young nation, Norway was first and foremost engaged in establishing the new institutions of a semi-independent state, but it was also important to strengthen the national awareness, even in children. How this could be done is shown by a book for young people edited by Per Christian Asbjørnsen in 1838 and entitled *Nor, a picture book for the Norwegian Youth, containing good and great acts carried out by Norwegians; Norwegian folktales and legends.*[1]

Asbjørnsen's book is significant in several ways. First, it shows that from the outset Asbjørnsen and Moe regarded the young readers as part of their public. Second, the contents point to what was to be held up as an ideal for children, especially boys, throughout the century: the heroic deeds of the ancient Norwegian kings and old Vikings. And lastly, I am sorry to say, many of the brave acts celebrated consisted in killing Swedes!

Writers of adult literature did not find it beneath their dignity to write for children. The great Norwegian poet of the period, Henrik Wergeland, for example, wrote many poems for children in order to help their education in national study as well as in religion and history, the last subject being at the time in Norway as elsewhere primarily the history of the kings. But when Wergeland versified the stories of Norwegian kings from the ninth to the fourteenth centuries to make them easier to remember, he seized the opportunity to disparage the union with Denmark, "those dark and evil times," while he expressed great hopes for the union with Sweden. More important, in 1841 he also wrote a national anthem for small boys:

> We a nation are, we too, though small
> No more than two feet tall.
> There many are, of such as us.
> Our native country is our great delight.
> In our hearts we know, in our eyes do sight
> How good and beautiful our Norway is.
> Our tongues in praise do ring
> In one of many songs that Norway's honor sing.[2]

The poet makes it quite clear that, even if the small boys do not quite understand the concept of freedom, they realize that it is something important which it will be their duty to guard:

> I wish to quickly grow
> --I have to wait, I know--
> so that I precious freedom bravely can defend
> that father praises without end.

There is no sting againt the Swedes here, but the wars against Sweden were still within living memory, and in 1850 Jørgen Moe published a children's book in which one of the characters is the old Grenadier Hans who had fought the Swedes under the command of Prince Christian of Augustenborg, whom his soldiers called "Gustenborgen."[3] The 10-year-old boy, Viggo, significantly called Viggo *Viking*, enjoys listening to Hans when he talks about his experiences of the wars. "Gustenborgen" is the great ideal, and his saying "Never turn your back until the retreat has been sounded" is repeated to Viggo so often that he follows this rule in dangerous situations when it would have been better to turn back. In a way, Viggo can be said to be brought up not only to be brave, but also to be prepared for his duty as a soldier.[4] However, no enemy is explicitly mentioned, and Viggo even claims that the Swedish soldiers are the bravest in the world.

The national awareness expressed in these works is no different from that which we find in the other Nordic countries. In Denmark, B. S. Ingemann in the 1820s wrote heroic romances of the medieval kings, based on old ballads, and in Finland J. L. Runeberg through his epos *The Tales of Ensign Stål* (1848-1860, written in Swedish and later translated into Finnish) celebrated the courage of the Finns and the Swedes in the war with Russia in 1808-1809. Later, these books would be read mostly by young people, but they were written for an adult public while the Norwegian works referred to were aimed directly at children.

After the middle of the century, Norway was growing less and less content with its status within the union with Sweden. The political development toward self-government worked its ways toward parliamentarism, which, when it was achieved in 1884, deprived the king of much of his power. But how was this to be reflected in children's books? Open hostility toward Sweden was inconceivable, and anyhow most of the ever-growing number of children's books were stories of everyday life. We have to look closely to find references to the national spirit, but if we analyze books where good behavior, diligence, and fear of God are the virtues preached, we may discover that reading Snorre Sturlason's sagas sometimes seems to be as important as reading the Bible.

Almost as an aside, we may be told that the sagas are the favorite reading matter of boys, that the crofter's son Ketil holds his own against the son of the parson because Ketil knows most of the sagas by heart.[5] A city boy staying on a farm may entertain the people working in the kitchen in the evenings by reading from Snorre.[6] Such ideas are even more emphatically expressed in poems:

> When my lessons I have done
> and to bed the little ones have gone
> my father's Snorre-book I'll get
> and next to mother I myself will set.
> Then aloud to her I'll read
> each and every ancient deed
> the splendid language of the Saga told
> where again we meet the kings of old.

The poet then repeats the more salient points in the history of the Norwegian kings. She has also written a special poem for one of her smaller sons, Haakon, who is encouraged to be as brave as the six kings who are his royal namesakes. He is to be Norwegian from head to foot, with a (possibly red) knitted cap, this most Norwegian of headgear, and a sheath knife.[7]

A fanciful demonstration of Norwegian superiority is shown by a young sailor who, after having been shipwrecked and captured by natives, makes himself respected by executing the difficult Norwegian dance *Halling*.[8]

But what about the girls? It does not seem that their upbringing included the reading of the violent sagas of kings, and as yet the authors did not encourage girls in the defense of their country. But at least one little girl proudly asserted her nationality when asked about it: "I am Norwegian, she said, and tossed her head like a true Norwegian."[9]

In Finland, the breakthrough for Finnish nationalism may be said to be the first publication in 1835 of the national epos *Kalevala*, which was later published in special abridged editions for young people. Riitta Kuivasmäki claims that this and other collections of Finnish folklore served the purpose of teaching young people to take pride in Finland's national treasures.[10] This fact became especially important when Finnish in 1863 was given equal status with Swedish, which in addition to Russian had been the language of the administrators and the upper classes.

Probably most famous in Nordic children's literature at this time was the Finno-Swedish writer Zacharias Topelius (1818-1898) whose stories for children were written from 1854 on and collected in eight volumes from 1865 to 1891. Because he wrote in Swedish, he is regarded as the creator of the first independent Swedish as well as Finnish children's literature.[11] His books were soon translated into Finnish, as well as into Danish and Norwegian.

Topelius wanted to teach children three main values: to respect their parents, to honor God, and to love their *fosterland* even if it was poor. This was very much in the spirit of the time, but only the last requirement needs concern us here. Topelius preached a *fosterlandskärlek*, love of the country that fostered you, which was imbued with a deep love of nature in all its changing seasons, the dark forests, the tall mountains, and Finland's thousand lakes. Just as important was his devotion to the poor and hard-working Finnish people.

In one of his best known stories, *The Birch and the Star*, we meet two children who after a devastating war have been adopted by people far away in a foreign country. But in spite of their protected life, they want to go back, being irresistibly drawn toward their *fosterland*. The only thing they remember about the small farm where they were born is a birch and a star. The perilous journey on foot takes them a year, but they do at last find that special constellation of a birch and a star that is like nothing else in the world.

Mary Ørvig sees the patriotic writing of Topelius, whether for children or adults, as a link in his consistent effort to awaken a Finland that despaired of the future.[12] He might sometimes look back with nostalgia at the courage of Finnish soldiers, usually old people who had once taken part in the war, and the little boy Pikku Matti is told that one day he may have to stand guard for his country. This *fosterlandskärlek* was such as to be easily assimilated by the other Nordic countries. Lars Furuland has shown how two lines by Topelius, originally adopted from *Kalevala*, came to be regarded as Swedish and used as the motto for a popular Swedish reader:

> Listen to the sighing of that spruce
> to whose roots your home is tied.[13]

If we look at books aimed directly at children, there appears to be little to choose from in Denmark and Sweden according to the histories of children's literature in these countries. Until the end of the nineteenth century, stories for children seem mostly to feature the stereotype tract, the cautionary tale, or straightforward educational information. Poetry praising the native country was often to be found in readers, as the quotation from Topelius shows, but the schoolbooks will not be discussed here.

The 1880s, the age of Henrik Ibsen and August Strindberg, was also the time of a new surge of nationalism which manifested itself through the interest in old artifacts and in the establishment of folk museums. Not until now were children's traditional songs and games regarded as an important part of the cultural heritage in Norway and Sweden. The first collection of this material was published in Sweden in 1886,[14] and in Norway in 1888,[15] while the Danes had included such songs in a collection of folk poetry.as early as the 1820s.[16] The Swedish and Norwegian editions were, however, picturebooks, aimed at children. Tone Birkeland states that this kind of song, passed down through generations, probably was the most important source of inspiration for illustrators of Norwegian picturebooks at the end of the century.[17]

Sweden differed from the other Nordic countries in its greater confidence in its own status as an independent nation: unlike Denamrk, it had not recently suffered heavy losses in a war, nor had it been the weaker part in a union. This may be the reason why, as Sonja Svensson has observed, at least one Swedish writer in 1894 thought it necessary to make an important change in Alphonse Daudet's touching story from 1873, *La dernière classe*. A little girl complains about how difficult it is to learn to write Swedish: "I can never manage to spell those wretched words." Her grandmother then retells Daudet's story in her own words, and when the girl hears of the little boy from Alsace, who will never more get the opportunity to learn to write his mother tongue, she ends by asking God to teach her to spell Swedish correctly.

One reason for this admonition, Sonja Svensson believes, lies in the then current problem of the large emigration from Sweden to America.[18] But the change may also have been made because the Swedish language had never been threatened, and therefore Swedish children were not expected to understand what the suppression of a language signified, while Norwegians, like the Finns, had for centuries been subjected to languages not their own.

As for Denmark, it had a negative experience of German nationalism. In 1848 Slesvig-Holstein demanded independence as a German state, and although the problem--after a short war--was solved by a compromise, this was only a brief respite. In 1864 Prussian and Austrian armies invaded Slesvig and moved further north into Jutland. In spite of brave resistance, Denmark was defeated, and Slesvig-Holstein lost. This war was the subject of the first Danish boys' book in 1899: *A Boy from "64"*.[19]

At the beginning of this story, Martin is six years old, and is engrossed in listening to his father and his neighbor reminiscing about the war in 1848 when they were soldiers together. When Martin's father later dies, Martin goes with his mother to live with his grandfather in Slesvig. This brings Martin close to the events of 1864, and after having admired the Danish soldiers trooping out with songs, he soon after has to witness their heartbreaking retreat. Martin is too young to be a soldier, but he proves his courage and is regarded as a spy by the Prussians. The author does not glorify the Danes as heroes, and his description of the events of war is restricted, though the Prussian soldiers are seen as ruthless and brutal. The book iswritten to remind children of what happened without any indication of a need for revenge. As an adult, Martin takes up a military career, which is, however, described in a peaceful setting.

Some of the sad events of 1864 also found their way into Norwegian children's literature. A boy called Peter Napoleon, because of his hero-worship of Napoleon, is very impressed when he discovers that the father of his friend Gunnar has been a volunteer in the war of 1864. Gunnar's father tells him about his own part in the war and shows him where he was hit by a Prussian bullet. He even allows Peter to see the order with which he was decorated, the Dannebrog-cross.[20]

We have now reached the last decade of the century, when the Norwegians, growing in self-confidence and often feeling humiliated by the Swedes, were in fact preparing for war. Marielouise Christadler, through an extensive analysis of French and German children's literature from the years preceding 1914, has revealed how at that time books were used for military propaganda,in Germany even explicitly talking of the necessity of war, "kriegerische Notwendigkeit."[21] This kind of bellicose propaganda was alien to the Norwegians and would probably have provoked the Swedes beyond endurance. On the other hand, French books written to remind children that France was one nation, including the lost provinces of Alsace-Lorraine, did not have relevance in Norway, which was not seeking to win back land lost to Sweden. G. Bruno's *Le tour de France par deux enfants* (1877), relating the story of two orphans from Lorraine looking all over France for their uncle, was probably of little interest outside France, and Hector Malot's *Sans famille* (1878) was published in Norway *for adults* in 1896, and became a children's book only in an abridged version later on. There was an Italian book from 1886, however, which was quickly seen as useful even to Norwegian children: *Cuore* by Edmondo De Amicis. After Italy became one kingdom in 1860, it was important to make Italian children understand that they all belonged to the same nation. To support this idea, De Amicis told stories about brave children from different parts of the country, some of them showing courage during hardships, others bravely taking part in liberation wars. With special permission from the author, *Cuore* was published in Norway in a somewhat edited version in 1889 and was reprinted several times. Best known was the moving story of the Lombardian boy. It was printed in a children's magazine, edited by Nordahl Rolfsen, who also made a point of using patriotic Norwegian material, including the history of battles where Swedes were beaten by Norwegians.[22] Rolfsen also used De Amicis's story in his reader for schools, where it has kept its place so well that to this day public libraries have elderly people asking for it.

The boy from Lombardia, being too young to be a soldier, offers his services as a scout. He climbs a tree and has just enough time to warn the Italian officer about the approaching enemy, when he is shot down and killed. His body is draped in the Italian flag, and the soldiers march past saluting the dead hero. "And he still slept there in the grass, draped in the banner [...] seeming to smile [...] as if he were happy to have given his life for his beloved country." The moral of this is that even children may die for their country, *la patria, fedrelandet*.

Norwegian patriotism now turned up in books apparently aboutother matters. A story about dolls and tin soldiers might, for instance, be a pretext to remind the readers of how Norwegian soldiers got the better of the Swedish Army at a skirmish in 1808, when the hero, Captain Jørgensen, chopped the head off an enemy, making it roll downhill.[23] Gunvor Risa remarks that this kind of literature was written to inspire in children the will to defense and love of their country.[24]

In 1895, Norway and Sweden were on the brink of war, when Norway, being obviously the weaker part, had to give way at the last minute. The following years were, however, used to prepare for war. This is when a champion for defense, the later colonel Henrik August Angell, enters the stage. In 1896, he turned to good account Montenegro's brave fight against the Turks in a book for young people. "God will help those who help themselves, but a coward deserves no help," he says. He emphasizes that if *The Sons of the Black Mountains*, as he called the book, had to bleed, they were bleeding for their own country, their own people, their own hearth. Even women had to fight alongside their menfolk for the freedom of their country.[25]

In 1904, a year of growing crisis, Captain Angell published *Brave Boys and Girls, Stories for Young People*. In the manner of De Amicis, he collected twenty one short stories in which a variety of children show different kinds of courage. The first story in the book is about a girl, *Bjørne-Kirsti* (Bear-Kirsti), who wards off a bear by attacking it with a scythe. Angell here stresses the achievements of *girls:* "As luck would have it, I shall first tell you about a small wench."

The author asserts the autenticity of his stories by referring to his own experience, sometimes having been present himself when the events took place, or at least having met or seen the children he wrote about, but sometimes repeating what others have told him. In the first part of the book, the children are *Norwegian,* whether a boy suppressing pain so as not to upset his mother, or a young sailor drowning to save others. Hans, who is looked upon as a weakling, gives his life when he tries to save another boy who has fallen through the ice on a lake while skating: "Who would have expected Hans, this quiet, almost diffident boy, to show such courage, and die such an honorable, fine death." And the captain adds: "The soldier, who defends the country of his fathers, is not charged first and foremost with killing, as many people believe, but with giving his own life, give it for others, for his country, for his father and his mother. The great and wonderful thing about defending one's country is to give one's life for one's brothers."

In the same way, the little Lapp girl who defies the forces of nature to get medicine for her mother wins his approval: "Well done, little Majsa! I thought I would scarcely myself like to take that road all alone in the middle of the night."

These young Norwegian people are shown fighting natural forces: wild beasts, storms at sea, snow and ice. But Captain Angell also writes about children he has met while traveling abroad. Sometimes they are poor children who have to leave home and fend for themselves, such as the little boy from Piedmont, or the Greek paper boy. But of more interest are the boy from Alsace who is executed by the Germans while shielding his father, and the girl Marie from Slesvig where Danish is replaced by German in schools, and children are punished for speaking Danish. Worst of all, they have to sing the song: "Ich bin ein Preusse, will ein Preusse sein." They replace it by singing: "Ich bin kein Preusse, will kein Preusse sein," and when Marie unflinchingly refuses to say she is a Prussian, she is eventually beaten so much that she has to give in. From then on she is an obedient pupil, being afraid that her parents will be punished if she is recalcitrant, but even if her mouth is German, her heart is Danish. The author is explicit in his message: Boys and girls, never let any part of our country be subjected to strangers. Defend the country of your fathers tooth and nail, with your life and your blood, love it in your heart and in your soul, in thought and action.

In 1905, Norwegian men were called up to guard the borders against Sweden, while the women were ready to turn out and do their duty as nurses. However, Captain Angell's appeal to the *Brave Boys and Girls* fortunately turned out to be superfluous, and the union between Sweden and Norway was peacefully dissolved.

Nationalism did not for that reason disappear from children's books, but having wound up the threads of nationalism throughout the nineteenth century and looked at some of the different ways in which patriotism may be expressed in children's literature, I will end here, on the happy note of the peaceful dissolution of the Swedish-Norwegian union, without any recourse to the old Viking spirit on either side.

NOTES

1. *Nor, en Billedbog for den norske Ungdom: indeholdende store och gode Handlinger af Nordmænd, norske Folke-eventyr og Sagn* (Christiania, 1838). All translations of titles and quotations are made by me.

2. Henrik Wergeland, "Smaaguttenes Nationalsang," *Arbeidsklassen,* 1841:23-24.

3. Jørgen Moe, *I Brønden och i Kjærnet: Smaahistorier for Børn* (Christiania, 1851). Issued before Christmas 1850.

4. See Åsfrid Svensen, "Når egenviljen halshogges: Jørgen Moes Beate og Viggo Viking," *Edda,* 1988, pp. 203-211. Svensen asserts that Viggo's education by Hans is a development towards the military preparedness of a soldier.

5. Marie Wexelsen, *En liden Julegave for Børn och Børnevenner* (Trondheim, 1858); Marie Wexelsen, *Ketil, en Julegave for de Smaa.* (Christiania, 1860).

6. Augusta Hagerup, *Kryb, saa gaar det* (Christiania, 1873).

7. Johanne Vogt, *En Børnebog til Julen* (Christiania, 1876).

8. Oluf Vilhelm Falck Ytter, *Haakon Haakonsen, en norsk Robinson* (Christiania, 1873).

9. Bolette Gjør, *Doktorens Pleiedatter* (Christiania, 1885).

10. Riitta Kuivasmäki, Only the best is good enough for the child: a survey of Finnish adaptations, Paper presented at the eighth congress of IRSCL, Cologne 1988.

11. Salme Aelmelaeus, "Från Topelius till Tove Jansson", in *Ungdomsboken i Finland förr och nu,* ed. Irja Lappalainen (Helsinki, 1970), p. 9.

12. Mary Ørvig, "Om Zacharias Topelius: efterord", in Zacharias Topelius, *Läsning för barn,* ed. Mary Ørvig (Stockholm, 1980), p. 58.

13. Lars Furuland, Läsebok för folkskolan," in *Läsebok för folkskolan,* reprint (Stockholm, 1979), pp. vi-vii.

14. Johan Nordlander, *Svenska barnboken,* ill. Jenny Nyström (Stockholm, 1886).

15. Elling Holst, *Norsk Billedbog for Børn*, by Elling Holst and Eivinds Nielsen (Christiania, 1888.)

16. J. M. Thiele, *Danske Folkesagn* (København, 1819-1823).

17. Tone Birkeland, Den norske billedboka (The Norwegian picturebook). Unpublished paper, 1989.

18. Sonja Svensson, *Läsning för folkets barn* (Stockholm, 1983), p. 128.

19. Niels K. Kristensen, *En Dreng fra "64"*.(København, 1899). See Inger Simonsen, *Den danske børnbog i det 19. aarhundrede* (København, 1966), p. 210; Chr. Winther, *Danske børnebogsforfattere* (Århus, 1955), p. 10.

20. Bernt Lie, *Peter Napoleon* (Christiania, 1900).

21. Marielouise Christadler, *Kriegerzielung im Jugendbuch: literarusche Mobilmachung in Deutschland und Frankreich vor 1914*, 2nd ed (Frankfurt am Main, 1979.)

22. *Illustreret Tidende for Børn*, 1885-1894.

23. Hallvard Bergh, *Hvordan Maria sankede pengene* (Bergen, 1889)

24. Gunvor Risa, "Eldre barnelitteratur," in *Den norske barnelitteraturen gjennom 200 år* (Oslo, 1981), p. 171.

25. Henrik August Angell, *De sortes fjeldes sønner* (Christiania,1896); Henrik August Agnell, Kjække gutter og jenter. *Fortællinger for ungdommen* (Christiania, 1904).

Views on Children's Literature in the Netherlands After 1880

Anne de Vries

In the 1970s an animated and sometimes heated discussion took place about children's literature in the Netherlands, in which much attention was paid to social and political aspects. The same discussion took place in other countries, but what may have been typical of the Dutch situation was the scant knowledge about the demands made on children's books in the past and the lack of interest in such knowledge. The pretense was that no attention had ever been paid to children's literature before, which did not exactly raise the level of the discussion. As one had to reinvent the wheel, views were elaborated in a rather superficial way.

I chose views on children's literature in the Netherlands as the subject for my doctoral thesis in order to gain greater insight into the evaluation of children's books. Knowledge of this subject is also a condition for understanding the history of children's literature (just like, for instance, data about the reception of important books by children and adults).

First, I examined the views that have been formulated in theoretical essays on the subject, the approaches that can be distinguished, and the factors from which these were determined. In addition, I examined to what extent the various approaches can be found in reviews. This part was meant only as a supplement to the above: but also as a way to determine what the views boil down to in practice and which approach had the greatest impact.

A comprehensive description of the practice of evaluation.was not a goal of my study

I limited myself to the period after 1880 because before then only a few theoretical essays on children's literature were published. During the Enlightenment, children's literature was seen as an instrument in moral or religious education. Because it was assumed that children would immediately imitate the characters, people wanted to give them stories about model children. The demands made on children's books were of a moral kind: the characters had to judge and act the way children were expected to do; they were allowed to make a mistake once in a while, but then the reader had to be shown "the sad consequences which every false step has for the culprit." Gradually, in the nineteenth century more demands were made on the literary value and the childlike qualities. In 1838, for instance, the critic E. J. Potgieter observed in a review that a noble goal was no license for poor art. Others demanded that a children's author be able to enter into a child's feelings and reflect what is going on in their minds.

Ironically, this means that the most important antithesis has already been described. For the whole period under investigation, two main approaches to children's literature are used, the exponents of which repeatedly reacted against each other: a pedagogical approach--in which the children's book is seen as a means of passing on moral, political, or religious value--and an aesthetic approach. In the aesthetic approach, some emphasize the children's book as a work of art, whereas others start from the child's experience. However, they have the same views on the function of children's literature, and in other respects as well their views hardly differ.

Alongside these main approaches is occasionally found a psychological approach, and after 1970 a "purely literary" approach based on an autonomous conception of literature.

The first theoretical essays on children's literature after 1880 came from teachers, who began to set up school libraries and wondered what books should be included in them. The most important figure was the later children's writer J. Stamperius (1858-1936), who demanded that children's books contribute to "the development of conscience and the education of the intellect" (a demand derived from the statutory aim of the public primary school). As far as the development of conscience was concerned, he considered most adventure stories, for instance the popular Indian novels by Gustave Aimard, to be absolutely unsuited. They contained too much violence "to awaken noble inclinations and to cultivate sound concepts of tolerance and love of one's fellow-man." As books that did not meet the second demand, Stamperius cited the work of Jules Verne in which science was interwoven too much with fantasy. Moreover, these stories contained too many physical phenomena which were no part of the of the primary school curriculum .

In 1899 Nellie van Kol (1851-1930) published an article in a literary journal, "Wat zullen de kinderen lezen?" (What should children read?), which brought the subject to the attention of a wider audience. In the next decade, many theoretical essays on children's literature appeared, many of which again used a pedagogical approach. A significant part was played by people who thought that children's literature could help create a better world. Inspired by her religious socialism, Nellie van Kol concentrated on the tenor of children's books, emphasizing the mutual tolerance of all religions, the fraternization of nations, and equal rights for men and women. Out of the same vision of a better world the representatives of the "Nederlandsche Kinderbond" (Dutch Children's Society) paid particular attention to fighting militarism and to cultivating respect for all living things. Others started from more traditional social standards. One of these is Ida Heijermans (1866-1943), who stated in a review: "Cigarette-smoking women painters who sleep in black silk pyjamas do exist! But in our girl's books they should not be aunts whom nieces idolize." Because the exponents of this approach, like the educationalists of the Enlightenment, assumed that reading had a direct moral impact, they emphasized moral standards when evaluating children's books. They also paid much attention to combatting unsuitable books, seeing the main danger in adventure novels and stories about naughty children.

The exponents of the aesthetic approach reacted strongly against any form of moralism. According to the author Theo Thijssen (1879-1943) there was only one demand that children's books must fulfil: "A children's writer must be a *writer*." In other words, only literary standards should apply in evaluation. He saw no reason for concern about "dangerous" books, but he could fully understand the preference many children showed for Indian novels and other adventure stories. For the author and painter Cornelis Veth (1880-1962) this was the main starting point. He thought that boys should not be begrudged their "real boy's books" and that they should not be troubled with moral strictures. Reading, he said, is only a form of play; the young reader is an art lover: "He does not read to learn. He reads not to learn."

Although Thijssen started from the book as a work of art and Veth took up the cudgels for the enjoyment a boy gets out of his books, their views hardly differ. For the other exponents of the aesthetic approach, too, literary demands were not there to serve an abstract literary value, but the experience of the reading child.

Almost the same views were defended by a deviant pedagogue, Jan Ligthart (1859-1916), who also took a stand in favor of "dangerous" books (adventure novels and stories about naughty children). He did not believe that reading had a direct moral impact. In his opinion, most pedagogues started from exalted moral principles, without taking the nature of the child into account. Therefore, he claimed, the goals they aimed for were illusions, and the danger of the so-called unsuitable books existed only in their fantasy.

According to Ligthart, these books even had a beneficial effect, because they fulfiled the emotional needs of children.

With regard to the concrete demands children's books should meet, the antithesis between the pedagogical and the aesthetic approach was concentrated on one point: the desirability or acceptability of an emphatic moral. The exponents of the pedagogical approach (Ligthart not included, of course) only made demands on the contents of the moral and paid no attention to how it was incorporated in the story. The exponents of the aesthetic approach had exactly the opposite views. They rejected moral lessons and ethical considerations because these were at the expense of vitality: they claimed that the moral must remain "hidden in the story," and they placed high demands on characterization and plot. Moreover, they did not appreciate explicit moral rules. They made a distinction between ethics and etiquette, and they stated that good and evil could not be reduced to rules and prescriptions.

In determining which approach had the greatest impact during this period, we are given little to go on by the reviews in newspapers and journals. Generally, they were very short, five to ten lines long, and contained only a characterization of the story and a vague assessment, without any arguments. A better standard was provided in the lists of recommended children's books, which were published regularly, especially after 1920. Because they did not contain elaborate reviews either, I examined to what extent controversial books, which may serve as a shibboleth, were recommended. In comparison with older lists, the number of adventure novels turns out to have decreased sharply; stories about naughty children are scarcely recommended either. I also examined the catalogues of the children's departments of twelve public libraries, in which I found these books in large numbers. In theory, therefore, anxious pedagogues had the greatest impact; in practice, people were much more broad-minded and did not begrudge children their favorite reading matter.

The most important development in the second period, from 1930 to 1960, was the increased interest in the emotional development of children, as a result of the research of Charlotte Bühler and others. However, the antithesis between the approaches remained the same. When the most important pedagogue of this period, D. L. Daalder (1887-1963), stated that books should fit in with the emotional needs of children, he added that we need not meet all their wishes: strict censorship was required to avoid bad influences. The need for adventure, for instance, should be met with stories about adventurers who have dedicated their lives to a just cause. Generally, he demanded from children's books that they provide children with a code: "This is proper and that is improper, this is decent and that is indecent, this is good and that is evil." He rejected an explicit moral, however, and he paid so much attention to literary aspects that one is justified in speaking of a "pedagogical-aesthetic" approach.

Alongside this, we again find a (purely) aesthetic approach and a psychological approach. Of the latter, the views of the children's librarian Louise Boerlage (1884-1968) are interesting. Like Daalder, she thought that reading matter should fit in with the emotional needs of children, but she proved less worried and called censorship unnecessary. She argued that we can let children read whatever we want, but they will only take in what fits inwith their emotions, what satisfies a need or fulfills a desire. She believed that children used their reading to explore their feelings, thereby anticipating reality. And because they went their own way in this, she saw censorship as not only unnecessary but also pointless: children would read what they wanted to anyway.

After the Second World War, there were clear developments in children's literature itself, but I did not detect a sharp break in the views on the subject. This shift did not appear until 1960, when even the exponents of the pedagogical approach no longer drew a sharp line between children and adults. Because children were taken more seriously, the pedagogical ideal changed: rather than provide them with a code of good and evil, it was now sufficient to create the conditions for independent choice.

After 1970, a split was visible in the approach to children's literature. This was a result of social developments in the 1960s, which caused a remarkable change of attitude and gave new impulses to the pedagogical approach. Once again, some people completely concentrated on moral and social demands. Working groups demanded children's books in which the traditional division of roles between men and women was broken down, in which sex was no longer taboo, and in which discrimination was combatted by a positive attitude toward other races and other cultures. Others elaborated a theory of committed children's literature, arguing that children's books had to show social reality in order to make children conscious of the balance of power in this world. They did not pay any attention to the emotional needs of children, and they rejected literary demands, which were alleged to be aimed at art for art's sake. They wanted to renew children's literature, not realizing that their views were merely an ideological variant of the views that the German pedagogue C. G. Salzmann had formulated two centuries before. If you want to provide children with virtue, Salzmann said, you should give them stories about virtuous children; the characters in such stories should judge and act the way children are expected to do; and so on.

It was not long before the views of the committed educationalists were criticized. The author Annie M. G. Schmidt reacted strongly against the "new Calvinism," which reduced reality to social problems. Her colleague Guus Kuijer supported Theo Thijssen's demand that "a children's writer must be a *writer*." According to Kuijer, pursuing pedagogical goals would never produce an interesting story: we cannot explain life to children, "because we are all living for the first time and we do not know how it should be done." In reviews, objections were raised to the fashionable commitment in children's books, with an accumulation of social problems that were hardly ever developed, so that children were unable to immerse themselves in these books.

For these reviewers, therefore, the literary arguments were there to serve the experience of the reading child. For the first time, there also were critics who appealed to an "autonomous" literary value. Some of them explicitly rejected the judgments of children, alleging that they were only emotionally involved in their reading and blind to literary quality. This perspective was rejected by someone who for years had organized a children's jury. The opinion expressed was that children actually do have an eye for literary quality, providing that it is relevant to them--that is to say, providing it lies within their horizon. If one does not take their way of reading into account, one runs the risk of recommending books that are in fact not children's books at all.

The approaches to children's literature can be reduced to views on the function of children's literature, which in turn can be reduced to views on the child, on the impact of reading, and sometimes on literature in general. In all respects, it is possible to distinguish between an Enlightenment tradition (pedagogical approach) and a Romantic tradition (aesthetic approach).

The exponents of the pedagogical approach emphasize what the child should become. Initially, the child was seen virtually as a tabula rasa. But when, after 1960, the pedagogues no longer drew a sharp line between children and adults, their approach remained the same. Then it becomes clear that views on the child can be reduced to views on humankind in general. In the Enlightenment tradition, the individual is seen primarily as a member of society. Because children are not yet ready for a role in society, the emphasis is on what they still have to learn. In the evaluation of children's books, moral (political, religious) standards are applied; even from the characters, a single step out of line is unacceptable.

In the Romantic tradition, the human being is seen as an individual. And as an individual a child already is somebody: it has its own emotions and its own thoughts, and therefore has a right to books that fit in with these. Consequently, those who espouse the aesthetic approach put higher demands on the artistic value of children's books. Because they also dissociate themselves from the "etiquette" of bourgeois society, they can identify very well with the preference for stories about naughty children and adventure novels (a preeminently Romantic genre about solitary heroes who display their character far from the civilized world).

The balance between these approaches was not always the same. From time to time, the Enlightenment tradition received new impulses from certain developments in society. Around 1900 one can distinguish a Second Enlightenment, which was connected, among other things, with the extension of youth in the "Century of the Child." After 1970 the Third Enlightenment occurred as a result of the social innovation of the 1960s.

The Romantic tradition has been steadier, although it appears most clearly in reactions to every new Enlightenment.

Do these observations correspond with the situation in other countries? I expect that the same antithesis can be found in most countries, but that the balance between the approaches will be different:. In one country, the pedagogical approach may have been more prominent, whereas in another the aesthetic approach may have dominated. In my opinion, a description of the views in those countries would give us a better understanding of the history of their children's literature.[1]

To a large extent, the approach to children's literature is determined by views on the impact of reading. The exponents of the pedagogical approach assume that reading has a direct moral impact. In other words, they maintain the impact of reading is determined by the book. Their view can be represented in Roman Jakobson's "communication model":

author-->text-->reader

Reading is seen as a linear process: just as one projects a film on the screen, so the book is projected at the reader. Some pedagogues point out that this process does not always go smoothly. Children must learn to read carefully, not only devouring the story but also paying attention to the lessons it contains. However, it is assumed that unsuitable books can have a pernicious effect from the very first reading.

The exponents of the aesthetic approach reject this view, arguing that the reader determines the impact of reading. In their view, therefore, the communication model would look like this:

author-->text<--reader

Reading is seen here as a creative process: every reader creates his own book, from his own experiences and his own emotions, and draws his own moral conclusions. These can, of course, be similar to the ideas of the author, but even then we cannot speak of a direct moral impact. Louise Boerlage claims that children only take in what they recognize. Thus, books only make them conscious of what they already know or feel unconsciously.[2]

My thesis covered the period from 1880 to 1980. I wanted to maintain a certain distance because it is almost impossible to rate new developments at their true value. Therefore, I was not unhappy that there was a break around 1980: the end of the period in which the evaluation of children's books was mainly determined by their "social relevance." Since then, no new development has taken place. At least that was what I thought in 1988, when I finished my thesis. Only two or three years later, there appeared to have been a new development after all. Although its extent cannot yet be estimated, my observations allow me to adjust my classification of the approaches to children's literature.

After 1980, literary standards became self-evident in the evaluation of children's books. Perhaps this stimulated the development of children's literature. At any rate, more children's books of a high literary quality appeared, with an original, personal style and an elaborated composition. And it has become more common that a children's book can be read at more than one level and hence asks for an interpretation.

This enlarges the chances of a purely literary approach in which critics concentrate on literary aspects and do not take the intended reader into account. As already mentioned, this approach appeared for the first time in the 1970s, but then it remained very rare. Ten years later it became more frequent, although it is still far from general. Usually critics and jurors do take children into account; they only seem to forget them when they are deeply impressed by a book.

This occurred with a few recent awards in the Netherlands. I will not discuss the awards or the books as such, but will confine myself to the argumentation. About one book the jury stated that it is "so complicated that it is almost necessary to read it to children." And about another: "The jury will not answer the question whether children are open for such a strongflow of emotions, and if so which children."

Both books were awarded two prizes: a "Zilveren Griffel" (Silver Slate-pencil) and the "Woutertje Pieterse Prijs." One of the jurors of the second award, Bregje Boonstra, who is one of the Netherlands' leading critics, concluded her review of the second book with this statement: "Like every children's book of importance it raises the question whether it is within the comprehension of children, and at the same time that question is irrelevant." This summarizes the essence of the purely literary approach in which it is the literary value that counts and not what a children's book has to offer to children:

The extremes meet. The exponents of this approach suddenly show a remarkable analogy to the moralists from the past, who concentrated so strongly on moral standards that they lost sight of children. As much as their demands may differ, the exponents of the pedagogical and the purely literary approach correspond to each other at one point: they apply only adult standards.

Therefore, in classifying the standards applied in the evaluation of children's books, we can start from two opposites, which are diametrically opposed to each other: pedagogical against literary standards, and purely adult standards against standards in which the reading experiences of children are taken into account as well. On the basis of these opposites, we can utilize the scheme visualized in the following figure:

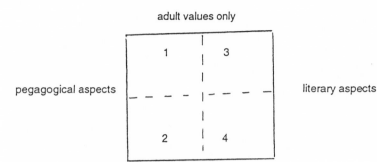

The figure shows four approaches to children's literature:

1. The traditional pedagogical (or moralistic) approach, in which the evaluation of children's books is determined by the moral, religious, or political values of the adults, because they assume that reading has a direct moral impact;

2. The psychological approach of Jan Ligthart and Louise Boerlage, who identified strongly with children and considered reading a necessary satisfaction of their emotional needs;

3. The purely literary approach, which aims at literary quality as an autonomous value and concentrates on composition, interpretation and originality;

4. The aesthetic approach, in which the literary demands are connected with the reading experiences of children, and in which much attention is paid to literary aspects that are relevant to them, for instance: plot, characters, and elements like humor.

An advantage of this scheme is that it leaves room for individual differences. As in every classification, reality shows much more variety than the scheme: besides differences in accent between the exponents of one approach, there are transition figures who show the characteristics of two approaches. As a result, the classification may appear to be more or less arbitrary.

In this new scheme, those differences can be drawn in. As already mentioned, some exponents of the aesthetic approach emphasize literary standards (the horizontal axis), whereas others give more attention to the experience of the reading child (the vertical axis). The first group can be placed at the right side of the fourth quadrant, and the second group in the lower half of this quadrant.

Some critics have a more complicated position, which can also be shown more clearly in this scheme. Generally, a critic does not apply the same standards for a lifetime, and some critics apply different standards on different occasions. For instance, both before and after the reckless statement that I quoted (that it is "irrelevant" whether a children's book is within the comprehension of children), Bregje Boonstra appears to find this question quite relevant after all in a number of reviews. Therefore, her position should not be represented by a point, but by a vertical line in the third and fourth quadrants.

In a less extreme way, this applies to many adherents of the aesthetic approach. Most of them do not take the reading experiences of children into account on every single occasion. When they reject a book on literary grounds, they do not always raise the question whether it might not be attractive for children after all. However, they never react against children and their way of reading. Therefore, their position can be represented by a vertical line at the right side of the fourth quadrant.

Finally, some critics use an even more complex (or less consistent) approach. For instance, D. L. Daalder stated that books should fit in with the emotional needs of children, but that strict censorship was required to avoid bad influences. In addition, he also paid much attention to literary aspects. His pedagogical-aesthetic approach can be represented by a triangle, of which the base is a vertical line in the first and second quadrant and the vertex lies in the third or fourth quadrant.

Which opposite is the most important? The answer to this question is very much a product of its time. Because literary standards are dominant at this moment, only the opposite between adult standards and the attention for the reading experiences of children is relevant, for which I use the terms *purely literary* and *aesthetic*. In conclusion, I want to examine the latter notion more closely.

Unlike *pedagogical* and *literary*, the term *aesthetic* seldom appears in the reviews and essays that I examined. I chose it myself as a label for the approach in which literary standards are combined with attention to the children's point of view. This corresponds to the etymological meaning of the term (derived from *aisthesis*, "perception," "sensation"), but it deviates somewhat from common usage in which "aesthetic" generally refers to structural aspects, and not to the experience of the reader. However, in reviews and essays about children's literature, the intended reader is quite commonly taken into consideration. This is not surprising, of course: with respect to children's literature, the distance between the critic (or scholar) and the intended reader is much larger than with respect to adult literature. Besides the distance between the professional reader and the public, there is a distance in cognitive and emotional development. Therefore, in the aesthetics of children's literature, the intended reader's experience is an essential piece of information, unless one presumes that it is irrelevant whether a children's book is within the comprehension of children.

As we have seen, this presumption is not exactly imaginary. The fact that I underline the etymological meaning of the term *aesthetic* therefore reflects a point of view. Both critics and scholars have to be aware of their distance to the intended reader; if they don't, they are at risk of taking no notice of one of the most important aspects of children's literature. If jurors create a standard of inaccessible children's books, scholars should be able to analyze not only the books as such, but also the reception by children.

NOTES

1. Until now I found only one example of similar research: a paper delivered by Edmir Perotti at the tenth Congress of IRSCL in Paris, 1991.

2. There can be no doubt that the second view on the reading process is right. On the basis of empirical data, there is no reason to assume that books have a direct moral impact. And what I found about reading experiences in autobiographies shows that the same book often has a different moral impact on different readers. Of course, this leaves the possibility open that reading has an educational value, also in a moral sense. However, this will only be possible with the right book at the right moment, for the right reader.

REFERENCES

Perotti, Edmir. Les échos de la "querelle." Littérature d'enfance: critique, éthique et estétique. Paper delivered at the tenth congress of IRSCL, Paris, 1991.

Vries, Anne de. *Wat heten goede kinderboeken? Opvattingen over kinderliteratuur in Nederland sinds 1880*. Amsterdam: Em. Querido, 1989. Ph.D. thesis, Free University of Amsterdam, 1989. With a summary in English. What is meant by good children's books? Views on children's literature in the Netherlands after 1880.

Vries, Anne de. "Vier benaderingen van jeugdliteratuur: een aangepast schema" (Four approaches to children's literature: an adapted scheme). *De Nieuwe Taalgids*, 1991:4, pp. 303-311.

Lame Old Bachelor, Lonely Old Maid: Harriet Childe-Pemberton's "All My Doing; or Red Riding Hood Over Again"

Roderick McGillis

Victorian children's books, as we would expect, reflect the age's concern with "The Woman Question." As Jack Zipes has argued, Victorian fantasy for the young contains "a strong feminine, if not feminist, influence in the writing of *both* male and female writers" (*Victorian Fairytales*, xxv). He notes that stories by such writers as Juliana Ewing, Mary Molesworth, Mary De Morgan, and Christina Rossetti contain "an intense quest for the female self" (xxvi). His interest is in the social and political emancipation of the female, her demand be heard, and her insistence that a better world will be possible only when men and women work together as equals. We can hear this utopian hope at least as early as 1825 in William Thompson's *Appeal of One Half the Human Race*: "Large numbers of men and women co-operating together for mutual happiness, all their possessions and means of enjoyment being the equal property of all--individual property and competition forever excluded" (cited in *The Woman Question*, Vol. 1, 36). A not dissimilar utopian design is evident in Margaret Fuller's *Woman in the 19th Century* (1845), and even in Sarah Lewis's *Woman's Mission* (1839). We can also hear this message, muted perhaps but nevertheless audible, in the stories that Zipes mentions and some of which he includes in his anthology *Victorian Fairytales: The Revolt of the Fairies and Elves* (1987). However, this insistence on social and political power slights the profound psychological "quest for the female self" which informs both the stories Zipes praises and two which he cites as examples of "female self-deprecation" (xxvi): Anne Ritchie's "Cinderella" (1868) and Harriet Childe-Pemberton's "All My Doing; or Red Riding Hood Over Again" (1882).

These two stories concern themselves with, among other things, female education and female participation in the world outside the safe confines of the home. They do so in such a way, however, that they challenge the dominant myth of growth and development presented to children by an androcentric society. Although the focus in these stories is on the mid- to late Victorian social milieu, both are aware of the intimate connection between the social self and the psychological self. Ritchie and Childe-Pemberton begin to examine the female's entry into the social order. I say "begin to examine" because neither writer can completely overcome the dominance of the male social order which is the only order open to them as writers. Their language is, to a great extent, male language, but they also offer acute examples of a literal language that is something of a return to what Lacan calls the Imaginary, that is, the pre-Oedipal stage in which no difference exists between signifier and signified.

For example, we all know that Cinderella meets her prince at a palace, a symbol of pleasure, art, and security. In Ritchie's "Cinderella," the young girl meets Charles Richardson at the Chrystal Palace, symbol of Victorian progress and achievement, but also a very real building, literally a palace for the people. Ritchie's first readers could, in fact, visit this palace. In Childe-Pemberton's story, the fairy tale woods are literalized in the very Victorian railroad train on which the young girl takes her journey. The train is, perhaps, a symbol of the masculine spirit, its aggressive and panting energy, chugging relentlessly through what was once placid (and feminine) countryside. But it is also literally true that young women and others might meet confidence men as fellow passengers on trains. My point is simply that these women writers choose to speak literally to their female readers. The very form of the stories, which incorporates the tradition of the motherly speaker, a tradition that dates back at least to the seventeenth century and that Mitzi Myers has studied in the late eighteenth century, creates an intimacy, a sense of experience shared.

Because neither story is well known, because space restricts me, and because Childe-Pemberton's story so clearly deals with female education, I concentrate on it here. Briefly, the story is a retelling of "Little Red Riding Hood" in a realistic late-Victorian setting. On hearing her 15-year-old niece complain that "Red Riding Hood" is only interesting to children and that it is unbelievable because it is unrealistic, a middle-aged aunt, whom we know only as Pussy, quickly defends the story by recounting a personal experience. This aunt, when a young woman, heedlessly chatted with a strange man on a train journey to her grandmother's and later, meeting him on her grandmother's estate, she invited him into the house. Her innocent openness and hospitality led to the robbery of her grandmother's house late one night.

During the robbery, grandmother received a shock that permanently weakened her health, and Pussy's fiance received a wound that caused him to lose a leg. Worse yet, Pussy confessed her blame in allowing one of the thieves to case the house prior to the robbery, and Herbert, her fiance, refused to marry her because he did not wish to saddle her with a cripple. Significantly, he never again lets Pussy's name cross his lips (*Victorian Fairytales*, 247). In short, because of her heedless and thoughtless ways, Pussy remains "a lonely old maid" and Herbert "a lame old bachelor" (247).

This outline might indicate that, as Zipes says, the story has an "accusatory tone and moralistic message" and that it "keeps within the bounds of a male discourse" (*Trials and Tribulations*, 31). We might read the story as a crude and obvious warning to young girls not to be taken in by strange men--"crude and obvious" because what Childe-Pemberton appears to do is to take a well-known fairy tale and render both its message and its form clear. She appears to remove the magic from the tale in order to emphasize its moral message. From the perspective of symbolic or male discourse, this is exactly what she does. She literalizes the story. In fact, she goes out of her way to emphasize the literal nature of her discourse. When the niece, Margery, complains that "Red Riding Hood" "can't possibly be explained to be true in any kind of way," Aunt Pussy speaks up and asks whether she is certain "that it cannot possibly be explained to be true in any kind of way." She then proceeds to tell her a story "out of my own experience" (212). In other words, she not only speaks personally, but she also renders literal what the traditional story only communicates symbolically. In light of the story's interest in male and female education--boys go off to school, girls are educated at home; Margery is learning mathematics, natural philosophy, and political science, subjects traditionally reserved for the male--this female project of literalizing the fairy tale should interest us.

Perhaps I ought to come clean and explain what I think this literal narrative in itself signifies. First, we should note that Margery is receiving something of a progressive education; that is, for a girl she is learning male subjects. She is learning, as Pussy says, "to set great store by whys and wherefores, causes and effects" (212). A quick glance might lead us to conclude that Margery slights the story of Red Riding Hood because it appears to her to lack a literal meaning or what she refers to as a "*true* meaning." Clearly, she does not take it seriously because it is "altogether too unlikely for anything" (211). In effect, she appeals to her aunt to make the story meaningful, to explain not the literal action of the story but the symbolic action. She is, as her aunt says, "beginning to put away childish things," and one of these things is the child's capacity to accept at face value the wonderful happenings of fantasy. When Margery asserts that "Red Riding Hood" cannot be explained "to be true in any kind of way," she means in a symbolic way; when her aunt demurs, she explains the story to be true in the kind of way I would call literal.

The story is literally true as Pussy's personal experience illustrates. What Pussy offers her niece is a mother's language: literal, personal, direct, and heartfelt. Although Pussy has "never learnt half the things" Margery learns, and although she knows "very little about mathematics and political economy," she has herself to offer her niece. Her experience is something Margery cannot find substitutes for in her books. In short, Margery is entering the adult world, or what more pertinently we might call the "father's" world, and her aunt offers her the comfort of maternal language and affection, perhaps even the hint of what Helene Cixous calls the "impregnable language," the language that will "wreck partitions, classes, and rhetorics, regulations and codes" (256).

From a Lacanian point of view, Margery has entered the symbolic order. According to Jacques Lacan, the very young child experiences union with the mother, or what Wordsworth describes as "The gravitation and the filial bond/Of Nature that connect him to the world" (*The Prelude*, 1850: 243-244). At the age of 18 months, however, the child begins to acquire the sense of "I," which at first, in the "Mirror Stage," is a "primordial" I. Later, the child begins to sense language and sexual difference, and this stage, Freud's Oedipal crisis, brings the father into the picture as a force that separates mother and child. In Wordsworth's version of the myth, which was well known to Victorian readers, the mother dies and the child is "left alone/Seeking the visible world, nor knowing why" (277-278). The loss of the mother coincides with the acquisition of language and the awareness of sexual difference, the father replacing the mother. I turn to a passage from Margaret Homans's *Bearing the World: Language and Female Experience in 19th-Century Women's Writing* (1986) to explain this coming of the father:

The father, who is discovered to have all along been in possession of the mother, intervenes in the potentially incestuous dyad of mother and child. Because what marks the father is his possession of the phallus, the phallus becomes the mark of sexual difference, that is, of difference from the mother.

The phallus becomes the mark of language's difference as well, which becomes equivalent to sexual difference. Whereas in the preoedipal relation to the mother, communication required no distance or difference, now, with the intrusive entry of the phallus, "the child unconsciously learns that a sign has meaning only by dint of its difference from other signs, and learns also that a sign presupposes the absence of the object it signifies" (Lacan) [...] Thus the child leaves behind the communication system he shared with his mother, which required no difference, and enters what Lacan calls the "Law of the Father", or the symbolic order (6-7).

To enter the "Law of the Father," the symbolic order, is to lose not only the mother, but also the phallus because the father prohibits its use. The child accepts with enthusiasm the symbolic order because language substitutes for what is lost; it provides something *like* what is lost. As Homans says, "Figuration, then, and the definition of all language as figuration gain their hyperbolical cultural valuation from a specifically male standpoint because they allow the son, both as erotic being and as speaker, to flee from the mother as well as the lost referent with which she is primordially identified"

(9). The child spends his (and the masculine pronoun asserts force here) time searching for the lost mother. In Romantic poetry this also takes the form of a search for a pure language, Keats's "mother-tongue." That is not sadly incompetent, but rather that is literally what it speaks. To end the quest, to find the mother or attain a perfect language, would be to put an end to the law of the father, to overcome the dominance or power of the male. This pure language, or the lost mother, nessesarily is approached only in a series of figures. These figures are supplied by the speaking subject. To be a subject, Lacan notes in his essay "Of Structure as an Inmixing of an Otherness Prerequisite to Any Subject Whatever," is to introduce "a loss in reality" (193). The pain of loss, then, finds compensation in figurative substitutes for that which is lost.

As may now be evident, the female finds herself both troped and trapped. She is the literal level that symbolic discourse constantly strives for, but that it must not achieve. She is perpetually sought after by male desire, but just the same she is perpetually absent. Lacan smugly notes: "There is no woman who is not excluded by the nature of things, which is the nature of words, and it must be said that, if there is something they complain a lot about at the moment, that is what it is--except that they don't know what they are saying, that's the whole difference between them and me" (cited in Homans, 9). Homans suggests, however, that the female might have a different relationship with the literal than a male does. It appears, she says, "that it would be equally satisfying for women writers to rediscover the presymbolic language shared with their mothers that writing as motherhood, as opposed to writing as the search for symbolic, phallic connections, might activate" (26). Childe-Pemberton's literalization of "Red Riding Hood," then, might reflect the female writer's attempt to rediscover the presymbolic language, to write as mother. The male writer substitutes figures for what he is lacking; the female writer who does not experience lack of the mother or the phallus, or whatever, to the same degree as the male does not need to speak figuratively. The woman writer knows what she is saying because she says it; for her, words and nature are the same thing. The male writer cut loose from nature by the law of the father knows less what he is saying because he constantly defers meaning by figuring it.

To come to the point, I appropriate Margaret Homans's suggestion that a daughter's psychological development differs from the one outlined by Lacan and also by, as Homans says, Wordsworth and the tradition of male discourse generally. Because a daughter's attachment to her mother is not the same as a son's, because she is less threatened by the father, she has less reason to embrace the Law of the Father wholeheartedly. She does accept this law, but "she does not do so exclusively" (Homans, 13). Consequently, the daughter "speaks two languages at once. Along with symbolic language, she retains the literal or presymbolic language that the son represses at the time of his renunciation of his mother" (13). Speaking two languages, the daughter experiences ambivalence. She is, of course, expected to enter the male world, yet she remains attached to the female world. A woman's proper duty, especially as conceived in the nineteenth century, is as a mother and a helpmate to her husband. She is not supposed to take up language and write, and when she does she writes like a man, one who conceives of "the idea of a mother-daughter language dangerous to writing" (27). For this reason, a story such as "All My Doing; or Red Riding Hood Over Again" ostensibly accepts the male stance. Just as the folktale "Red Riding Hood" presents its sexual warning symbolically, Childe-Pemberton's retelling presents Pussy's violation by the male through figures: the robbery of grandmother's house and the "penetration" of her bedroom, the loss of Herbert's leg, and Pussy's name. Pussy's ruin results from her ignorance of the male's designs on her. Childe-Pemberton and her narrator Pussy draw attention to the symbolic dimension of the story when Pussy remarks that "the loss of a limb implies a great, great deal more than the loss of the limb itself" (247). Yet the sexual symbolism suggested here--loss of a limb equals the loss of virility--has its literal aspect. The loss of a limb *does* imply more than simply the loss of a limb; it implies a readjustment of one's whole life. Symbolic and literal language conjoin here.

This story of a heedless girl who suffers a life of independence and loneliness and who appears to accept society's judgment of her as the cause of her male friend and lover's single and incomplete life speaks in two languages. Not only is its literalization of the traditional story significant in itself, but also the apparent acceptance of the Law of the Father is more apparent than actual. The story of how two people who love each other fail to make a life together is an indictment of a society dominated by male values. Even the fact that Pussy remains unmarried is not as terrible a fate as the Victorian sense of a woman's fulfillment in marriage might indicate. As early as 1792 in *Vindications of the Rights of Woman*, Mary Wollstonecraft argues that marriage renders women like children, and she urges independence for the female. Even earlier, in her children's book *Original Stories from Real Life* (1788), she urged young girls to improve their minds since "it is the proper exercise of our reason that makes us in any degree independent" (386). Certainly, she does not advocate the single life, but her portrait of the widow "raised to heroism by misfortunes" in the *Rights of Woman* (138) suggests that the single life need not be the unfulfilled life. And by 1845 Margaret Fuller could write: "In this regard of self-dependence, and a greater simplicity and fulness of being, we must hail as a preliminary the increase of the class contemptuously designated as 'old maids'" (*The Woman Question*, 58). In light of this valuation of independence--even to the point of the female remaining single--we might examine the apparent lesson to be derived from Herbert remaining "a lame old bachelor" and Pussy remaining "a lonely old maid."

The comma in my title--lame old bachelor, lonely old maid--signifies lack. Obviously, what the old bachelor lacks is companionship, female companionship; what the old maid lacks is also companionship, male companionship. In fact, they lack each other. The story, in which these two lonely figures live, makes it abundantly clear that this is lack, absence, deferral, separation, loss. Pussy's family is constantly "in a hurry, and nobody ever attended to anyone else" (215). Her father, she says, eats his meals standing "like the hatter in 'Alice in Wonderland', his teacup in one hand and his slice of bread and butter in the other" (214). The reference to the hatter nicely suggests that the father is caught in a dull round, defeated by time, and is perhaps overly attentive to the judicial and class system of his age. In any case, he is often absent even when he is present. For example, Pussy tells of entering the diningroom one morning to find her father "hearing one of the children say the multiplication table, eating his breakfast rapidly the while, and scanning the morning paper into tha bargain" (215). Her mother has told her that her father wishes to see her, but when she approaches him she finds he has no time to tell her what he wants. Deferral is the order of the day and of most days in this family and its world.

In contrast, nothing is deferred at Pussy's grandmother's house. Here is a small world in which comfort is the order of the day, of all days. Pussy's grandmother, like so many of the grandmother figures who populate Victorian children's books, is single. She lacks a husband, but this lack is hardly a lack. This is how Pussy descibes her:

She was a large, handsome, good-natured woman, who liked everything about her to be handsome and on a large scale; she habitually wore good silk dresses, and had her rooms filled with choice flowers; her cook was good, and her carriage and horses always smartly turned out. She wore handsome rings, and had her pocket-handkerchiefs scented with the best eau-de-Cologne. Yet she was hardly to be called an epicure, was my grandmother; she only liked to be comfortable and have nice things about her; and no one was more anxious that others should be comfortable too, and take their share of nice things. (225)

The word most often used to describe her and her living conditions is "comfortable." She lives with her daughter Rosa who spends her time "worrying, and fretting, and bustling about the comfort of the house" (225). Although both grandmother and Rosa are anxious that others are well taken care of, neither of them suffers. The Victorian ideal of female self-renunciation, articulated, for example, by John Ruskin in *Sesame and Lilies* (1865), does not appear to enter their heads. This is a very comfortable household indeed, and the three women manage well without men about the house. In fact, when men enter the house disaster follows. Had Herbert not been staying the night, the robbers would not have shot him in making their escape. And obviously had Pussy not invited the strange man she first met on the train into her grandmother's house, the robbers would not have come at all. Men destroy this comfortable woman's world.

In the traditional story of Red Riding Hood, at least as the Brothers Grimm tell it, a man saves the day. The woodcutter arrives to rescue Granny and Red from the belly of the wolf. Here Herbert assumes the woodcutter's role; perhaps the wooden leg he ends up with is a grim reminder of the original story. Although Herbert assists in scaring away the robbers, he is ineffectual in saving Pussy from the dire consequenses of the break-in. In fact, he perpetuates these consequences by renouncing his relationship with her. The story, we might say, ends for Pussy as it ended for Perrault's Red: the man's world has swallowed her. The male experiences life as lack, and the woman represents this lack. And she does so by bearing it, by carrying the blame for the necessary loss that others, that is, the male, must suffer. This story's Red Riding Hood, Pussy, carries this blame because she has been hoodwinked by a man, a thief, a betrayer, and one who violates female space. Pussy judges herself heedless and thoughtless, and yet she realizes that her betrayer played upon her innocence. She accepts blame for the catastrophe, and yet she resists blame. She, like her creator, experiences ambivalence: Is she perpetrator or victim?

Pussy's initial reaction to the robbery, the shock her grandmother received, and Herbert's wound is self-recrimination: "I realised how the blame of it all lay primarily at my door. *I* it was who heedlessly introduced the plausible stranger into the house. *It* it was who had blindly allowed him to make a plan of the rooms under pretence of sketching the oak" (239). Her locution "I it" neatly communicates how the experience has desexed her. She regrets not having heeded her mother's caution not to speak with strangers and not having taken her brother's words to heart about considering consequences before she either acted or spoke.

This bringing together of the mother and eldest brother is interesting. Taken alongside the mother's education of Margery in male subjects (and we might recall that Pussy comments that she might proceed differently were she in charge of Margery's education), this parallel of the mother's advice with the son's suggests the weakness of mothering in the book. When mothers educate their daughters in male discourse, they comply with patriarchy's systematic diminishment of the female. Pussy's relationship with Margery provides a corrective to mother-daughter relationships which are in coercion with patriarchy. Instead of providing Margery with books, Pussy gives herself; she is the text Margery reads (cf. Myers, 39, 49).

Unlike her niece, Pussy has no mother to comfort her, although her Aunt Rosa's capableness and control offer her a model of female ability to cope with a crisis. After hearing that the police have a good chance of apprehending the robbers, Pussy resolves to bear witness against them, and especially against the one who had duped her. She reasons: "after all, he, and he only, was the real cause of my grandmother's illness and Herbert's wound." She recognizes that he has violated her: "he had traded on my thoughtlessness and had taken advantage of my innocence" (242). Her sense of selfhood reemerges in her fierce indignation against the man who has deceived her: "he had made a tool of *me* [...] he had inspired *me* with confidence and belief in his perfect honesty [...] he had contrived out of my very simplicity to make *me* the accomplice of his crimes!" (242). Her identity is strong enough to withstand the "rather unpleasant remarks" passed on her conduct which she hears during the trial of the culprits.

What might have happened to Pussy were this all her story had to relate is anyone's guess. Her testimony at the trial of the felons helped gain a conviction against the man who had violated her trust and her person. This, she says, ends her story "so far as the robbery is concerned" (244). However, she still has to tell what happened to herself, her grandmother, and Herbert. We already know the surface details here: Pussy remains a lonely old maid, grandmother never recovers her health, and Herbert lives on a lame old bachelor. If Pussy's voice as narrator of the story is any indication, she has not lived an unrewarding and empty life. She tells her tale with gusto, obviously enjoying the role of storyteller, and amused at her youthful bustle and self-importance. But what in the final part of her telling would account for her mature sense of self-worth? Aside from recounting the effects of Herbert's wound in the last paragraphs of the story, Pussy also recalls her grandmother's reaction to the robbery. What accounts for the depth of grandmother's shock is the red cloak that Pussy so loved and that connects her to the Red of "Red Riding Hood."

True to her realistic and literal telling, Pussy precisely describes this red cloak near the beginning of the story. But what catches us is the alteration Childe-Pemberton makes from the original in which Red receives the cloak from her granny. In this version, Pussy herself buys the cloak using money she has received from an "old bachelor uncle" (214). This may be the clue that the young Pussy has, like Margery at 15, entered the symbolic order where fashion dictates identity. Clothes make the person. In Pussy's case, her scarlet cloak, "with a pair of red stockings, just showing above laced boots, the smallest of small black hats on my head, and my hair drawn back into a chenille net" make her look "not very unlike Red Riding Hood herself." In this get-up, she says, "people took me to be younger than I was" (214). And the "dapper little man" on the train whose age "was impossible to guess at" takes her for a ride (220). Because of her vanity, because of her acceptance of identity as fashion, she easily falls victim to the charms of a man who sees her only as a mark, a mark of easy money, easy gratification of his own desire for gain.

During the robbery of her grandmother's house, one of the thieves put on Pussy's scarlet cloak, and the appearance of this cloaked figure in her room is what so deeply affected her grandmother. She repeats over and over again: "I thought it was Pussy! I thought it was Pussy! The dreadful face under the hood! The face of a murderer!" (244). As Pussy explains, what her grandmother reacted to was not the robbery, but rather an "attempt to murder." The man's face in her granddaughter's hood signifies death to her. The discovery that the person in the hood was not Pussy unhinged grandmother's mind. The discovery that her granddaughter was really a man was too shocking to bear. Of course, Pussy is not a man. But her grandmother's experience, mistaken though she was literally, serves as a warning. The red cloak and all it represents--Red Riding Hood, fashion, male dominance, death to female identity--must be relinquished. The cloak speaks to us in the two languages of the daughter: symbolically and literally. As a symbol, the red cloak connects this story with the story of Red Riding Hood and with the blood that is let in the rather bloodless account of the wolf's eating of the little girl and her grandmother, but just the same it literally signifies the fashionable world of female economy which Pussy has accepted. We might say that this Victorian retelling of "Red Riding Hood" both literally and symbolically endorses the moral warning of the traditional story.

This story also appears strongly to endorse the Victorian emphasis on the efficacy of suffering. Two trials are apparent: one, the trial by jury of the thieves, and the other, the psychological trial of Pussy and the others who were in the house the night of the robbery. This second trial, though dire, brings Pussy to a realization of her love for Herbert and to an understanding of her youthful folly. Interestingly, however, when Pussy confesses her innocent complicity in the robbery, her grandmother "chuckled [...] with the comfortable chuckle that reminded me of the days of her health." Pussy is taken aback, but her grandmother "*would* persist in laughing about it" (246). The laugh of Medusa? True, Granny does speak of the value of experience and of its cost. This platitude sits well perhaps with the epigraph to the story from F. W. Farrer, which speaks of "manly resolution" as the ideal result of loss. But Granny's laugh and Pussy's storytelling bespeak a womanly resolution, a resolution, in the words of Xaviere Gauthier, to "*make audible* that which agitates within us" (163). Motherly speech, audible speech, oral speech, women's speech: this is what we hear in "All My Doing; or Red Riding Hood Over Again." The power of this speech resonates beyond its sound as Pussy indicates at the end of the story when she says (ostensibly to Margaret, but since she does not name her we may assume she speaks to her audience in general) the "slightest word has an echo far beyond what you can hear" (248).

What we can hear, of course, is contradictory: symbolic language and literal language, self-deprecation and self-assertion, acceptance of Victorian norms and resistance to those norms. If, as Perry Nodelman suggests, children's literature "is a feminine literature" (33), then such contradictions are to be expected. They are the inevitable result of an ambivalence. Women and children are familiar with disenfranchisement, with, as they say, the experience of being marginalized, and the literature produced by and for them manifests a desire to revise the power structure that excludes them. This literature must be subversive. And yet this literature written, for the most part, by women for women and for children, this motherly writing, reflects social responsibility, the responsibility a mother has to teach her child the means of survival in the social world that has been for so long the world of the father. This contradictory impulse, this ambivalence, leads to the two languages of women's writing, and if Nodelman is right, of children's literature.

What would be interesting to discover is whether this same ambivalence appears in children's own writing. Also, to hear the literal and symbolic languages Homans explicates in stories such as "All My Doing; or Red Riding Hood Over Again" is easy because of the overtly literal setting for the fairy tale. To find such a strategy of literalization and, of course, to value it in the many fantasies written by women for children might well allow us to recover much that has lain silent and unavailable from that period. It might also allow us to read those works that have survived--for example, Frances Browne's *Granny's Wonderful Chair*, Jean Ingelow's *Mopsa the Fairy*, or Frances Hodgson Burnett's *The Secret Garden*--as poignant expressions of two languages, the language of No and the language of Yes: the No of the Father and the Yes of the Mother. The father's No puts an end to secrets, explains everything as figuration; the mother's Yes keeps thesecret intact and returns us to the humus from which we came. To be lonely is surely preferable to being lame.

REFERENCES

Cixous, Helene. "The Laugh of the Medusa," in Elaine Marks and Isabelle de Courtivron, eds. *New French Feminisms*. New York: Schocken, 1981, pp. 245-264.

Gauthier, Xaviere. "Is There Such a Thing as Women's Writing," in Elaine Marks and Isabelle de Courtivron, eds. *New French Feminisms*. New York: Schocken, 1981, pp. 161-164.

Helsinger, Elizabeth K., Robin Lauterbach Sheets, and William Veeder. *The Woman Question: Society and Literature in Britain and America 1837-1883*. Vol. 1. Chicago: University of Chicago Press, 1989 (1983).

Homans, Margaret. *Bearing the World: Language and Female Experience in 19th-Century Women's Writing*. Chicago: University of Chicago Press, 1989 (1986).

Lacan, Jacques. "Of Structure as an Inmixing of an Otherness Prerequisite to Any Subject Whatever," in Richard Macksey and Eugenio Donato, eds. *The Structuralist Controversy*. Baltimore: Johns Hopkins University Press, 1977 (1970), pp. 186-200.

---. "The Mirror Stage as Formative of the Function of the I as Revealed in Psychoanalytic Experience," in Dan Latimer, ed. *Contemporary Critical Theory*. New York: Harcourt Brace Janovich, 1989, pp. 502-509.

Myers, Mitzi. "Impeccable Governesses, Rational Dames, and Moral Mothers: Mary Wollstonecraft and the Female Tradition in Georgian Children's Books," *Children's Literature*,1986:14, pp. 31-59.

Nodelman, Perry. "Children's Literature as Women's Writing," *Children's Literature Association Quaterly*, 1988:13, pp. 31-34.

Wollstonecraft, Mary. "Original Stories from Real Life" (1788), in Robert Bator, ed. *Masterworks of Children's Literature*. Vol. 3. New York: Stonehill, 1983, pp. 351-406.

---. *Vindications of the Rights of Woman* (1792). Harmondsworth, Middlesex: Penguin, 1985.

Wordsworth, William. *The Prelude: A Parallel Text*. J.C. Maxwell, ed. Harmondsworth, Middlesex: Penguin, 1971.

Zipes, Jack. *The Trials and Tribulations of Little Red Riding Hood*. South Hadley, Mass.: Bergin & Garvey, 1983.

---, ed. *Victorian Fairytales: The Revolt of the Fairies and Elves*. New York: Methuen, 1987.

The Role of Women Writers in Early Children's Literature: An Analysis of the Case of Mrs. Barbara Hofland

Dennis Butts

In late eighteenth- and early nineteenth-century England, many women began writing for children--Lucy Cameron (1781-1858), Maria Edgeworth (1767-1849), Maria Hack (1777-1844), Hannah More (1745-1833), Mrs. Sherwood (1775-1851), and Mrs. Sarah Trimmer (1741-1810), to name some of the most prominent.

They often produced rather didactic books in the form of moral tales, in which they usually intended to propagate the traditional moral, religious, and social values of their time. (Hannah More and Mrs. Trimmer actually wrote to defend the British status quo against the atheistical revolutionary doctrines of the French Revolution.) Their tales usually concentrate on the world of domestic reality rather than on that of exotic fantasy or overseas adventure. They focus upon everyday family life and work, showing in Hannah More's *The Shepherd of Salisbury Plain* of 1795, for example, how it is possible to be happy, even if you are only a poor shepherd with a sick wife and a large family, as long as you practice the Christian virtues.

In writing such tales, however, some women writers, either deliberately or unconsciously, raise questions about the family, work and the role of women in the society of their day, which often challenge the values their stories seem to support.

Barbara Hofland is a superb example of the woman writer whose children's books reveal more than she always lets out overtly, and who has more to say about the situation of women in the early nineteenth century than more radical feminists would suspect. An extremely popular author of children's stories at the beginning of the nineteenth century, regularly producing simple moral tales of middle-class family life and impeccable Christian morality, Mrs. Hofland often shows what Patricia Thomson has called "the insidious percolations, often against the author's will, of the new ideas that were beginning to undermine the Victorian domestic idyll."[1]

For this the vicissitudes of Mrs. Hofland's long, hard, and ultimately heroic life are almost certainly responsible, for it was a life that contained triumphs and disasters which she not only drew on for the materials of her books, but which also helped her develop, unconsciously perhaps, strong feminist insights.

Barbara Wreaks, as she was first called, was born in Sheffield in 1770, the daughter of an ironmonger who died when she was only 3, leaving his widow to bring up Barbara and a younger boy. Barbara's mother remarried, and Barbara was brought up, happily evidently, by a maiden-aunt. She seems to have acquired some kind of education, for she was well acquainted with the Bible and with Shakespeare and most of the English poets, as well as a good deal of history and geography.

She was a lively and talented girl, and began to appear in the pages of the new Sheffield newspaper, *The Iris,* from 1794 onwards. These were turbulent times, however, and it is a tribute to Barbara's liberal sympathies and courage that when the editor of *The Iris*, James Montgomery, was imprisoned in 1795 for printing an allegedly seditious ballad, Barbara published a sonnet in praise of the editor's lawyer.

All this time Barbara was earning a living running her own milliner's shop, but she sold this business when she married a prominent Sheffield businessman, Thomas Hoole, in 1796. The couple spent two idyllic years together, as Hoole's business prospered, and they soon had a baby daughter. But tragedy was never very far away from Barbara, and in June 1798 the daughter died, to be followed in March 1799 by the death of Thomas Hoole, leaving the young widow with a baby boy of four months to support. The collapse of Hoole's business shortly after his death left her virtually penniless, and, to make matters worse, money that had been left to Hoole's infant son Frederic was lost when the trustees went bankrupt too.

The young widow was resilient, however. Taking her infant son with her, she went to live with her mother-in-law in Attercliffe, and there with her old friend James Montgomery she began to put together a collection of her verses, which was published in 1805 and achieved the remarkable sale by subscription of over two thousand copies. This sucess was a tribute more to the widow's personality perhaps than to the quality of her poetry, which, apart from some "Lines occasioned by the death of a little relative," is rather disappointing.

With the money raised from the sales of the poetry, however, Mrs. Hoole was able to send her son to the Moravian school at Fulneck and to open a girls' boarding school in Harrogate. Encouraged, too, by the success of her poems, she wrote her first children's story, *The History of an Officer's Widow*, in which she told the story of a family and their struggles together after their father died of war wounds. John Harris, London's leading publisher of children's books, gave her £6 for it and published it in 1809, the same year she opened her school in Harrogate.

Other children's books soon followed, and even better was the arrival of a handsome suitor in the person of Thomas Christopher Hofland, a talented but impecunious landscape artist, who met Barbara when poverty forced him into teaching art for a time. Although Barbara's friends had doubts about the match, there was no doubt about Hofland's ability--he had exhibited at the Royal Academy since 1798--and Barbara fell deeply in love with the attractive and engaging artist. They were married in 1810.

At first all went well. Hofland exhibited paintings at the Leeds Art Exhibitions, and his "View of Windermere" was accepted by the Royal Academy. But, although Barbara's writing was going well, the school proved a disappointment, not only because of so many difficult pupils but also because of the equally difficult parents' reluctance to pay their children's fees. Even more worrying was the state of Hofland's health. He was ill in January and again in March 1811. It cannot have been difficult for Barbara and her husband to feel that their problems could best be put behind them by making a fresh start elsewhere. In November 1811 they sold up in Harrogate and before the year was out had settled in London.

The move obviously gave a fresh impetus to Hofland's career. He won a prize of 100 guineas for a seascape in 1814, and in 1815 he had no fewer than six pictures accepted by the Academy. Mrs. Hofland's own career prospered too, and during their first year in London she had no five books published, including her most successful *The Son of a Genius* (1812), which reached a fourteenth edition by 1826 and was frequently reprinted in America and France. She was praised by Queen Charlotte and became friendly with such writers as Maria Edgeworth.

In *The Son of a Genius*, Mrs. Hofland told the story of a talented but imprudent artist who wasted his gifts and almost ruined the lives of his wife and children because of his erratic and unstable temperament. When we read this, it is difficult not to suspect that Mrs. Hofland was beginning to reflect some of the experiences of her own second marriage. Hofland had been brought up as a leisured gentlemen, and in many ways he still regarded himself as one, despite the fact that he had to earn a living as an artist. He was, for example, frequently away from home, not just on painting expeditions but on fishing jaunts. Then again, although he undoubtedly had artistic successes, they were irregular, perhaps because of his poor health. Although Mrs. Hofland's friends had their suspicions about this, Mrs. Hofland never voiced them. The saddest thing of all, however, is that as Hofland's career failed to develop in the way he had hoped--his tragedy is not unlike that of his friend Benjamin Haydon--so he became extremely difficult to live with, and at his worst moments even abused his wife .

In 1816, Hofland produced an illegitimate son--from what source we do not know, perhaps someone he met on one of his expeditions--whom his wife took in, nursed, and treated as her own child for the rest of her life. Whether it was to avoid embarrassment over this or for business reasons, the Hoflands moved to Twickenham in the same year and began work on an important commission for the marquis of Blandford, heir to the duke of Marlborough. The marquis had bought the mansion of Whiteknights near Reading, and having spent large sums on its garden and library--paying over

£2,000 for a fine edition of the *Decameron*, for example--he engaged the Hoflands to produce a book describing his showplace, with illustrations by Hofland to accompany a text written by Mrs. Hofland. For nearly three years husband and wife worked on the project, making sketches, engaging engravers and printers, producing a very handsome volume. But by the time the book was finished in 1819, although the marquis had now become the duke of Marlborough, he was virtually bankrupt, so the Hoflands never got a penny from him, except for the money they got for selling off unwanted copies of the book themselves.

So Hofland's career continued in its erratic way. In 1821, an exhibition of his paintings in New Bond Street failed, and his outbursts of temper became more noticeable to outsiders. Nonetheless, Mrs. Hofland continued to support him cheerfully. "We never heard her utter a complaint or expose any weakness of her husband," said a friend.[2] The pattern of their lives settled into a routine of occasional artistic successes by the husband sustained by the steady production of literary works by Mrs. Hofland, often two or three books a year, children's tales, textbooks, essays for the Annuals--anything that would bring in money. By the 1830s, she often found the physical effort of writing painful because of a shoulder injury received in 1818, but still she kept on writing.

All this time she had been cheered and sustained by the love of her son Frederic, who, after school at Fulneck, had gone on to Cambridge and then taken Holy Orders. Working as a curate in Holborn, he did marvelous work among the poor. He was one of those Christian priests whose simple goodness shines out amidst some of the worst aspects of nineteenth-century England. But in the autumn of 1832 he fell ill, and the mother who had already buried his babysister and his father, now had the task of nursing him through the last weeks of his life.

Even now she was not finished. There were still books to be written, correspondence with old friends like James Montgomery to be kept up, a husband to be looked after. In 1840 Hofland fulfilled a lifetime ambition when he visited Italy, but his health continued to deteriorate on his return, and he died in 1843. Despite her loss, Mrs. Hofland went on working, on another children's book, her forty-third, and made a last visit to Sheffield where she again met her old friend Montgomery. "I have got quite safe to my native town," she wrote to a friend. "I was tired but a day's quietness restored me, and I am now as well as possible, save my breath; and of that I must not complain. My Heavenly Father deals with me very gently; life has been stormy with me, but I trust my sun will set peacefully."[3]

She returned home to finish her children's story in the summer of 1844, but then an attack of erysipelas was aggravated by a fall (she was now in her seventy-fourth year) and she did not have the strength to resist a second attack when it came. She died on November 4, 1844 and was buried in a vault in Richmond Parish Churchyard.[4]

Mrs. Hofland's arduous and heroic life is not untypical, except in its details, of the lives of many women writers of her time.[5] Indeed, one of the reasons why her books were so popular, sometimes going into a dozen editions, is that many readers recognized the picture of life they presented. For Mrs. Hofland is in many ways an extremely orthodox and representative woman of the period, lower middle class, a moderate member of the Church of England (neither a Dissenter nor an Evangelical), liberal in her sympathies but not particularly radical. She is a firm believer in marriage and conventional family life. Mrs. Ellis's plea in *The Women of England* (1839)[6] for good household management as both a practical and a moral duty is one she would have agreed with; and there is no question of any young girl, wife, or mother in her books asking for anything like women's rights! When young Maria in *The Clergyman's Widow* declares her ambition to become a good wife, Mrs. Hofland adds approvingly, "No pernicious doctrine of modern philosophy had contaminated the purity of her understanding".[7]

Above all, Mrs. Hofland shares the belief of many of her contemporaries in the validity of the Protestant Work Ethic, as a reading of any of her simple stories for children reveals. Although she wrote the same kind of moral tales as Maria Edgeworth and Mrs. Sherwood, almost all her books abound in references to work and to money.

The *Son of a Genius,* for example, contrasts the tragedy of Lewis, the artist of genius but unstable temperament, with the story of his young son who supports his mother and sister by selling little drawings in Leeds Market for two shillings each, and, through virtue and industry, finally achieves the happiness and prosperity that his father's lack of steady application failed to provide. The same lesson is repeated in such stories as *The History of an Officer's Widow* (1809), *The Blind Farmer and His Children* (1816), and *Elizabeth and Her Three Beggar Boys* (1833). Mrs. Hofland clearly wished her young readers to see a close relationship betwen the upholding of such Christian virtues as trust in God, patience, moderation and self-control, and their reward not simply in spiritual blessings, but on this earth now.

So, while most of Mrs. Hofland's moral tales are based upon the assertion of the primacy of moral and Christian qualities, an important thread of economic activity is almost always associated with them. (It is impossible, of course, not to relate this to the circumstances of her own life, her early widowhood, poverty, and the long years supporting her second husband.) Thus, her three books about widowhood--*The Clergyman's Widow* (1812), *The Merchant's Widow* (1814) and *The Officer's Widow*--all show women wresting with financial problems after their husbands' deaths. *The Blind Farmer* depicts the economic struggles of a farmer's family after he loses his farm, and *Elizabeth and Her Three Beggar Boys* is about a working-class housewife who adopts three boys and brings them up despite her own poverty. *The Daughter-in-Law* (1812) and *The Sisters* (1813) both deal with the problems caused by extravagant stepmothers, and *Alicia and Her Aunt* (1822), *The Affectionate Brothers* (1816), and *Ellen the Teacher* (1814) all center on young people whose parents die young or leave them to fend for themselves.

There is thus in Mrs. Hofland's books written for young people and children at the beginning of the nineteenth century always plenty about work. Nearly all her characters have jobs, and this almost endless curiosity about what people do for a living gives her books a dimension missing from many earlier writers and pointing forward to the later achievements of Dickens, George Eliot, and Thomas Hardy.

Clergymen, teachers, and governesses were fairly commonplace in contemporary literature, and it is not surprising that Mrs. Hofland also describes the working lives of artists, soldiers and merchants. But she also describes people working as brickmakers and potters, as silver platers and milliners, as apothecaries and servants and glove-makers, giving specific information about earnings, for example.

It is important not to claim too much. The *majority* of her characters' occupations are predominantly middle class, or the kinds of occupations such as schoolteaching, which middle-class people took in distressed circumstances. The accounts of factory work are limited, and the amount of detail also varies enormously. Nonetheless. Mrs. Hofland's treatment of work is still impressive, especially if we compare it with that of such contemporaries as Jane Austen, for example.

It is, however, when she writes of women and work that Mrs. Hofland writes with most conviction and no little originality. Domestic crises tend to be at the heart of her fiction--the death of a father ,a husband's instability, the loss of the family livelihood--and what she is interested in is how people respond in that crisis. She is, of course, a firm advocate of love, marriage, and family life. Some of the most touching moments in her stories arise when she depicts the love and cooperation between members of a family at the time of great distress such as the loss of a parent. (Charlotte M. Yonge's *The Daisy Chain* and Mrs. E. Nesbit's *The Railway Children* may owe something to Mrs. Hofland here.)[8]

In a number of stories, however, harassed wives like Mrs. Lewis in *The Son of a Genius* or Mrs. Daventry in *The Merchant's Widow* reveal strengths and abilities quite unsuspected by their husbands. Mrs. Lewis contrives to support her family when her artist-husband fails to do so, but Mrs. Hofland tells us that she has to do it secretly in order to avoid hurting his pride. Mrs. Daventry, the widow of the merchant who underestimated her business ability, reveals her strength as she gradually recovers from grieving over his death:

When at last the affectionate mother was enabled to lift her head to Him who seeth in secret, and who turneth not a deaf ear even to those "sighings of the sorrowful soul which cannot be uttered", she began to recover those faculties of mind which might be said to be suspended; she was aware that her affairs were in a disordered state, and that it was her duty to inquire how far she was justified in continuing her present establishment, though a reduced one? Rousing herself she sent for the principal clerk engaged in her late husband's services, and inquired of him "if any letters had been lately received from her uncle, and whether they contained remittances of any consequence?"[9]

The transition from bereavement to religious consolation, and from religious consolation to the more practical matter of the remittances--all within a single paragraph!--is absolutely typical of Mrs. Hofland's psychological insight as well as her values.

Similar suggestions of female competence are rendered with even more force in *Ellen the Teacher*. Captain Delville gives up his army career when he marries and sets himself up in business. But he is unsuccessful, and so his young wife begins to investigate:

hitherto mild, gentle, and engaging, she had appeared rather amiable than strong, interesting than useful; but she now felt herself called upon for peculiar exertion as a mother and a wife; and conscious that she possessed talents which possessed utility, she busied herself in assisting her husband to arrange hisaffairs, examine his resources, secure his friends, and multiply his connections [...] Her situation was trying and delicate; for she found her husband more ignorant of the routine of business than she supposed possible, and grievously indolent; yet the very consciousness of his unfitness for it rendered him peculiarly tenacious of his own authority; so that while she conducted everything in *fact*, she was condemned to affect ignorance, to apply for instruction, to praise exertion which never existed and flatter powers it was nearly impossible to awaken.[10]

Given the social conventions of the age and the circumstances of her second marriage, it is not surprising that Mrs. Hofland should have seen the frustrations of talented women so clearly, nor that she should at times have written so feelingly about them. Though deeply committed to marriage and the role of the wife as homemaker, she could not help suggesting other roles for the heroines of her children's books. Mrs. Hofland's books uusually articulate the conventional views of women of her day, but she frequently and stealthily offers alternative views in ways which it has been suggested that some later children's writers, such as Louisa May Alcott, also do, for example.[11]

In the most remarkable of her stories dealing with women and work, she comes near to offering an absolutely radical solution. The moral of her tale *Decision* (1824) is the need for discipline and self-control, and this message is articulated through what looks like Mrs. Hofland's familiar plot of a family's economic distress and then gradual recovery.

Mr. Falconer, a gentleman of wealth and property, lives extravagantly, and when his business collapses, his daughter Maria learns that her father has squandered his wife's fortune as well as his own. Alhough she is sorry for her father's plight, she is indignant at his mismanagement. "At this moment

I cannot forgive my father--I have no patience with him," she tells her mother in very unladylike terms. "Has he not schemed, wasted, fooled away two noble fortunes?"[12]

It is Maria who decides that their remaining money and property must be used to pay their outstanding debts, and then, astonishingly, the 19-year-old girl declares her intention of becoming an iron-merchant! Despite friendly protestations--"But your exquisite voice, your elegant person, Maria !"--she packs her plainest clothes and moves to a nearby manufacturing town where she rents a warehouse and begins selling steel to the poorer artisans in smaller quantities than the great iron-masters find profitable. (Brought up in the steel town of Sheffield, Mrs. Hofland would know all about the problems of the little "mesters" with a small smithy at the back of the house.)[13]

Despite the roughness of the work and the genteel protests of her parents, Maria prospers because she is meeting a real need. She brings straightforward common sense to the task, deciding, for example, to use a nightcap to cover her hair and to wear thick leather gloves to handle the iron bars. Business expands, and when she is lent 200 pounds she decides toenter the German market too. Mrs. Hofland enthusiastically tells us that "Maria entered with renovated vigilance into the various duties of her situation, and presented to the observant eye decided proof of how much woman is capable." She is especially praised for "the knowledge and acumen she displayed in all her matters of business," and, we are told, by firmness, integrity, and "womanish exactness" attained a "prosperity which she evidently enjoyed."[14]

Significantly, Maria continues in her business long after it would have been possible for her to sell the concern and return to her former way of life. Although she is disappointed in one love affair, she also turns down two proposals of marriage. The reader familiar with other tales of Mrs. Hofland and her contemporaries confidently expects Maria to marry the German businessman she meets, and then, when she declines his proposal, to accept the hand of her first love when he returns to her, a widower. But Maria in fact turns down both proposals, preferring to go on living with her aged mother.

For the truth is that Maria, an early example of the career woman, is married to her job, to use the well-worn phrase, and although Mrs. Hofland would have denied it, *Decision*, her story for young people, is almost a subversive book.

NOTES

1. Patricia Thomson, *The Victorian Heroine* (Oxford, 1957), p. 7.

2. S. C. Hall, *A Book of Memories of Great Men and Women of the Age from Personal Acquaintance* 3rd ed., (London, n.d.), p.123.

3. Thomas Ramsay, *The Life and Literary Remains of Barbara Hofland* (London, 1849), p. 201.

4. For details of Mrs. Hofland's life, as well as Thomas Ramsay op.cit., see also Dennis Butts, Mistress of Our Tears (London: Scholar Press, 1992).

5. See, for example, the cases cited by Ellen Moers, *Literary Women.* (London, 1977).

6. Mrs. Ellis, *The Women of England* (London, 1839).

7. Barbara Hofland, *The History of a Clergyman's Widow and Her Young Family* (London, n.d), p. 157.

8. C. M. Yonge, *The Daisy Chain* (London, 1856); E. Nesbit, *The Railway Children* (London, 1906).

9. Barbara Hofland, *The History of a Merchant's Widow* (London, 1867), pp. 21-22.

10. Barbara Hofland, *Ellen the Teacher; A Tale for Youth* 3rd ed. (London, 1822), p.16.

11. See, for example, E. L. Keyser, "Domesticity Versus Identity; a Review of Alcott Research," *Children's Literature in Education,* 16 (1985), pp. 165-175.

12. Barbara Hofland, *Decision; a Tale* (London, 1840), p. 64.

13. Ibid., p. 81.

14. Ibid., p. 189.

Part IV

GENRES, MODES, STYLES

National Myths in Three Classical Picture Books

Reinbert Tabbert

In memory of Joseph H. Schwarcz, author of *Ways of the Illustrator*

The English love their *Peter Rabbit*, the French their *Babar*, and the Germans used to get involved with their *Häschenschule* (i.e., school of little hares). *Peter Rabbit* was published in 1901, *Babar* in 1931, and *Häschenschule* in 1924, and each of them is still in print. So here are three animal picture books that have proved to be classics.

As Peter Berger[1] and Leonard Marcus[2] have pointed out, in the course of the nineteenth century animals passed out of the lives of most European families. Toy substitutes entered the nurseries, and fictional substitutes entered the newly founded realm of the picture book. These picture-book animals tended to be more individualized characters than those of the fable tradition. Many of them merged with various child images that had developed since Rousseau had proclaimed the shift from Original Sin to Original Innocence.[3]

There is yet another context that is worth considering. In a sense, Peter Berger may be right when he argues that "the pettiness of current social practices is universalized by being projected on the animal kingdom."[4] However, quite a few of the animal picture books are not only less universal in their outlook than traditional fables, but also betray characteristic features of national cultures.[5] An awareness of such cultures had originated in the course of European Romanticism and the Napoleonic Wars. "We all belong to a given culture," the English writer Peter Dickinson has said. "We know (the inwardness of) it through a series of generally held and shared notions which, in order to have a word for them, I shall call 'myths'."[6] This idea may be supplemented by a sentence of his German colleague Michael Ende: "I think that without some kind of an ideal, of an image of a hero, there is no myth and without myth there is no culture."[7]

Myths of a given culture are quite obvious in such picture books as the Australian *Waltzing Matilda* by Desmond Rigby (1970) and the Ghanaian *The Brassman's Secret* by Meshack Asare (1981), however recent their dates of origin. In the three animal picture books this essay focuses on, they are rather implied.

Biographical Conditions of the Three Books

A biographical reason for the impact of the three books may be that all of them are first books. "It must be inevitable," the Australian writer Hesba Brinsmead has remarked, "that one puts into one's first book a lot of archetypal material that has banked up in one's psyche for a long long time. This, I think, is why so many first books reach out to so many people."[8] In the long run, they may even become classics, for as Margaret Meek believes, "the classic children's book is one where the private sensibility of the author, a kind of primitive autism is widely shared by children as a group. The way a classic tale is told calls out a strong sense of recognition in a tribe, in this case the young."[9] However, just as the privateness of the author's vision may be transcended by expressing predilections of the culture he belongs to, the appeal of his story may be narrowed to an audience of that very culture. In other words, there are classics with a universal impact and classics with a national, if not regional, impact.

The story of the origin of *Peter Rabbit* has often been told.[10] This book can certainly be read as the outcome of a specific life situation. Beatrix Potter, born in 1866 into a prosperous London family, seems to have suffered from the fact that her life was not only well sheltered, but also well controlled. The days in a London nursery were boring. What she enjoyed most were the long summer holidays in Scotland or in the Lake District which she spent together with her younger brother exploring fields and meadows, collecting and drawing all sorts of animals. "It sometimes happens," she wrote later, "that the town child is more alive to the fresh beauty of the country than the child who is country born."[11]

As an adult, Potter continued her studies of nature in London museums and dreamed of illustrating a book on fungi. But in spite of her thorough knowledge of the subject, she was not taken seriously by the experts. It was then that she hit upon the idea of turning one of the illustrated letters in which she had told animal stories to the children of her former governess into a picture book. *Peter Rabbit* was an immediate success.

Let me remind you of what it is about. In spite of his mother's warning, Peter sneaks into Mr. McGregor's garden where he stuffs himself with vegetables, but then is pursued by Mr. McGregor until at last he finds the gate and runs home. While his obedient sisters enjoy their blackberry supper, Peter has to go to bed early and drink camomile tea. This is the story of a woman who was expected to like Flopsy, Mopsy, and Cottontail, but who desired to be like Peter. A sound knowledge of nature prevented her from slipping into sentimentality. "Rabbits," she observed once, "are creatures of warm volatile temperament but shallow and absurdly transparent. It is this naturalness, one touch of nature, that I find so delightful in Mr. Benjamin Bunny, though I frankly admit his vulgarity."[12]

L'Histoire de Babar is a product of the artist not as an isolated child, but as an isolated parent.[13] Jean de Brunhoff was born in 1899 and he married in 1924. In the early 1930s, he contracted tuberculosis which forced him to spend some time in a Swiss sanatorium, away from his family who most of the time lived in Paris. This precarious situation seems to have caused the young painter to take up the character of a little elephant whom his wife had used in stories for their two sons and turn him into the hero of a picture book. "That Jean had intimations of death must be true," Maurice Sendak has said.[14] According to Sendak, the theme of the book is: "a father writing to his sons voicing his natural concern for their welfare."[15]

Babar is a happy little elephant who, when his mother is cruelly shot by a hunter, leaves the jungle and runs straight into a big town resembling Paris. A friendly old lady gives him money to buy clothes and introduces him into educated society. His cousins Arthur and Celeste come to see him, and when they are called home by their mothers he follows them, just in time to succeed the king of the elephants who has died. Celeste becomes his queen. Thus, a father's concern for his sons' welfare leads to promises of happiness.

Die Häschenschule, a picture book by Fritz Koch-Gotha based on the somewhat amateurish verses of Albert Sixtus, is informed by a sense of nostalgia. Fritz Koch, born in 1877 near the town of Gotha, had made a successful career as a newspaper illustrator in Berlin before he published his first picture book in 1924. The style of detailed character studies which he and other newspaper artists had practiced before World War I was being replaced by a sketchier and more anonymous kind of style in accordance with the hectic years of the Weimar Republic.[16] So he turned to illustrating books, and the simple plot of *Häschenschule* also allowed him to turn to reminiscences of his own petit-bourgeois childhood among the wooded hills of Thuringia.[17]

The book opens with Mother Hare sending her boy and her girl to school in the forest. There an elderly schoolmaster has set up his strict regime teaching the little hares all sorts of useful things, tampered by more pleasant ones. The raison d'être of his insistence on discipline is the image of the treacherous fox. In the end, the pupils prove to be immunized against it, and the two model children return home to have their lunch together with mother and father. The educational principles revealed in this "school of little hares" are definitely not those the modern educationists of the Weimar

Republic are known for, but rather those Koch-Gotha experienced in his own childhood in Imperial Germany.[18]

After this first biographical approach to the three picture books, we may conclude that the German specimen is more entangled in its national and historical context than the two others. Hence, it is bound to have a less universal appeal and to be more easily dated.

The Settings

The main child characters of the three books have in common that they set out for a locality that must have had a strongly emotional meaning for the respective artist: the garden for Beatrix Potter, a town like Paris for Jean de Brunhoff, and the forest for Fritz Koch-Gotha. There are several praises of gardens in Potter's work, as for instance in her *Tale of Johnny Town Mouse*: "And when the sun comes out you should see my garden and the flowers--roses and pinks and pansies--no noise except the birds and bees and the lambs in the meadows."[19] For de Brunhoff's Babar a beautiful landscape is a good reason to build a town. Thus, in *Le Roi Babar* he says: "Ce paysage est ci beau, que chaque jour, en me réveillant j'aimerais le voir. C'est ici qu'il faudra construire notre ville."[20] Koch-Gotha's cartoon panopticum of Germans cannot do without forests. There is a sketch of a stout and schoolmasterly hiker telling a boy about some huge trees. "It is not enough to admire a forest, you must also inquire, by singing that lovely song, who has put it up."[21] The "lovely song" he refers to is one of those numerous German songs that focuses on forests.

As far as the settings of the three books are concerned, it is particularly obvious that the artists' inclinations are in unison with predilections of their national cultures. "God Almighty first planted a garden and, indeed, it is the purest of human pleasures," the English philosopher Francis Bacon said.[22] So many of his countrymen have followed God's example that in 1956 Victoria Sackville-West could notice: "Our island can boast of the greatest number of the loveliest private gardens in the world."[23] "Paris, the largest city proper of continental Europe," the *Encyclopaedia Britannica* points out, "has radiated an enchantment irresistable to millions around the world."[24] And as the center of centralist state, one may add, it is France in a nutshell. Walter Benjamin's fragmentary essays on *Paris the Capital of the 19th Century* abound with quotations confirming this idea.[25] Germany has never had a city of similar attractiveness. Although most of the people live in towns, Elias Cannetti has emphasized, "in no modern country in the world a forest feeling has remained so much alive as in Germany [...] The German still loves to go into the forest, where his ancestors used to live, and feels at one with the trees."[26] The poet Hans Magnus Enzenberger calls "the forest in the head"[27] a collective lie, which has its origin in German Romanticism and cannot even be destroyed by acid rain.

What else is a "collective lie" but a myth denounced from a critical point of view. If the English garden and the French capital are similar myths they are perhaps less problematic because they are less dominated by the past. In fact, isn't Frances Hodgson Burnett, author of *The Secret Garden*, right when she says: "As long as one has a garden, one has a future--and as long as one has a future, one is alive."[28]

The Characters

WIth regards to the characters of the three picture books, three aspects are of particular interest:

1. The implications of both their animal and their child nature.
2. The presentation of their clothes.
3. The manipulation of the reader's involvement.

Beatrix Potter seems to have chosen rabbits as characters for her first picture book not so much because of their popularity in British folklore and nursery lore, but rather because she was familiar with them from her own household. Her unsentimental view of them[29] made at least her hero appear to be similar to a common British child. If "Flopsy, Mopsy and Cottontail" sounds a trifle too pretty and cuddly, "Peter" definitely does not.

At the beginning, a reluctant Peter is dressed up by his mother. When he is pursued by Mr. McGregor, he successively loses his shoes and his jacket. "Now at last he is a proper rabbit!" a child observer responded to that situation.[30] So when the danger, and hence our sympathy, is greatest, the true nature of the hero is revealed. Similarly, at the beginning of Kenneth Grahame's *Wind in the Willows* the emotional impact of spring makes Mole bolt "out of the house without even waiting to put on his coat."[31] Thus, dressing up animals in children's books allows authors to use nudity as a fitting image of their true nature. It is this kind of "naturalness," I believe, that is particularly appreciated in British culture.[32]

Our emotional interest in Peter is reinforced by structure and symbolism. True, he seems to be the protagonist of a cautionary tale in the Struwwelpeter tradition. Yet his spirit of adventure and his longing for good things to eat are more engaging, because they are more "natural" than his sisters' obedience. Then there is the well-structured appeal to the British sympathy for the underdog and the victimized.[33] Tripartite structures are used to emphasize the danger. After his two meals Peter hopes to find parsley, but he meets: Mr. McGregor. The poor refugee is first threatened by a rake, then by a sieve, and finally by his persecutor's heel. He feels left alone by a busy mouse, is made uncomfortable by a white cat, and, again, is pursued by that horrible human being. Yet there is also support. Three sparrows, the common people among the birds, implore him not to give up when he gets caught in a gooseberry net, and they also welcome his rescue. Moreover, Peter is silently accompanied by (to quote Wordsworth) that "pious bird with the scarlet breast, our little English robin."[34] If the English robin, whom everybody knows from Christmas cards, is associated with Jesus Christ, that association is also possible in the case of poor Peter. When he creeps into the garden, the garden gate seems to form a cross over his back, and when he has finally left it, his jacket and his shoes are put up on a real cross, with the pensive robin on one of its arms.

Now, I do not want to turn *Peter Rabbit* into a passion play for children. But I do believe that its illustrator uses a secularized form of Christian symbolism, as it is not uncommon in Protestant countries, in order to make us sympathize with her little hero. In the tradition of the cautionary tale Peter may be called "naughty," yet we feel that he is hardly less of a "*good* bad boy" than his American cousin Tom Sawyer.[35]

Elephants are less cuddly than rabbits, but they have a reputation for being patient and wise.[36] Their countries of origin also make them participate in an aura of the exotic, which was quite appreciated by French intellectuals in the first decades of our century.[37] Thus Babar is not only an animal and a child, but also a "noble savage."

Different from Peter Rabbit, Babar seems to be his true self when he is finally dressed up in handsome clothes. The keyword is "elegance" (a synonym of which is "urbanity"[38]). The original text reads: "Satisfait de son élegance, Babar va chez le photographe."[39] Beatrix Potter, in *The Tale of Tom Kitten*, makes a cat mother dress up her naughty boy in "elegant uncomfortable clothes,"[40] and in *The Tale of Jemima Puddle-Duck* she makes a stupid duck meet an "elegantly dressed gentleman"[41] who turns out to be a treacherous fox. Thus, for the English author elegance is associated either with uncomfortableness or with falsehood, while for the French author it signifies the unison of outward appearance, social values, and good feeling in the sense of the proverb "Fine feathers make fine birds." That nudity is close to barbarism may be deduced from Louis Pergaud's famous novel about two gangs of boys, *La Guerre des Boutons* (1912).

It has been pointed out that there is no French equivalent for the English word "child."[42] The original meaning of "enfant" is "infant," referring to a very young creature who is not yet able to speak. Correspondingly, at the opening of the book Babar is an infant, and as soon as he wears his clothes he appears to be an adult. The process of education, which is implied rather than elaborated upon, seems to correspond to what the Fench novelist Michel Tournier has said about the traditional concept of that process: "L'enfant [...] est une petite bête, sale, viceuse et stupide [...] L'éducation doit en faire un être présentable."[43]

If reasonableness is a guiding principle of the book, nevertheless emotion plays an important part in bringing about the reader's involvement. The little elephant's loss of his mother grants a close relationship between reader and hero from the outset. At the same time, it enables the author to replace the natural mother by a civilized old lady who turns Babar into her social equal. Babar's childhood reminiscences keep up the link with the land of his origin, and the death of the elephant king provides the necessary condition for the final triumph of civilization in the shape of an educated elephant.

Just as the birds help to further our interest in Peter Rabbit, so in the French book a similar function is fulfilled by technical implements: the camera and the lift, the motor-car and the balloon. The fascination of technology that Jules Verne had helped to explore for teenage readers, Jean de Brunhoff even offered to a picture-book public.

It is most likely that Albert Sixtus and Fritz Koch-Gotha used hares for their picture book because of the popularity of those animals in German folklore. In the course of seasonal festivals, the Easter Hare comes second only to Father Christmas. Yet the choice is also understandable in view of a story that propagates caution and submissiveness.[44]

There is a meaningful ambiguity about the animals' clothes. In the beginning, Mother Hare admonishes her children to keep themselves tidy. However, their schoolmaster appears to be oblivious of his clothing and, on the other hand, the arch-enemy of the hare community, the fox, is dressed as smartly as a dandy. With his special appeal to girls,[45] there is also someting erotic about him, similar to the wolf in "Little Red Riding Hood." Taking into account the demonstrations of the schoolmaster's competence and of the fox's falsehood, the conclusion can only be: "Appearances are deceptive." The image of the treacherous fox, which seems to have stuck most vividly in the minds of people who were introduced to the book when they were young, is reminiscent of well-known myths of delusion in German literature and history.[46] There is Goethe's "Erlking" (whom Michel Tournier has called "le symbole même de l'Allemagne"[47]), there is Heine's "Loreley," and there is above all Hagen in the "Nibelungenlied" putting a spear in the back of innocent Siegfried[48], just as some German generals after World War I declared that their army had been stabbed in the back by the "red" revolutionaries of 1918. This political variety of a popular literary myth must have been in the minds of the author and illustrator as well as of the adult readers when *Häschenschule* was launched in the early 1920s.

As opposed to the fox, the schoolmaster is a pillar of honesty. He is so intensely dedicated to the subjects of his teaching that his features seem to become adapted to them. Thus, he is almost a bird when teaching music and a ball of energy when training the boys in racing for their lives.

The child characters are not allowed the same degree of individuality as the two most important adults. Of course, they function as objects of identification for young readers. The emotional involvement they provide becomes evident when the well-ordered sequence of fifteen pictures, each accompanied by eight lines of verse, is split up into five units. Then each of those units leads to what may be understood to be of particular interest: the arrival at school, the lesson about the fox, the punishment of a naughty pupil, survival training, and the cosiness of a petit-bourgeois home after the children have proved resistant to the allurement of the red fox. This is the appeal of the grim, relieved by promises of homeliness. When I asked Germans of my own generation about *Häschenschule*, they tended to sigh that it was a mirror of their own childhood, and when I presented the three books to my students, they regretted the absence of love in *Häschenschule*.

One further aspect is worth noticing. The expertly painted pictures of dressed-up animals are counterpointed on the text pages by green silhouettes of either real animals or real human beings. So the concept of a discrepancy between reality and appearance even structures the makeup of the whole book. In a picture book of 1940, Koch-Gotha used the same device in order to contrast a group of village boys playing soldiers with glimpses of real war.[49] In that case, there is a purpose to the pictorial arrangement which is all too obvious.

If Peter Rabbit and Babar are individuals who prove their individuality by various activities, the children in *Häschenschule* are presented as collective beings subjected to powerful adults. The English and the French story are kept moving by an animal signifying a child idealized either for its"naturalness" or for its civilization. The emphasis in the German story is on an animal representing an adult demonized as an arch-enemy.[50]

A Variety of Responses

The three picture books have challenged artists to produce variations of their predominant themes. John Burningham has transformed Peter Rabbit into Harquin the Fox, who in spite of his parents' warnings goes down to the valley where he not only enjoys a tasty chicken, but also leads a group of threatening huntsmen into the slimy marsh.[51]

As to Babar, I have come across a picture book from Thailand[52] which I cannot read but which, as far as I can judge from the pictures, has faithfully transferred the French story into a Thai environment. *Häschenschule* has been deliberately travestied by Janosch in his *Tale of the Clever Little Hares*,[53] in which the menacing fox is outfoxed by the tiny hare James and his four brothers and sisters. Thus Burningham has reinforced Potter's tendency by allowing his "good bad" hero a glorious triumph, and Janosch comes to a similar result by reversing the tendency of *his* model. Only Babar seems to be untouched by the change of times.

When we shift the focus from creative responses to critical responses, the picture is quite different. There are various sympathetic appreciations of both *Peter Rabbit*[54] and Babar,[55] of which I find those by Maurice Sendak[56] particularly rewarding. But there is also a painfully disillusioning analysis of *Babar* by the Chilean critic Ariel Dorfman,[57] who very plausibly argues that what is presented as a praise of civilization also implies a praise of colonialism. Had he known the Thai version of *Babar,* there would surely have been an additional shade of bitterness in his comment. *Häschenschule* has been defended on the ground that it offers to children what they value highly, a sense of order and a sense of security.[58] But since the late 1960s, it has been more usual in Germany to reject the book for its conservative ideology or for its authoritarian concept of education.[59]

As far as the responses of present-day children are concerned, my results are restricted to the written answers of fifty six 8-year-old pupils in a South

German town who had been read out the German version of the stories and simultaneously shown color slides of the pictures.[60] Of these fifty six, fourteen had known *Babar* before, thirteen *Häschenschule* and two *Peter Rabbit*. For twenty nine, *Babar* was the book they liked best (that is more than half), for eleven it was *Peter Rabbit*, and for six it was *Häschenschule*. The main reason for choosing *Babar* were as follows: He becomes king (17); he comes to the old lady (9); he falls in love (5); and the wedding is beautiful (5). These reasons can be summed up as promises of happiness. *Peter Rabbit* is preferred by some because Peter is hunted (5); he escapes the hunter (5); and the story is full of suspense (2). So it seems to be the element of suspense which makes this book attractive. The few children who liked *Häschenschule* mentioned the following reasons: The fox does not kill the hares (5); and the pictures are beautiful (5). So here an emotional as well as an aesthetic reason is given.

For thirteen children *Peter Rabbit* was the book they liked least, for nine it was *Babar*, for another nine *Häschenschule*, and twenty five did not make up their minds. The main reasons for rejecting *Peter Rabbit* were as follows: Mr. McGregor is so wicked to Peter (3); Peter has to run away (3); and the pictures are not nice (2). *Babar* is not liked because his mother is shot dead (4); he is in the city (4); he puts on clothes (4). Objections to *Häschenschule* were: the fox (5); there is no suspense (3).

As shown in this essay, there are implied myths in the three picture books which are part of the national cultures the books have originated from. Happily, the results of my investigation, however limited, do not allow the conclusion that young readers are fixated on books of their own culture. It was a relief to discover that *Häschenschule* was favored by only a very small number of German children, though I slightly regret that there were not more to cherish *Peter Rabbit*.

NOTES

1. John Berger, "Why Look at Animals?" *About Looking* (New York: Pantheon, 1980), pp. 1-26.

2. Leonard S. Marcus, "Picture Book Animals: How Natural a History?" *The Lion and the Unicorn*, 1983-1984:7/8, pp. 127-139.

3. Peter Coveney, *The Image of Childhood* (Harmondsworth, Penguin, 1967).

4. Berger, p. 13.

5. I know this is a tricky category. "Do such things as 'national cultures' really exist? This is one of those questions, like the freedom of the will or the identity of the individual, in which all the arguments are on one side and instinctive knowledge on the other." See George Orwell, *The English People* (London, Collins, 1947), p. 12.

6. Peter Dickinson, "The Day of the Tennis Rabbit," *The Quarterly Journal of the Library of Congress,* Fall 1981, p. 208.

7. Michael Ende in Eppler, Ende, and Tächl. *Phantasie, Kultur, Politik* (Stuttgart: Thienemann, 1982), p. 40 (my translation). See also the general discussion of myths in literature in K. K. Ruthven. *Myth* (London: Methuen, 1976).

8. Hesba Brinsmead in Walter McVitty, *Innocence & Experience. Essays on Contemporary Australian Children's Writers* (Melbourne: Nelson, 1981), p. 159.

9. Margaret Meek in "Choosing a Modern Classic," *Times Literary Supplement,* November 25, 1983.

10. Margaret Lane, *The Tale of Beatrix Potter* [1968] (Fontana, 1986), pp. 39-76; *The History of the Tale of Peter Rabbit* (London: Warne, 1976); and so on.

11. Lane, p. 29.

12. From Beatrix Potter's *Journal,* cited by Maurice Sendak, *Caldecott & Co* (New York: Farrar, 1988), p. 67.

13. See Bettina Hürlimann, *Europäische Kinderbuch in drei Jahrhunderten* (Zürich-Freiburg: Atlantis, 1963), pp. 189-193

14. Sendak, p. 99.

15. Ibid.

16. See Regine Timm, *Fritz Koch-Gotha* (Munich: Rogner & Bernhard, 1972), pp. 104-106.

17. Wilhelm Bricot, *Die Häschenschule* (Bremen: Wassman, 1985), p 24.

18. Here is a summary of the educational objectives in Imperial Germany: "What was desired was a system of education that would make the great bulk of the population not only literature but also pious and moral, vocationally and economically efficient and above all obedient and desciplined," see *Encyclopaedia Britannica.* Macropaedia 6 (Chicago, 1976), p. 378.

19. Beatrix Potter, *The Tale of Johnny Town Mouse* (London: Warne, 1918), p. 34. See also B*eatrix Potter Nursery Book* (London: Warne, 1984), p. 21 and *The Tale of Pigling Bland* (London: Warne, 1913), p. 35. In *The Tale of the Flopsy Bunnies* (London: Warne, 1909) Peter Rabbit has become a gardener himself.

20. Jean de Brunhoff, *Le roi Babar* (Paris: Jardin des Modes, 1933), pp. 4-5. Just as the elephants, the monkeys have a town of their own. See *Les vacances de Zéphir* (Paris: Jardin des Modes, 1937).

21. Timm, p. 33. Joseph von Eichedorff, a poet of Romanticism, has been particularly sucessful in fostering the German love of forests, as for example with

his song "O Täler weit, o Höhen": "O broad valleys, o hills, o beautiful green forest, you pensive refuge of my joys and sorrows! [...] A quiet impressive statement is written in the forest of how to live and love aright..." *The Penguin Book of German Verse*, ed. Leonard Forster (Harmondsworth: Penguin, 1974), pp. 311-312).

22. The English poet Abraham Cowley has turned this idea into an interesting antithesis: "God the first garden made, and the first city Cain." See *The Penguin Dictionary of Quotations* (Harmondsworth: Penguin, 1960), pp. 18 and 121.

23. Victoria Sackville-West, in Brian Harrison, *Britain Observed* (Stuttgart: Klett, 1984), p. 137. See also Alex Natan, *Britain Today* (Munich: Hueber, 1965), p. 296: "It has been estimated that there are 19 million amateur gardeners, from shipping tycoons to trade unionists."

24. *Encyclopaedia Britannica,* Macropaedia 13, (Chicago, 1976), pp. 1004-1005.

25. Walter Benjamin, *Das Passagen-Werk* (Frankfurt: Suhrkamp, 1982), pp. 524 and 652: "Tout ce qui est ailleurs est à Paris" (Victor Hugo, 1881). "Avec ce titre magique de 'Paris', un drame, une revue, un livre est toujours sûr du succès." (Théophile Gautier, 1856). See also "As an artist, a man has no home in Europe save in Paris" (Friedrich Nietzsche in *Penguin Dictionary of Quotations,* p. 271).

26. Elias Canetti in Hans-Magnus Enzenberger, "Der Wald im Kopf," *Mittelmass und Wahn* (Frankfurt: Suhrkamp: 1988), p. 190. See also Bartholomäus Grill, "Deutschland--ein Waldesmärchen" *Die Zeit*, December 25,1987.

27. Ibid.

28. Cited by Walter Pape, *Das literarische Kinderbuch* (Berlin-New York: de Gruyter, 1981), p. 394.

29. See note 12.

30. Cited by Imke Behr, Die Bilderbücher von Beatrix Potter. Diplomarbeit (Hamburg: Fachhochschule für Bibliothekswesen, 1975), p. 29.

31. Kenneth Grahame, *The Wind in the Willows* (London: Methuen, 1961), p. 1.

32. Maurice Sendak has related his own motif of naked child figures to the influential English poet and artist William Blake: "My conception of personal experience as exposure--of your soul, but also literally of your body--really stems from my love for William Blake and *Songs of Innocence and Experience* where people are naked. They're not naked to titillate people; they're naked because they're yielding up their most personal moment when they give themselves up to their dream or their fantasy or their wish." In an interview with Jerome Griswold. German version: Jerome Griswold, "Sendaks Bilder zu Randall Jarrells Kinderbüchern," in Reinbert Tabbert, ed. *Maurice Sendak--Bilderbuchkünstler* (Bonn: Bouvier, 1987), p. 48.

33. Orwell, pp. 14-15.

34. "The Redbreast Chasing the Butterfly," *The Poetical Works of Wordsworth,* ed. Thomas Hutchinson (London: Oxford University Press, 1956), p. 128.

35. Leslie Fiedler, *No! in Thunder* (Boston, 1960), p. 263.

36. See for example Bertold Brecht's praise of the elephant in "Herrn K.s Lieblingstier," *Kalendergeschichten* (Berlin: Weiss, 1949), pp. 170-171.

37. Cf., for example, the authors Michel Leiris, Blaise Cendrars, and Franz Hellens.

38. "Elegance" in *Webster's Third New International Dictionary,* Vol. 1. (Chicago: Encyclopaedia Britannica, 1966), p. 733.

39. Jean de Brunhoff, *Histoire de Babar* (Paris: Jardin des Modes, 1931), p. 13.

40. Beatrix Potter, *The Tale of Tom Kitten* (London: Warne, 1907), p. 18.

41. Beatrix Potter, *The Tale of Jemima Puddle-Duck* (London: Warne, 1908), p. 22.

42. Richard Howard, "Childhood Amnesia," in Peter Brooks, ed., *The Child's Part* (Boston, Beacon, 1972), p. 165.

43. Michel Tournier, *Le vent paraclet* (Paris: Gallimard, 1977), p. 58.

44. See Bricot, p. 26.

45. *Die Häschenschule* (Hamburg: Hahn, n. d., p. 12): "Und die kleine Gretel denkt: 'Wenn er mich nur nicht mal fängt!'".

46. See Zohar Shavit, *Poetics of Children's Literature* (Athens, Georgia: The University of Georgia Press, 1986), pp. 14-15.

47. Tournier, p. 115.

48. As to the importance of Nibelungen myths for Germany in the nineteenth and twentieth centuries see an exhibition catalogue *Die Nibelungen. Bilder von Liebe, Verrat under Untengang,* ed. Wolfgang Storch (Munich: Prestel, 1987).

49. Richard Fietsch and Fritz Koch-Gotha, *Mit Säbel und Gewehr. Lustige Bilder vom Soldatenspielen* (Stuttgart: Loewes Verlag, 1940).

50. There is an interesting correspondence between the cultural connotations of the French and German picture book on the one hand and what American novelist Thomas Wolfe, a germanophil, wrote in a letter of 1930, on the other hand: "I am at length in the Black Forest [...]--a landscape of rich dark melancholy, a place

with a Gothic soul [...] These people, with all that is bestial, savage, supernatural, and also all that is rich, profound, kindly and simple, move me more deeply than I can tell you. France at the present time has completely ceased to give me anything. That is no doubt my fault, but their books, their art, their cities, their people, their conversation--nothing buttheir food at the present time means anything to me." See *The Letters of Thomas Wolfe*, ed. E. Nowell (New York: Scribner's, 1956), pp. 261-262.

51. John Burningham, *Harquin: The Fox Who Went Down to the Valley* (London: Cape, 1967).

52. I have a copy of it.

53. *Janosch's kleines Hasenbuch* (Munich: dtv junior, 1977). Translated by Anthea Bell: "The Tale of the Clever Little Hares," in Janosch, *The Big Janosch Book of Fun and Verse* (London: Andersen Press, 1980), pp. 99-123. A recent animal picture book which is more in accordance with present-day school life in Germany than Koch-Gotha's or Janosch's books is Ingrid Uebe/Helga Spiess, *Der kleine Brüllbär geht zur Schule* (Ravensburg: Maier, 1989). The main characters are no longer hares, but a friendly, if somewhat moody b,ear boy and a very independent tiger girl.

54. For example, Marcus Crouch, *Beatrix Potter* (London: Bodley Head, 1960); Rumer Godden, "From Beatrix with Love," *The New York Times Book Review*, May 8, 1966, pp. 4, 5, 45; Peter Neumeyer, "A Structural Approach to the Study of Literature for Children," *Elementary English*, 1967:44, pp. 883-887; Judy Taylor, *Beatrix Potter. Artist, Storyteller and Countrywoman* (London: Warne, 1986).

55. For example, Edmund Leach, "Babar's Civilization Analysed," in *Only Connect*, ed. Sheila Egoff et al. (Toronto: Oxford University Press, 1969), pp. 176-182; Marc Soriano, *Guide de littérature pour la jeunesse* (Paris: Flammarion, 1975), pp. 103-104; Ann M. Hildebrand, "Jean de Brunhoff's Advice to Youth: The Babar Books as Courtesy," *Children's Literature,* 1983:11, pp. 76-95; Annie Pissard, "Long Live Babar!" *The Lion and the Unicorn,* 1983-1984:7/8, pp. 70-77.

56. Sendak, pp. 71-76, 95-105.

57. Ariel Dorfman, *The Empire's Old Clothes* (New York: Pantheon,1983), pp. 17-64.

58. Sybil Schönfeldt, "Weltentdeckung im Bilderbuch," *Schriftenreihe für die evangelische Frau,* no. 249 (Nürnberg: Lätare Verlag Stein, n.d)., pp. 8-16.

59. Gerhard Haas, "Das Tierbuch," in *Kinder- und Jugendliteratur,* ed. Gerhard Haas (Stuttgart: Reclam, 1984), pp. 180-181; Bricot op. cit.

60. I would like to thank Brigitte Knopf, who teaches at the Hochbuchschule in Reutlingen, for organizing the contact with her colleagues and the children.

Reconstructing the Homeland: Loss and Hope in the English Landscape

Tony Watkins

It is a truth (not *universally* acknowledged) that we live by fiction rather than by fact. Stories, says Fred Inglis, are "our essential instruments for turning the intense inanity of events into intelligible experience";[1] and "novels are the disciplined and public versions of the fictions we must have if we are to think at all."[2]

It follows from this account that, in order to answer the existential questions that we or our children may ask: Where have we come from? What are we? Where are we going? we must use stories, for even philosophical and social theories are narratives[3] about the way the world was, is, and will be.[4] These stories contribute to the formation of the cultural imagination, a network (as Clifford Geertz and, more recently, Paul Ricoeur have argued) of patterns and templates through which we articulate our experience: "In the same way that our experience of the natural world requires a mapping, a mapping is also necessary for our experience of social reality."[5] By the same token, the stories we write for children constitute, as Margaret Meek puts it, a "symbolic outlining of sets of possibilities for defining how things are in the world and how they might be." But, of course, it is a "symbolic outlining acceptable to adults."[6]

Thus, stories help children make sense of the world and they contribute to children's sense of *identity*, an identity that is simultaneously personal and social. That is, narratives shape the way children find a "home" in the world. But the concept of home can have philosophical resonances that go well beyond the idea of a physical space in which children live. For example, we can distinguish three different but related senses of home that operate at the level of the cultural imagination. First, "home" can refer, as Patrick Wright puts it, to "the interior space in which some recognition can be given to the endowments and potentials which have no opportunity for realisation in the world as it is."[7] Ernst Bloch goes further. In discussing the principle of hope which lies at the heart of utopia, he perceives an even more profound meaning in the concept of "home":

> What is envisioned as home (Heimat) in childhood is in actuality the goal of the upright gait toward which human beings strive as they seek to overcome exploitation, humiliation, oppression and disillusionment. The individual alone cannot attain such a goal, which is only possible as a collective enterprise.[8]

A third meaning of "home," and one that has a powerful effect in shaping our children's identity through the cultural imagination, is constructed through the images we supply and the stories we tell of the land in which we live: our "homeland." Raymond Williams demonstrated the importance of the images of "the country and the city"[9] for an understanding of English culture, and children's writers, especially writers of fantasy, are a rich source of such images of landscape and townscape. Some works of fantasy construct images of an imaginary homeland that help sustain myths of national identity, community and common heritage.[10] We should not be surprised that such works of fantasy are profoundly political in this way, for, as Robert Leeson has argued: "Fantasy is the most philosophical, the most ideological, the most political of forms of writing [...] And it is from fantasy that the young reader may most readily, in the long term, absorb ideas about how the world ought to be."[11] One line of such English fantasy for children is the "country-bred fantasy" of writers like Kenneth Grahame, J. R. R. Tolkien and Richard Adams. There is, of course, a danger in grouping these writers together under some such title as the "Arcadians," because they do not share exactly the same attitudes towards the English landscape.[12] However, they *do* all tell stories that contribute to children's everyday consciousness of the "homeland." But if we ask, "What *meanings* of the homeland do such books offer children?", we run into profound difficulties. At the risk of oversimplification, the situation appears to be something like this: on the one hand, we have the "preferred meanings" established by the "interpretive community" of academics and others in the field of children's literature; on the other hand, we have the meanings that are revealed as adults and children actualize these narratives and mobilize their meanings to make sense of their lives. I do not mean to imply that the two sets of meanings are necessarily distinct and different, but I am trying to suggest something of the complexity of the situation. For as Tony Bennett argues, the literary text: "is historically redetermined during the process of its reception, figuring not as the source of an effect but the site on which plural and even contradictory effects may be produced during the course of its history as a received text."[13]

In order to understand a little of the cultural significance of writers such as Grahame, Tolkien, and Adams, we can use the concepts "nostalgia," "heritage," and "utopia" (three "keywords,"[14] perhaps, for understanding English culture generally). It is obviously impossible to give a proper account of these concepts in this essay, but we can *suggest* how they illuminate our understanding of such works and their cultural reception. Many academic commentators would agree that there is astrong feeling of nostalgia in the works of these writers. Clearly, nostalgia can operate at the personal and individual level, but it can operate at the national cultural level as well. Significantly, nostalgia means, literally, "homesickness" or "a painful yearning to return home."[15] Bryan S. Turner has argued that, as social and cultural discourse in contemporary culture, nostalgia is experienced as a sense of historical decline and loss

involving a departure from some golden age of "homefulness" [...] a sense of the absence or loss of personal wholeness and moral certainty [...] the sense of loss of individual freedom and autonomy with the disappearance of genuine social relationships [...] and the idea of a loss of simplicity, personal authenticity and emotional spontaneity."[16]

Nostalgia seems to be a persistent feature of Western culture, and it is associated with "the loss of rural simplicity, traditional stability and cultural integration following the impact of industrial, urban capitalist culture or feudal social organisation." In this century, nostalgia can be seen as part of the response to "the dynamic and future-oriented nature of modernity" which has led to the dislocation, devaluation, and disenchantment of everyday life.[17]

In *The Wind in the Willows, The Lord of the Rings* and *Watership Down*, nostalgia manifests itself as an anti-industrial stance (although there is considerable ambivalence in Grahame's depiction of the motor-car), combined with a deep respect for a hierarchical feudal system in which "individuals gain identity and obtain security within the organic society established according to tradition and natural qualification."[18] But it is also a society in which females are either absent or kept firmly in place as homemakers. The books are male versions of nostalgia, articulated through deep structural oppositions of "adventure" and "home." These nostalgic longings, with all their ideological implications, are blended with mythic images of the English landscape: the opening chapter of Grahame's book gives what has been called "a full rich portrait of the earthly paradise"[19] of the Thames near Cookham; in Tolkien, the English Midlands are transformed into The Shire, "rich and kindly," and "a pleasant corner of the world"; and Adams,"transforms a stretch of [...] familiar, Home Counties countryside into a vast, seemingly mythic, realm."[20] What happens when such conservative texts "enter history" in the process of their reception? It is then that the complexity of the cultural meanings of the texts is revealed.

Texts can be conscripted into the service of the "National Heritage" that serves to reinforce an idealized picture of the national home--through what Robert Hewison calls "the Heritage Industry."[21] National Heritage, Wright has argued, involves "the extraction [...] of the idea of historical significance and potential from a denigrated everyday life and its restaging or display in certain sanctioned sites events, images and conceptions."[22] Part of the National Heritage is a National Geography that lies "hidden away" just beyond the reaches of an industrialized Britain. The sites of this geography promise *another world*, "a dichotomous realm existing alongside the everyday,"[23] which can provide "that momentary experience of utopian gratification in which the grey torpor of everyday life in contemporary Britain lifts and the simpler, more radiant measures of Albion declare themselves again."[24] These sites can be reached by courtesy of the English Tourist Board. In 1983, the Board ran a series of advertisements featuring the characters from *The Wind in the Willows*. Toad, Mole, and Rat drive in a vintage car to explore "the real England" of ancient monuments and small villages with pastoral and comic pastoral names: "Sheepwash," "Butterwick," "Buttocks Booth". The advertisements promised the following: "Hidden just beyond the noise of the motorway you'll find secret places that have barely changed for hundreds of years."[25]

Such advertising can be seen as simply turning nostalgia into a commodity, exploiting it as a resource for tourism, and thus serving the ideological interests of the capitalistic industry of the National Heritage. There is something to be said for such a view. And yet, as Patrick Wright reminds us,

Like the utopianism from which it draws, national heritage involves positive energies which certainly can't be written off as ideology. It engages hopes, dissatisfactions, feelings of tradition and freedom, but it tends to do so in a way that diverts these potentially disruptive energies into the separate and regulated spaces of stately display.[26]

As tourists, we may go on holiday, as Fred Inglis argues, to restore "our lost complicity with nature." What fuels the "powerful dream of the perfect holiday" is the *hope* that "all shall be well and peace of mind restored as by coming home."[27]

So we are faced with the complexity of the cultural meanings of such nostalgic fantasy for children. Texts of nostalgia can also act as texts of utopia, thus playing a highly ambivalent role as forms of social criticism: "By converting the past into a Utopian homestead, nostalgia may lay the foundations for a radical critique of the modern as a departure from authenticity."[28] Like all texts, texts of nostalgia operate as "the site on which plural and even contradictory effects may be produced."[29] In a similar way, John Thompson, in distinguishing between beliefs and ideologies, has argued that"the ways in which beliefs are actualized [...] the ways in which meaning is mobilized in the Social World is of crucial importance. Certain expressions may serve to sustain relations of domination in one context and to disrupt them in another."[30] As for Tolkien and Adams, Jack Zipes has argued that Tolkien was a

producer of utopias who presented solutions and answers to the problems confronting humankind. He harked back to the past because he esteemed traditional religion and conservative forms of government. His perspective was definitely regressive but not reactionary, for his sympathies remained with the common people whom he regarded as exploited by capitalism and technology.[31]

It was not surprising, then, that Tolkien's work was eagerly taken up by the counterculture of the late 1960s. David Glover draws attention to what he calls the "wide-ranging syncretism" of the counterculture with its "profoundly anti-bureaucratic and anti-organisational emphasis [...] Tolkien and McLuhan rubbing shoulders with Marcuse and Mao."[32] King Arthur was hailed as "the People's King, the King who was and once again shall be" ruling over "a very green land, a land of trees and hills and castles [...] a human yet spiritual land."[33]

It is perhaps more extraordinary that Richard Adams' novel for children, *Watership Down*, which has been described as "conservative fantasy [...] of the "collective consciousness" of the traditional middle-classes,"[34], should have enjoyed such popularity among the student subculture of the 1970s. In *Watership Down* we are presented, yet again, with images of the English rural landscape, a landscape lovingly described in terms of its cartography, its history, its traditions, and its wealth of natural life:"The rabbits sheltered in dim-green, sun-flecked caves of grass, flowering marjoram and cow parsley: peered round spotted hairy-stemmed clumps of viper's bugloss, blooming red and blue above their heads: pushed between towering stalks of yellow mullein."[35] The political "parable" of the novel has been described by Christopher Pawling in these terms:

Hazel & Co. triumph over the "anarchy"/"decadence" of Cowslip's warren and "totalitarianism" of Woundwort. They win through because their group is a "meritocracy" which harnesses the energies and talents of each individual member in a productive and rational manner [...] But Adams is no libertarian (his democracy is clearly founded on a combination of "breeding" and "intelligence") and it is obvious that Hazel is a "natural leader" from the outset.[36]

Yet the novel, for all its apparently regressive ideologies, proved very popular with students. The nature of its appeal is obviously difficult to determine, but the book can be seen to possess qualities of a critical utopian kind. These qualities represent "an 'ecological' variant of latter-day Romanticism"[37] through which Adams, like Tolkien, can attack a technology which is not harnessed to "meaningful human goals."[38]

Thus, texts, even of nostalgia, may contain elements of utopia that offer us a "distance from present reality, [and] the ability to avoid perceiving present reality as natural, necessary, or without alternative."[39]

In summary, I have assumed with Clifford Geertz and Paul Ricoeur that, "because human life is symbolically mediated, any concept of the real is interpretive."[40] Narratives shape our reality. The stories we offer our children can help them shape their sense of identity, help them find a home in the world. But the meanings of a text depend on the history of its reception and the way meanings are mobilized in human praxis. We have seen that texts of nostalgic rural fantasy may be appropriated to serve ideological interests. As Fredric Jameson reminds us," a practice of ideological analysis, must in the practical work of reading and interpretation be exercised *simultaneously* with [...] a decipherment of the Utopian impulses of these same still ideological cultural texts."[41] Texts may be appropriated in the service of what Bloch calls, "concrete utopias,"[42] opposed to the present narrow conceptions of what it means to be human. The meanings of such works of fantasy as have been discussed here lie in their *use* in making sense of the world. For our children, they may offer, in the words of Jack Zipes,

wish-images and wish-landscapes [that] measure the distance we have yet to go to achieve real happiness. The wish landscapes seem to transcend reality yet, in fact, leave indelible marks in our consciousness and in cultural artefacts: they are the traces of utopia that constitute the cultural heritage [and they] point to the ultimate realization of a promised land that has yet to find its appropriate form.[43]

That is the land of "hope" and a far, far better "home" than we have ever known.

NOTES

1. Fred Inglis, *Popular Culture and Political Power* (London: Harvester-Wheatsheaf, 1988), p. 15.

2. Fred Inglis,.*The Promise of Happiness: Value and Meaning in Children's Fiction* (Cambridge: Cambridge University Press, 1981), p. 310.

3. Inglis, *Popular Culture and Political Power*.

4. A similar point is made by Agnes Heller. She argues that our "historicity" (our "everyday historical consciousness") is constructed aand sustained through storytelling. See Agnes Heller, *A Theory of History* (London: Routledge and Kegan Paul, 1982), pp. 52ff.

5. Paul Ricoeur, *Lectures on Ideology and Utopia* (New York: Columbia University Press, 1986). See also Clifford Geertz, *The Interpretation of Cultures* (New York: Basic Books, 1973).

6. Margaret Meek, "Symbolic Outlining: the Academic Study of Children's Literature," *Signal*, 1987:53, p. 110.

7. Patrick Wright, *On Living in an Old Country: The National Past in Contemporary Britain* (London: Verso, 1985), p. 11, explains Heller's concept of "home".

8. Ernst Bloch, *The Utopian Function of Art and Literature: Selected Essays*, trans. Jack Zipes and Frank Mecklenberg (Cambridge, Mass.: MIT Press, 1988), introduction p. xxvii.

9. Raymond Williams, *The Country and the City* (St. Albans: Paladin, 1975).

10. For the relationship of popular fiction to such myths, see J. Yanarella, Ernest J. and Lee Sigelman, *Political Mythology and Popular Fiction* (New York: Greenwood Press, 1988).

11. Robert Leeson, "Children's Books and Politics," *Books for Keeps*, 1984:25, p. 5.

12. A danger that Humphrey Carpenter is aware of in his *Secret Gardens* (London: Unwin, 1987).

13. Tony Bennett, "Marxism and Popular Form," *Literature and History*, 1981:VII/2, p. 56 (author's emphases).

14. My indebtedness to the work of Raymond Williams is obvious.

15. Fred Davis, *Yearning for Yesterday: a Sociology of Nostalgia* (New York: Free Press, 1979), p. 1.

16. Bryan S. Turner, "A Note on Nostalgia," *Theory, Culture and Society*, 1987:4, pp. 147-56.

17. Wright, pp. 16-20.

18. Timothy E. Cook, "Democracy and Community in American Children's Literature," in Yanarella and Sigelman, p. 55.

19. Carpenter, p. 155

20 C. Booker, *The Seventies* (Harmondsworth: Penguin, 1980), p. 254, cited in Christopher Pawling, "Watership Down: Rolling Back the 1960s," in Christopher. Pawling, ed, *Popular Fiction and Social Change* (London: Macmillan, 1984).

21. Robert Hewison, *The Heritage Industry* (London: Methuen, 1987).

22. Wright, p. 69.

23. Ibid., p. 78.

24. Ibid., p. 76.

25. See Tony Watkins, "Making a Break for the England: The Rover-Bakers Revisited," *Children's Literature Association Quarterly*, 1984:1, pp. 34-35.

26. Wright, p. 78.

27. Inglis, *Popular Culture and Political Power*, pp. 157-158.

28. Turner, p. 154.

29. See note 13.

30. John B. Thompson, "Language and Ideology: A Framework for Analysis," *Sociological Review*, 1987:35/3, pp. 516-536.

31. Jack Zipes, *Breaking the Magic Spell: Radical Theories of Folk and Fairy Tales* (London: Heinemann, 1979), p. 158.

32. David Glover, "Utopia and Fantasy in the Late 1960s," in Christopher Pawling, ed, *Popular Fiction and Social Change*, p. 191.

33. *International Times,* 1971:98 quoted by Glover, p. 191.

34. Pawling, p. 232.

35. Richard Adams, *Watership Down* (Harmondsworth: Penguin, 1984), p. 268.

36. Pawling, p. 227.

37. Ibid., p. 217.

38. Ibid., p. 216.

39. Ricoeur, introduction by George H. Taylor, p. xxx.

40. Ibid., p. xxxi.

41. Fredric Jameson, *The Political Unconscious: Narrative as a Socially Symbolic Act* (London: Methuen, 1981), p. 296.

42. The term is used by Ernst Bloch to refer to "relative historical gain, revolutionary transformations and formations [...] stepping stones and indications of what the human individual and the world could become." See Bloch, introduction by Jack Zipes, p. xxvii.

43. Zipes, p. xxxix.

Literature for Young People and the Novel of Adolescence

Dagmar Grenz

Around the turn of the century, a new genre emerged in the German-speaking countries: the school novel, which portrayed the sufferings of a youth in school or a military academy.[1] This new genre was a rejection of the Bildungsroman of the eighteenth and nineteenthth centuries, of which Goethe's *Wilhelm Meister* was considered the classic example. Whereas here the hero still manages, in his clash with the world, to arrive at a reconciliation between the self's and the world's demands,[2] the turn of the century's novels of adolescence often end with the death of the still young protagonist, and no discovery of identity or meaning takes place. This break in German literature with the well-developed tradition of the Bildungsroman[3] is to be seen as an expression of the crisis in contemporary bourgeois society, which had disallowed a discovery of identity in the classical sense long since.

The novel of adolescence underwent a revival in Germany in the 1970s, now influenced, though, by an American novel of the early 1950s: J. D. Salinger's *The Catcher in the Rye*. Further influences came in the late 1960s and early 1970s from the students' and women's movements, so that, for example, in contrast to the turn of the century's novel of adolescence, a female protagonists appear along with male leading characters.[4]

The novel of adolescence is a novel with a young hero who is in the midst of an existential crisis.[5] This genre, then, is one that we would naturally also expect to find in young people's literature (by which I understand literature intended for young people), and perhaps even to be at home in it. That is not the case, however. The turn of the century's novels of adolescence were part of adult literature, although they were read by both adults and young people, and they exercised no influence (at least none that is known) on literature for young people. Salinger's *The Catcher in the Rye*, a book often read by young people, was not written (or published) as a novel especially for young people either.[6] The same is true of the German novel of adolescence of the 1970s. Unlike those of the turn of the century, however, these novels had a lasting effect on contemporary young people's literature. In the late 1970s and particularly in the 1980s, the genre of the novel of adolescence became an important component of literature for young people.[7]

The starting point of this essay is the question to what degree does the novel of adolescence specific to young people (meaning the novel that was especially written or published for a young audience) differ from the novel of adolescence of literature in general? We may also ask whether, in the sphere of this genre, a convergence between literature for young people and literature as a whole has been consummated to an extent that would allow us to speak of a structural leveling of the differences.[8] If that were the case, it would mean that the novel of adolescence specific to young people would occupy an important position not only in young people's literature, but also in the context of modern contemporary literature as well, along with Salinger's *The Catcher in the Rye*, Ulrich Plenzdorf's *Die neue Leiden des jungen W.*, P. Schneider's *Lenz*, and so forth.

My thesis is as follows: the novel of adolescence specific to young people, despite its convergence with adult literature's novel of adolescence, does not achieve its polyvalence and radicality (as measured against the contemporary context). The modernity of the novel of adolescence specific to young people, in comparison with adult novel of adolescence, is always a tempered one.

In the following pages, this thesis is developed by comparing several novels of adolescence specific to young people with those of adult literature. In a concluding section, the example of the contemporary novel of adolescence is given to draw conclusions regarding the relationship of young people's literature to modern contemporary literature for adults.

Ulrich Plenzdorf's *Die neuen Leiden des jungen W.* (The new sorrows of young W.), published in East Germany in 1973, and the young people's book by Irina Korschunow, *Die Sache mit Christoph* (The matter with Christoph, 1978),[9] evince a common motif: in both of these novels of adolescence, the young dropout or outsider who escapes from home and finally sees no way out of his problems anymore meets his death in an accident. The accident becomes a form of unconsciously committed suicide.

This shared motif is fashioned in conspicuously dissimilar ways. Plenzdorf links Edgar's story with Goethe's *Sorrows of Young Werther* though a montage of quotations and the paralleling of the plot action and the constellation of characters.[10] This extends the scope of the novel's meaning: Werther's criticism of the rationalistic posture and labor division of bourgeois society applies to East Germany's socialist society as well, which, by abolishing private ownership of the means of production, claims to have also put an end to the alienation of the self from his work. And Werther the lover, too, who abandons himself wholly to the unconditionality of his emotions, gradually becomes an identification figure for Edgar, who at first, brashly cool, rejects Werther's manner of loving completely.

While Plenzdorf's work portrays the existential crisis of a young person and at the same time criticizes society, in Irina Korschunow's book, Christoph's death is finally ascribed to his personality structure, thus taking back the social criticism expressed at various points. Christoph appears to be too thin-skinned for this world: "It was all too hard for him," for that reason it is "good that he's dead."[11]

Christoph's suffering is not simply individualized, however. The narrative point of view--and this is the most essential difference from Plenzdorf--relativizes it as well. The story is told from the viewpoint of Christoph's friend Martin, who in the course of the book increasingly distances himself from Christoph's world-weary attitude, his lack of prospects for the future and his cool reserve toward others. For him, Christoph's death becomes a "salutary educational experience,"[12] the trigger for a process of rethinking that leads him from a temporarily skeptical and doubting frame of mind to a fundamental affirmation of life and society. We can sat that Korschunow's novel, criticizes the doubting and foundering hero of the contemporary novel of adolescence from the standpoint of the classical Bildungsroman. Finally, the end of the novel, can only be considered tasteless: between Martin, his friend, and Ulrike, Christoph's girlfriend, a love relationship develops following his death; and Martin is certain that he will be more loving to Ulrike than Christoph was.

J. D. Salinger's *The Catcher in the Rye* and B. Wersba's *Ein nützliches Mitglied der Gesellschaft (Run Softly,Ggo Fast)* are also about young protagonists who break out of their previous environments.[13] Here, however, it is not death that comes at the end, but the discovery of a new identity.

Wersba's *Run Softly, Go Fast* is a good, ambitious book for young readers: it is suspenseful and entertaining; the narrative point of view includes both the remembered past and the present; the discussion of events in the late 1960s evinces an openness toward the goals and life-styles of the period's Hippie movement; and finally, the father-son conflict is depicted from the son's point of view without trying to make it seem better. Yet Wersba's book, although it appeared almost twenty years later, is much more traditionally written than Salinger's *The Catcher in the Rye*, with a narrower scope of meaning, unambiguous psychological explanations, sometimes implausible character conceptions and patterns of action, and, in the end, a harmonizing basic tenor.

The problem facing Davy, the young protagonist, can be clearly defined: it is the conflict between a strong father, who is averse to liberating his son, and the son, who is fighting for his release. In this confrontation, Davy's situation always takes a turn for the better. In the decisive situations of his life, he encounters "savior figures," who turn up like *dei ex machina* and put him on the right path: a friend who encourages him to stick to his artistic ambitions against his father's will and move out of the house; and, later,

Maggie, who extricates him from the Hippie drug scene, frees him from his loneliness and sexual problems, and, finds a gallery owner who puts on Davy's first exhibition Throughout, Maggie's capacity for understanding and love appears virtually boundless. Through his artistic talent, Davy is able, in spite of his dropout's existence, to develop self-confidence in his relationship with his father, a typical representative of the self-made man. He does so much more easily than the average Hippie of the time, who at best dabbled in the arts. When Davy has a bad experience, it remains an episode; even then he is never shown foundering in it. This is already established by the first-person narrative, which describes, retrospectively, the most important events--from Davy's fifth year until his father's death--and joins them together interpretively into a life story which has, finally, a meaning: namely that of the separation from his father and the finding of his own identity. At the end, 19-year-old Davy receives his first noteworthy recognition as an artist, has a new home with a virtually ideal girlfriend and is able to relativize his father conflict by raising it to the plane of the ever-recurring conflict of generations in which both sides are both right and wrong.

The reasons for the existential crisis of Salinger's young protagonist Holden Caulfield are more complex than those for Davy's, and they do not allow of solution as easily. Indeed, they cannot, even be reduced to an unambiguous formula.[14] Holden is afraid of becoming an adult because, for him, contemporary America's competitive society is characterized by "phoniness." He is afraid of sexuality, which he correlates with the corrupt adult world, and he is afraid of development, of change in general. What he would like most would be to save himself and the children, as his image of the catcher in the rye shows, from the "fall" into adult life. The parents play no prominent role in his crisis. Instead, Holden's situation is characterized, by a general uncertainty and fundamental unrelatedness. The unrelatedness reveals itself clearly in his many futile attempts or plans to get in touch with people and in his ideal of living as a deaf-mute in an isolated log cabin. His fear of sexuality, because it is part of his fundamental fear of becoming an adult, cannot, unlike Davy's, be cured by a single night with the "right" woman: On the contrary, although the girl he could apparently come to love, Jane Gallagher, does preoccupy his thoughts and feelings time and again, he does not manage to enter into contact with her. The chosen narrative perspective also renders a more radical portrayal of Holden's crisis situation possible. The narrative covers only three days--the period from Holden's flight from college until his return home. The first-person narrator, looking back on these events from a distance of several months, moves for the most part on the plane of the experiencing self, remaining so "caught up" in its point of view that he cannot, even later, arrange the events into a structure with an overriding meaning.

At the end, Holden has undergone a change of consciousness. After the discussion with his younger sister Phoebe, the first real contact that he enters into with a human being, his sense of responsibility for Phoebe causes him to give up his plan to escape and, at the same time, his desire not to develop. He is willing to face adult life.[15] How this will look remains open; the only thing that is certain is that he will be going back to a college. The narrator's current situation demonstrates how deep the existential crisis went: Following his return home, he experienced a total physical collapse and is now in a sanatorium for his convalescence.

The polyvalence of the depiction corresponds to the complexity of Holden's problem: only when the closely woven web of allusions and motifs is deciphered (the ducks in Central Park, for example, the red hunting hat, Allie's baseball mitt, the Egyptian mummies in the Museum of Art, the motif of falling or almost falling),[16] does the text's complex (and for that reason not definitively ascertainable) cargo of meaning disclose itself to the reader.

In conclusion, I would like to look briefly at novels of adolescence with female protagonists.[17] Here, too, a clear difference between the novel of adolescence specially intended for young people and the one belonging to general literature is to be observed. This is also true of a book that, in my view, is the most accomplished of all: *Kamalas Buch* (Kamala's book) by the Swedish writer Inger Edelfeldt.[18] It depicts in the third-person, from the main character's point of view (and really restricted to this perspective, too) the suffering that life causes her or she causes herself: her complete incapacity to develop a self of her own with individual needs, wishes, and goals. The inner emptiness of her profoundly depressive personality predestines her to become a victim of today's normative ideas of what a young girl should be like. Since she does not, in her view, fulfill these norms, they become for her a source of constant dissatisfaction not only with her own outward appearance, but also with her unhappiness itself, with which she reproaches herself, too, because only happy women, after all, can be beautiful and successful with men. Her orientation to the man is total: she has internalized his point of view fully, seeing herself always through the eyes of the "dream prince" who will someday come as her savior, and whom she, because he is already present in her imagination, must please even now. Without a man she does not feel, as it were, entitled to exist.

The unrelatedness of the female main character, her inability to move (as though paralyzed, she looks upon her increasingly dirty apartment, which she for a time nevertheless no longer dares to leave), her self-hatred that extends to the wish for self-mutilation, her murder fantasies--all of these are described in restrained, soberly observant, economical language. This language (like the limited point of view) remains in the language of the girl character and yet is unobtrusively stylized in its urgency. Even the pauses between sentences are eloquent. Comic or tragic-comic events are presented succinctly, without further comment, and at times an impressive figurativeness evolves out of the everyday language, as if it were the most natural thing in the world, In the counterimage of the girl Kamala who grew up among wolves, successfully renounces human civilization, and becomes the other self of the main character's split personality, a last remnant of desire for another, self-determined life is held on to--admittedly at the cost of a divided self, and without the ability to concretize the desire with content.[19]

This novel, which convincingly portrays the complete failure of female self-discovery, even though or perhaps more because the female principal character rigorously complies with sex role expectations, is provocative in the context of contemporary young people's or girls' literature; in the general literary context, however, it is not. The external determination of the woman by her confinement to her sex role was already portrayed in general literature at the beginning of the 1970s, and in more radical fashion than Inger Edelfeldt's. Verena Stefan's *Häutungen* (Sheddings), for example, in answer to the internalization of the male point of view by the woman, questions heterosexuality in general as regards love relationships between women as the only humane ones still possible. In spite of this simplifying way of looking at things, and also in spite of a language that, in its attempt to break through male-oriented patterns, sometimes verges on kitsch, the radicalness of the criticism of existing relations between the sexes is impressive. Ultimately, it leads to a new vision that dissolves old role definitions and tracks down possibilities for behavior beyond those definitions. At the same time, of all the books compared here, Verena Stefan's *Häutungen* and Inger Edelfeldt's *Kamalas Buch* evince the least structural difference.[20]

In the preceding, I have used for comparison novels of adolescence from adult literature which, because of their manner of portrayal e(ven when it is more complex than that of young people's literature) can also be read and are read by younger readers. They were works belonging, if not always to the highest literary category, then certainly to literary fiction. The exception is the book by Verena Stefan, which on the strength of its experimental character, however, occupies a special position. Along with these, there are novels of adolescence in adult literature, which, because of various factors such as their length, the complexity of the topics addressed, complicated verbal and narrative structures, paucity of action, tha narrative viewpoint of an adult self influencing the portrayal of the crisis of adolescence, would be much more difficult for young people to read. Here, the gulf separating adolescent and adult literature is significantly greater, with adult literature's degree of modernity sometimes being very much higher.[21]

In Th. Bernhard, for example, adolescence is depicted less from the youth's point of view than from that of his remembering, reflecting adult self, which incorporates contemporary history. The youth's experiencing self is not so much a searching self as a humiliated one. It is at the mercy of inconceivable insults and deformations that the adult self, with the uncompromisingness of hate, again and again circles afresh and probes in intricately hypotactic complex sentences that--as it were, without pauses for breath--are undivided into paragraphs and chapters (See Th. Bernhard, *Die Ursache. Eine Andeutung*, The cause. An intimation, 1975). In B. Frischmuth's *Die Klosterschule* (The convent school, 1968) simple sentence and narrative structures are chosen, which are nonetheless extremely disconcerting. Although the story is told from the point of view of a schoolgirl, the language is shaped by sentences that the nuns drill into the pupils in the boarding school. The self is deindividualized and "anonymized'," and there is no prospect of sympathizing with a suffering self, only a cool distance toward the deformation of a large number of female individuals. H. Fichte's *Versuch über die Pubertät* (Essay on puberty, 1974) in its framework a novel of adolescence told by a first-person narrator, a homosexual, not only dissolved the narrative continuum in favor of various time levels and scenes of action,but also abolished the borders between fiction and essay as well. The look at his own puberty is expanded by the interpolation of interviews with two other homosexuals and the inclusion of the first-person narrator's exotic experiences in Bahia and Haiti. The at times hard, drastic topic is presented plainly and directly,as in the sadomasochistic orgies of the homosexual scene or the dissecting of the dead in a forensic institute in Brazil. Lastly, a theater play, *Klassen Feind* (Class enemy) by N. Williams is perfectly understandable for young readers, but the drastic language, which knows no limits, the extreme destructive urge of the young characters, and finally the messages of the play as a whole (society has written off the youths, their waiting for a teacher is in vain; and none of them dares to come to class anymore) are of a radicalness and uncompromisingness not to be found in contemporary literature for young people.

As the text comparisons presented here demonstrate, young people's literature did take up the novel of adolescence as a genre and, along with it, the problem complex of the modern ego that is uncertain of itself, which already entered literary fiction in 1774 with Goethe's *Werther*.[22] Measured against the contemporary novel of adolescence in adult literature, however, the novel of adolescence written (or published) specially for young people does not achieve the same degree of modernity in that it is on the whole more traditionally written: It evinces a tendency toward greater unambiguity and toward harmonization; it follows the Bildungsroman more than the novel of adolescence; and when it does take on the model of the novel of adolescence, it more readily adopts that from the turn of the century than that of contemporary literature. As a result, it can be said that none of the contemporary novels of adolescence for young people achieves the rank of Musil's *Törless,* and not that of the still relatively traditionally written novels *Unterm Rad* (Under the wheel) by Herman Hesse or *Freund Hein* (Friend Hein) by E. Strauss either, or that of a Salinger, a Plenzdorf, or a P. Schneider. Even as accomplished a book for young people as *Kamalas Buch* by Inger Edelfeldt breaks new ground only in the context of young people's literature, and not in that of literature in general. The "accomplished" contemporary novel of adolescence for young people, compared with general literature, in most cases achieves only the rank of "superior" light fiction.[23]

For this reason, we can only speak of dissolving the border between literature for young people and that for adults in the sphere of the novel of adolescence if, in the comparison, we do not (as is usually the case) have literary fiction in view, but rather light fiction for adults.[24] On this level, the relation of literature for adults to that for young people is less a problem of differing ages than one of literary competence. Neither most adults nor most young people possess the literary competence required to decipher modern literary texts.

Literary fiction that is read by many adults and by many young people (like Goethe's *Werther* or Salinger's *The Catcher in the Rye*), is probably a stroke of luck. It is literature that can be read on various levels--on the level of a naive identification with the unhappy lover, with the rebelling dropout; and on the literary level, on which the more complex strata of significance are realized.

The thesis that the contemporary novel of adolescence for young people usually achieves only the rank of high-quality light fiction in no way indicates a devaluation of young people's literature. Nor does it necessarily inply the requirement that young people's literature, if it is to be "good,, must itself be literary fiction. In the assessment of young people's literature, after all, not only literary criteria play an important role, but reader-oriented criteria as well.[25] Nonetheless, critics of children's and young people's literature should be aware of the difference between the "superior" book for young people and literary fiction. These critics should not, as often seems to be the case, obscure it, as if, when dealing with literature for young people, one is from the start moving in a completely different world in which fundamentally other literary measures obtain (allowing the "superior" book for young people to seem the *non plus ultra*). Critics of children's and young people's literature should keep the development of contemporary literature for adults in view. Only in that way can they test, in a particular case, whether the distinction between the book for young people and literature for adults is, in view of the young audience, a necessity, or whether it is a question of an outdated tradition that has become a needless barrier between literature for young people and literature for adults.

NOTES

1. See E. Strauss, *Freund Hein* (Friend Hein, 1902); H. Hesse, *Unterm Rad* (Under the wheel, 1906); R. Musil, *Die Verwirrungen des jungen Törless* (The confusions of young Törless, 1906); F. Huch, *Mao* (1907); R. Walser, *Jakob von Gunten* (1909); narratives such as *Die Turnstunde* (The lesson in gymnastics, 1899) by R. M. Rilke and *Abdankung* (Abdication, 1906) by H. Mann or the chapters about Hanno in Th. Mann's *Buddenbrooks* (1901); if one also takes into consideration the drama, F. Wederkind's *Frühlings Erwachen* (Spring Awakening, 1891) belongs to this group of texts, too. Concerning the novel of adolescence at the turn of the century, see A. von Hermanni, "Adoleszens (sic!) und Identität als Romanthemen. Ein Beitrag zum besseren Verständnis eines jugendliterarischen Typus, *Fundevogel*, 1984:4/5, pp. 33-36 and the literature mentioned there; as well as R. Minder, "Kadettenhaus, Gruppendynamik und Stilwandel von Wildenbruch bis Rilke und Musil," in his: *Kultur und Literatur in Deutschland und Frankreich. Fünf Essays* (Frankfurt am Main, 1962), pp. 73-93.

2. This takes a utopian turn, however, even in the first Bildungsroman, *Wilhelm Meister*. See J. Jacobs, *Wilhelm Meister und seine Brüder. Untersuchungen zum deutschen Bildungsroman* (München, 1972), pp. 87f.

3. This applies only to literary fiction, of course; light fiction continued to take recourse to the pattern of the Bildungsroman.

4. One of the few novels of the turn of the century which present a young female protagonist is *Ruth* by Lou Andreas-Salomé (1895). The same author also wrote *Im Zwischenland. Fünf Geschichten aus dem Seelenleben halbwüchsiger Mädchen* (In between. Five stories about the state of feeling of teenage girls, 1902).

5. See H. H. Ewers, "Zwischen Problemliteratur und Adoleszenz-roman. Aktuelle Tendenzen der Belletristik für Jugendliche und junge Erwachsene," *Informationen des Arbeitskreises für Jugendliteratur*, 1989:15 (1989), pp. 4-23.

6. Concerning the resonance of Salinger's *The Catcher in the Rye* see P. Freese, *Die Initiationsreise. Studien zum jugendlichen Helden im modernen amerikanischen Roman mit einer exemplarischen Analyse von J. D. Salingers "The Catcher in the Rye"* (Neumünster, 1971), pp. 178ff.

7. Concerning the novel of adolescence in contemporary literature for young people see Hermanni; W. Kaminski, *Jugendliteratur und Revolte. Jugendprotest und seine Spiegelung in der Literatur für junge Leser* (Frankfurt am Main, 1982); and the very informative article of H. H. Ewers, which includes a bibliography.

8. This thesis is advocated by Ewers, p. 10.

9. U. Plenzdorf, *Die neuen Leiden des jungen W.* (Rostock: Hinstorff, 1973; Frankfurt: Suhrkamp 1973; Suhrkamp Taschenbuch, Frankfurt 1976); I. Korschunow, *Die Sache mit Christoph* (Würzburg: Arena, 1978; München: dtv pocket, 1980).

10. See H.-R. Jauss, "Klassik--wieder modern?" *Der Deutschunterricht*, 1978:30/2, pp. 35-51, especially pp. 45ff.

11. Korschunow, *Die Sache mit Christoph* (München, 1980), p. 75, p. 121.

12. Ewers, p. 14.

13. J. D. Salinger, *The Catcher in the Rye* (New York: Little, Brown, 1951); in German: *Der Fänger im Roggen* (Reinbek, 1986; first German edition Zürich, 1954); B. Wersba, *Run Softly, Go Fast* (New York: Atheneum, 1970); in German: *Ein nützliches Mitglied der Gesellschaft* (Ravensburg: Otto Maier, 1984; first German edition Baden-Baden: Sinnal, 1972).

14. An extensive structural analysis and interpretation are to be found in Freese, pp. 178-281.

15. My interpretation of the ending of the novel follows Freese, pp. 267ff.

16. See Freese.

17. Novels of adolescence with a female protagonist which address themselves to young people are, for example, *Rita Rita* by R. Herfurther (1984) or the novels of D. Chidolue: *Das Fleisch im Bauch der Katze* (The flesh in the belly of the cat, 1980); *Aber ich werde alles anders machen* (But I'll do everything in a different way, 1981); *Diese blöde Kuh* (This stupid girl, 1984); *Lady Punk* (1985); *Bist du irre?* (Are you mad? 1986). See D. Grenz, "Zeitgenössische Mädchenliteratur--Tradition oder Neubeginn?" *Sprache und Literatur in Wissenschaft und Unterricht*, 1988:62, pp. 2-21; B. Pyerin, "Ideal und Wirklichkeit. Emanzipatorische Mädchenbücher," *Informationen des Arbeitskreises für Jugendliteratur*, 1989:15/2, pp. 30-37. Neither article deals not specially with the novel of adolescence, but rather with the girls' book.

18. I. Edelfeldt, *Kamalas Buch* (Stuttgart: Spectrum, 1988); original edition *Kamalas bok* (Stockholm: Almqvist & Wiksell International, 1986). As I was told by the Swedish publishing house, *Kamalas Buch* as well as Edelfeldt's *Briefe an die Königin der Nacht* (Letters to the queen of the night, 1986; Swedish original 1985) were not published as books for young people, but as part of adult literature. Since in Germany *Kamalas Buch* was published as a book for young people and I'm examining the literature for young people here I consider the book as part of German youth literature. Concerning the change from one literary system to another, see note 24.

19. I interpret the ending in a different way from Ewers, p. 14. For further references see H.-H. Ewers, "Verrückt will man nicht werden. Krisenprotokoll einer 'normalen' jungen Frau," *Eselsohr*, 1988:5, p. 17.

20. Further novels of adolescence with a female protagonist which belong to adult literature are, for example, C. McCullers, *A Member of the Wedding* (1946); German editions *Das Mädchen Frankie* (1951); *Frankie* (1974); K. Struck, *Klassenliebe* (Class love, 1973); R. Schneider, *Die Reise nach Jaroslav* (Journey to Jaroslav, GDR1974/FRG 1976); O. F. Walter, *Wie wird Beton zu Gras. Dast eine Liebesgeschichte* (How does asphalt turn into grass. Almost a love story, 1979).

21. That does not imply that the gulf which separates literature for adults from that for young people necessarily increases adult literature's degree of modernity.

22. See Ewers. p. 14.

23. J. Thiele who compares the picture book and modern art comes to similar results. See J. Thiele, "Wurzelkinder und Honigpumpe. Zum Verhältnis von Kunstmoderne und Bilderbuch,"in *Kinderliteratur und Moderne,* eds. H.-H. Ewers et al. (Weinheim-München: Juventa, 1990).

24. That's why on this level a change from one literature to the other can take place without great difficulty (for example, *Kamalas Buch*; cf. note 18).

25. See M. Dahrendorf, "Zum Hiatus zwischen Kinderliteratur und literarischer Moderne," in *Kinderliteratur und Moderne*, eds. H.-H. Ewers et al. (Weinheim-München: Juventa), 1990.

The Origin and Function of Laughter in Children's Literature

Maria Lypp

Nowadays the laughter of the young reader as a response to a humorous text seems to be a central element of children's literature. This has not always been so. The question is how the convention arose that children's literature must follow the child's disposition for unconstrained laughter.

The following essay considers two periods that were significant to the emergence of humorous children's literature: the sixteenth and the nineteenth centuries. Children's literature was dominated in its early phase by a superior sort of laughter, a triumphal laughter at an inferior object. Only later did humor concerned with surprising transformations, in a playful way, between different forms emerge. This latter kind of humor, which inspires the reader's imagination, is closely related to the fantastic. Therefore, it coincided, with the admission of the fantastic into children's literature, that is, with the concept of childhood of the Romantic period. The beginning of the nineteenth century is thus an important epoch in the study of humorous children's literature.

Nevertheless, the Romantics' high regard for childish fantasy is not the primary root of humor in this context. Even before the pedagogues concerned themselves with the specific nature of childhood, humor was enlisted in the service of education. The pedagogical writings of the humanists, the fables and animal epics of the Reformation period, which were specifically addressed to children, also addressed the uneducated classes of society. This means that pedagogical discourse had to adapt to existing cultural standards. The ordinary people had their carnival, fools, and farces. In addition, polemical and political writings contained satirical elements. This pervasive humor marks the sixyeenth century as the first epoch of humorous children's literature.

This was the period of what we can call poetical-pedagogical fools' discourse. Two literary genres are involved: the fable and the parodical inversion of didactic literature, the so-called Grobian literature. Aesop's fables, which formerly had been used for instruction in rhetoric, became in the sixteenth century didactic stories for children's edification and entertainment. As such, they were highly regarded, even by educators, for their humor. Martin Luther admitted "the cheerful children's book of Aesop's fables." In the preface to his anthology of these stories, he reflects extensively on the topic of laughter. He sees the comical element as an essential ingredient of the fable, since, as in art in general, the world of the fable represents reality in a transformed guise. Here the disguise is comical; Luther calls it "a merry lie" that leads to its moral indirectly. The principal character, who speaks the truth while hiding behind a mask, is the fool. Interestingly enough, the poet himself, Aesop, is depicted with the features of a fool. Indeed, in Burkard Waldis's anthology, the most comprehensive edition of the fables in the sixteenth century, Aesop is pictured on the title page as a fool, sitting backward on a rocking horse, surrounded by laughing children. Luther claims that Aesop was not a historical figure at all but was invented as a comic character to enliven moral stories for the young. The masquerade is more than mere decoration. It represents the only means to reach the young public and the common folk. The comic element is essential in order to bring across the moral point.

As is well known; in the humanistic period the fool was a central figure who possessed various contradictory qualities and functions (for instance, in the works of Murner, Brant, and Erasmus). The figure of the fool was an element of common discourse in which children could participate; it was an official terrain to which children had access. The affinity of the fool with the child stems from the ambivalence between simplemindedness and wisdom: the fool is child and teacher in one person. This kind of association of contrasts is the fundamental element of humor.

If the fable is considered to be a comical genre--a point of view that is foreign to us today--then it is not because of its contents, which are rarely comical, but because of its strange ambivalence. Here the animal world and the world of humans are identified; they represent two contexts that in reality stand in sharp contrast. In the fable the two worlds are not hierachically ordered; the one does not negate the other. In this situation laughter is not scorn. Dieter Henrich calls this kind of laughter *primary* and claims that it is inherent in all humor.

The fables also contain another kind of laughter, which *is* based on the contrast between superior and inferior, between right and wrong. This is a destructive kind of laughter. Social criticism in the sixteenth century often resorts to the allegorical style: pamphlets of the Reformation refer to the Pope as a donkey and to monks as calves. Animal comparisons were a preferred weapon in political debate. Therefore, the animal epics, such as *Reinecke Fuchs* and *Froschmeuseler* by Georg Rollenhagen, were understood as thinly disguised political criticism. They were called "a mirror of our times."

A current research trend in children's literature tries to restrict the humor involved to so-called childish humor, which excludes satire, irony, and parody as being too complicated for the child's mind. A glance at the sixteenth century shows that satire was naturally included in the repertoire of the fables and animal epics of the period. The satire not only was directed against the general circumstances of the time, but also concerned itself specifically with education. In this context we also find irony.

In the educational literature concerned with good manners, especially table manners, there is a literary form that attempts to reach its aims not by admonishing but by frightening. It turns the social conventions upside down and postulates indecent behavior. This negative teaching is pure satire. Grobian is the personification of bad behavior. He is a ruthless egocentric, and his vulgarity guarantees him a high rank in the society of swine. In Samuel Scheidt's version of Dedekind's Grobianus, Grobian appears as a magistrate, who goes so far as to justify at length the breaking of society's rules. For example, one should not wash one's hands before eating, since while one is absent from the table somebody else might take the best place. Or one should not refrain from venting wind from the stomach, as otherwise it might rise to the head! The literary technique of inversion is very old. It appears in folkloristic "tall tales." Humanistst also used it extensively in the form of ironical praise. Humanistic and folkloristic elements are combined in Grobianism to form a carnivalistic spectacle, where satire is employed for educational purposes. Grobian is the archetypal negative hero of children's literature and the original taboo-violating comical figure. The grotesque exaggeration of the physis, the dramatization of the corporeal, is a recurrent theme in humorous children's literature. This is because of the child's bodily growth and the regulating of bodily functions by education.

Grobian has sometimes been seen as an ancestor of *Struwwelpeter*. However, the differences between these two seem to be more significant than the similarities. In contrast to Struwwelpeter, Grobian is not punished. His triumphal message is: remain a Grobian! Education is left to irony. The punishments that are meted out to the characters in the Struwwelpeter stories are exaggerated out of any realistic proportion and thus become grotesque. In the Grobian tales, laughter is an integral element of education; in the Struwwelpeter stories, laughter serves to make the rigor of education bearable. The punishments are extreme but nevertheless comical: Zappelphilipp's family is buried under the tablecloth, or Hans-look-in-the-air falls into the water. Everyday educational conflicts can be laughed at in their exaggerated representation.

The concept of childhood as a special status, for which a systematic education was necessary, developed historically in the period between the appearance of the Grobian and the Struwwelpeter stories. In the pedagogy of the eithteenth century laughter was suspect. Enlightenment strove for moderation of the emotions and taught avoidance of all extremes. In the uncontrolled outburst of laughter, this emotional discipline is temporarily suspended. The moral concepts were supposed to appeal to the child's reason, not to his emotions. For this purpose, a sophisticated language was developed in which complicated ethical ideas were simplified according to the child's mental capacity. In this carefully ordered moral structure, an aberration may be tragic; it is never an occasion for laughter. Indeed, according to the prevailing optimism of the Enlightenment, such moral deficiencies are neither necessary nor irremedial. The children in children's journals, constantly studying and contemplating, had no occasion for laughter; they saw no rent in the moral fabric, only unrelenting progress.

All this is not meant to convey the impression that all enjoyment and pleasure was banned from children's literature of the Enlightenment. On the contrary, these advanced to a status equal to that of the pedagogical elements. However, the comical was not intended. Under the weight of the dominating moral themes the mere offer of naturalistic or geographical subject matter could already be a relief: we find, for instance, such titles as *Fun with Insects* or *Fun with Astronomy*. The variety of an almanac--a game, a riddle, even a single colored engraving--offers a welcome contrast to the systematic instruction.

Besides these carefully measured entertainments there existed an underground, perhaps involuntary, humor, that was not subject to anxious pedagogical censure. It might appear, for example, in an innocuous ABC reader. A completely heterogeneous set of objects are pictured together in order to illustrate the use of a letter of the alphabet. Are an octopus, an orange, and an oven related only because they all start with the letter O? Or do they form some kind of comical society? Sometimes a rhyme might be used to bring some order to such an odd collection. We then find texts reminiscent of the English nonsense rhymes of a later period. The play on words associated with learning to read is an involuntary parallel to the nursery rhyme. However, all popular entertainment was rigorously eliminated from the educational literature of the eighteenth century: Hanswurst, Eulenspiegel, the Schildbürgers. The fact is that there were two distinct literatures in this period--and the common people's literature was scorned by the pedagogues as vulgar. Certainly, young people could buy these books in the street and did so widely. Carnivalistic laughter survived as a kind of inofficial humor.

The revival of laughter in the children's literature of the nineteenth century went hand in hand with the emergence of a vision of childhood with eminently positive features. One speaks of "the happy time of childhood." The adult discovers in the laughter of children his own lost laughter. In his introduction to Karl Simrock's *Deutsches Kinderbuch* (1857), Corridi writes: "Every time I open this book I feel inspired to leap, to dance, to cry out loud." He considers Simrock's anthology of old children's rhymes "a monumentous event in universal history." He conceives of a children's world, with its own traditions and history which are importany to the history of humankind in general. The child "binds the things of heaven and earth together like beads on a string, and springs happily about with his new toy." The fascination of the play on words is discovered. The play with language, the primeval cultural experience of the small child, becomes the heart of children's literature.

Originality, simplicity, intuition--all these are qualities that have been attributed to folk culture since Herder. The affinity of children and common people in the thinking of the Romantics is well known. The common factor is no longer their ignorance; rather, it is their naive genius. Punch, transported by Franz Pocci from folk theater to the children's stage, is the archetypal comic genius. He integrates the primary instincts, the lust of eating and drinking, with a complete indifference to all forms of education; he is a naive subversive. As a servant of noble masters, he knocks exalted passions and elevated ideals from their pedestals. He is an old acquaintance from the Commedia dell'arte, as well as a child full of strength and humor. Pocci, as a typical Romantic devoted to the vanished poetry of the medieval world of knights and magic, saw its ironic illumination on the Caspar theater as a chance to preserve it. The past becomes a playground, and in this way comic children's literature becomes a means of preserving not only the adults' biographical past, but also the historical past. The Punch and Judy show is not simply addressed to children; it is also full of literary allusions and elements of parody that only adults can appreciate. Thus, the revival of laughter in children's literature had a special significance for adults. It provided an escape from the complexities of the modern world, as is especially apparent in the life and works of Lewis Carroll.

Both the amusement associated with the play of language in children's rhymes and the puppet theater, with its play on anachronistic values, are based on surprising ambivalences of meaning, that is, on free humor. The nineteenth century also exhibits a strong tendency to another kind of humor, a norm-violating humor, or a humor of liberation. Its roots lie not in children's literature, but in popular graphics. Caricature, especially in the period immediately preceding the Revolution of 1848, now came into full bloom. Many well-known artists worked for satirical journals, and at the same time produced illustrations for the *picture sheets*--a widespread form of entertainment addressed to young and old, but towards the end of the century increasingly targeting children. For example, the "Munich Picture Books" was the title of a series edited by the publishers of the Munich picture sheets.

The close connection between political journalism and children's literature restored to humor the sharp contrasts, the conflict with social circumstances, hierarchies, and norms, which it had had in the sixteenth century. The parallels are striking. Once again children's literature began to participate in general humorous culture, especially in political satire.

Animals reappeared in comical roles and assumed a prominent rank in children's literature which they have maintained up to the present day. One of the most successful picture books in the middle of the nineteenth century was *Speaking Animals* by Adolph Glassbrenner and Carl Reinhardt. In the Victorian age, the traditional animal fable becomes increasingly sentimentalized. In contrast, the animals in the picture books represent bourgeois characters, for instance, the cock in tophat and tailcoat, a cigar in his beak. The familiar surroundings of everyday life are rendered in great detail. For children, the fact that these ridiculous figures represented adults increased the comical effect.

Nevertheless, the humor in these children's books is not specifically childish. The permeability of children's literature for general humor is remarkably illustrated in the fairy tale of "The Race Between the Rabbit and the Hedgehog." This story was published in fairy—tale anthologies, but the original version, attibuted to Wilhelm Schröder, was intended as political satire. Schröder was concerned with the "hedgehog's mask" of human beings.

His introduction leaves no doubt that his aim is to demask the ruling aristocracy. In the sequel, *Life and Death of a Hedgehog*, the hedgehog becomes a minister, and the hedgehog economy a political scandal-- reminiscent of Reinecke Fuchs.

Under the influence of political satire, animals in children's books also assumed completely new functions, crossing the boundaries of traditional fables. Instead of representing human beings in disguise, animals became the human's antagonists. In Carl Reinhardt's picture book *Hanswurst's Treasure Box,* the animals are enormous, threatening, and malicious creatures, who are a danger to people, especially to adults. In their amusing escapades, they are close relatives of *Max and Moritz.* The animal folk in *Noah's Ark* by the same author are depicted with a similar lack of respect. In this slapstick version of the biblical story the animals mock Noah cruelly. As punishment Noah turns them into craftsmen: "The craftsmen appeared after the flood and disappeared with the invention of the railroad."

These animals represent both children and the common people, though as a metaphor for disobedience and no longer in a Romantic sense. Sometimes children's books become a vehicle for the oppositional contraband of their authors. Adolph Glassbrenner and Theodor Hoseman, for example, disguise their vision of democracy in the fiction of a children's state, *Marzipan Island.* In this funny story, the children's society is taken over by King Knirps and his tyrannic crew, but with the help of the angels the children succeed in freeing themselves of oppression. We laugh at the triumph of utopian society.

The humor of disobedience and opposition in caricature, with its grotesque exaggeration, paves the way for humor in realistic children's stories. At the beginning, we have *Struwwelpeter* and *Max and Moritz*, both of which, because of their drastic character, are limited to the style of the picture sheet. The line is continued with the Casper figure of Pinocchio, who wishes to become a child (this is a halfway station between the farce of the puppet and the real world of the child). It culminates in the tales of the mischievous Tom Sawyer. By the end of the nineteenth century, the little rogue is a well-established literary figure. In a sense, the impudent rogue character was prefigured in a story of Heinrich Hoffmann, "Lazy Bastian." Bastian goes to sleep in the forest instead of attending school. As a consequence of his never having learned to read, we see him performing the silliest pranks in a variety of professions. In one case he brings a fine lady sparrows instead of laces (in German there is a play on words here: sparrows = Spatze, laces = Spitze).

At the onset of the twentieth century, a striking variety of humorous forms emerged. From the simple tittle-tattle of a nursery rhyme to fireworks- like displays of language all shadings of expression are offered to children, so that a mere list of titles might be mistaken for the dictionary of a foreign language: Gackeliene, Puttiput, Mieckchen, Pieckchen. Funny animals are combined with funny names to constitute comical zoologies beyond number. Fantastic animals, defying science, existed at least as early as 1900; there were hybrids of a giraffe and a dog, or a pig and a crocodile. Besides these linguistic and zoological acrobatics, pure playing on words and form, there are stories in which the humor of liberation dominates, in the style of Wilhelm Busch, where saucy girls are the principal characters. Finally, Eulenspiegel, Münchhausen, and Don Quixote have become the representatives of classical humorous children's literature. Each is originally a figure in adult literature, and each has his own fascinating history of adaptation. Although interesting in their own right, limitations of space prevent further elaboration on these subjects here.

A number of conclusions are possible:

1. There are not two distinct kinds of humor--one for children and one for adults. Children's literature has received important impulses from the general culture of humor throughout history, in particular from folk literature and political satire.

2. Laughter is established in contemporary children's literature. It is pedagogically desirable and profitable for the publisher.

3. This situation is not unproblematic. The comical has become conventional. The child-reader is confronted with a repertoire of fixed stereotypes; his or her reaction to them is more often conditioned than spontaneous.

4. Mickey Mouse, Casper, Pumuckl, Pinocchio, Pippi, Eulenspiegel, Münchhausen--all are signs for fun, a good time meant exclusively for children. This reduction diminishes the stature of these historical comic figures.

5. Although the accessibility of comic literature for our children is centainly welcome, we cannot ignore the leveling effect of this abundance-- the tendency to a big, rather than an arbitrary, playground for fun.

6. The historical perspective shows that fun used to be taken more seriously. Contemporary humor often lacks surfaces of friction. The world cannot be turned upside down because in liberal education all authority has withered, and there is no binding educational canon that can be parodied. All threatening elements have long been eliminated from our fairy tales; kings and witches are no longer majestic figures of power; they are now mere buffoons.

7. Most important is the lack of general culture of humor such as that which nourished the children's literature of the past.

8. For this very reason, today children's literature has an important cultural role: it is the sanctuary where laughter, in particular archaic and carnivalistic laughter, is not only allowed but also positively encouraged. In this way, laughter may be preserved for society in general.

Select Bibliography

Arbuthnot, May Hill, Margaret Mary Clark and Harriet G. Long. *Children's Books Too Good to Miss*. Cleveland: Case Western Reserve University Press, 1966.

Ariès, Philippe. *Centuries of Childhood: A Social History of Family Life*. Transl. Robert Baldick. New York: Vintage-Random House, 1962.

---. *Western Attitudes towards Death from the Middle Ages to the Present*. Trans. Patricia Ranun. London: Marion Boyars, 1976.

Arnold, Klaus. *Kind und Gesellschaft in Mittelalter und Renaissance*. Wurzburg: Ferdinand Schoningh, 1980.

Ashton, John. *Chapbooks of the Eighteenth Century*. London, 1882.

Attebery, Brian. *The Fantasy Tradition in American Literature. From Irwing to Le Guin*. Bloomington: Indiana University Press, 1980.

Avery, Gillian. *Nineteenth Century Children. Heroes and Heroines in English Children's Stories, 1780-1900*. London: Hodder and Stoughton, 1965.

---. *Childhood's Pattern*. London: Hodder and Stoughton, 1975.

Bader, Barbara. *American Picturebooks from Noah's Ark to the Beast Within*. New York: Macmillan, 1976

Bolin, Greta, Eva von Zweigbergk and Mary Øvig. *Barn och böcker. En orientering*. Stockholm: Rabén & Sjögren, 1972.

Bottigheimer, Ruth. *Grimm's Bad Girls and Bold Boys: The Moral and Social Vision of the Tales*. New Haven: Yale University Press, 1987.

Bravo-Villasante, Carmen. *Weltgwschichte det Kinder- und Jugendliteratur. Versuch einer Gesamtdarstellung.* Hannover: Schroedel, 1977.

Brüggemann, Theodor and Hans-Heino Ewers. *Handbuch zur Kinder- und Jugendliteratur von 1750 bis 1800.* Stuttgart, 1982.

Butts, Dennis. *Good Writers for Young Readers.* St. Albans: Hart-Davis, 1977.

Cadogan, Mary and Patricia Craig. *You're a Brick, Angela! A New Look at Girls' Fiction from 1839 to 1975.* London: Gollantz, 1976

---. *Women and Children First. The Fiction of Two World Wars.* London: Gollanz, 1978.

Carpenter, Humfrey and Mari Prichard. *The Oxford Companion to Children's Literature.* London: Oxford University Press, 1984.

Cott, Jonathan. *Pipers at the Gate of Dawn: The Wisdom of Children's Literature.* New York: Random House, 1983

Coveney, Peter. *The Image of Childhood, the Individual and Society.* Harmondsworth, Penguin, 1967.

Crouch, Marcus. *Treasure Seekers and Borrowers. Children's Books in Britain 1900-1960.* London: Library Association, 1962.

---. *The Nesbit Tradition. The Children's Novel 1945-1970.* London: Benn, 1972.

Daalder, Dirk Leonardus. *Wormcruit mer suycker, historisch-critisch overzicht van de Nederlandse kinderliteratuur mer illustraties en portretten.* Amsterdam: Arbeiderspers, 1950.

Dahrendorf, Malte. *Kinder- und Jugendliteratur im bürgerlichen Zeitalter. beträge zu ihrer Geschichte, kritik und Didaktik.* Königstein: Scriptor, 1980.

Darton, H. F. J. *Children's Books in England, Five Centuries of Social Life.* Rev. ed. Cambridge: Cambridge University Press, 1982.

DeMause, L., ed. *The History of Childhood.* New York: Harper and Row, 1975.

Egoff, Sheila. *The Republic of Childhood. A Critical Guide to Canadian Children's Literature.* 2nd ed. Toronto: Oxford University Press, 1975.

Escarpit, Denise. *La littérature d'enfance et de jeunesse en Europe. Panorama historique.* Paris: Presses universitaires de France, 1981.

Ewers, Hans-Heino, ed. *Kinder- und Jugendliteratur der Aufklärung.* Stuttgart, 1980.

---. *Kindheit als poetische Daseinsform*. München: Wilhelm Fink, 1989.

--- et al., eds. *Kinderlitteratur und Moderne*. Weinheim-München: Juventa, 1990.

---, ed. *Komik im Kinderbuch. Erscheinungsformen des Komischen in der Kinder- und Jugendliteratur*. Weinheim-München: Juventa, 1992.

Eyre, Frank. *British Children's Books in the Twentieth Century*. London: Longman, 1971.

Fisher, Margery. *Intent Upon Reading. A Critical Appraisal of Modern Fiction for Children*. Leicester: Brockhampton Press, 1964.

Flaker, Aleksander. *Modelle der Jeans Prosa*. Kronberg: Scriptor, 1975.

Fraser, James H, ed. *Society and Children's Literature*. Boston: Godine, 1978.

Green, Roger Lancelyn. *Tellers of Tales. British Authors of Children's Books from 1800 to 1964*. London: Ward, 1965.

Grenz, Dagmar. Mädchenliteratur. *Von den morlichbelehrenden Schriften im 18. Jahrhundert bis zur Herausbildung der Backfischliteratur im 19. Jahrhundert*. Stuttgart, 1981.

Haas, Gerhard, ed. *Kinder- und Jugendliteratur. Zur Typologie und Funktion einer literarischen Gattung*. Stuttgart: Reclam, 1974.

Hagemann, Sonja. *Barnelitteratur i Norge inntil 1850*. Oslo: Aschehoug, 1965.

---. *Barnelitteratur i Norge 1850—1914*. Oslo: Aschehaug, 1970

---. *Barnelitteratur i Norge 1914—1970*. Oslo: Aschehoug, 1974.

Haviland, Virginia. *Children and Literature. Views and Reviews*. London: Bodley Head, 1974.

Hürlimann, Bettina. *Three Centuries of Children's Books in Europe*. London: Oxford University Press, 1967.

Inglis, Fred. *The Promise of Happiness: Value and Meaning in Children's Fiction*. Cambridge: Cambridge University Press, 1981.

Kaminski, Winfred. *Jugendliteratur und Revolte. Jugendprotest und seine Spiegelung in der Literatur für junge Leser*. Frankfurt am Main, 1982.

Kiefer, Monica. *American Children Through their Books 1700-1835*. Philadelphia: University of Pennsylvania Press, 1948.

Klingberg, Göte. *Till gagn och nöje--svensk barnbok 400 år.* Stockholm: Rabén & Sjögren, 1991 (Studies Published by the Swedish Institute for Children's Books; 38)--With a summary in English: For Instruction and Delight. The Swedish Children's Book--400 Years.

Krüger, Anna. *Die erzählende Kinder- und Jugendliteratur im Wandel. Neue Inhalte und Formen im Kommunikations- und Sozialisationsmittel Jugendliteratur.* Frankfurt am Main: Diesterweg, 1980.

Landsberg, Michele. *The World of Children's Books. A Guide of Choosing the Best.* London: Simon & Schuster, 1988.

Lane, Selma G. *Down the Rabbit Hole. Adventures and Misadventures in the Realm of Children's Literature.* New York: Atheneum, 1972.

Leeson, Robert. *Children's Books and Class Society. Past and Present.* London: Writers and Readers Publishing Cooperative, 1977.

Lehtonen, Maija and Marita Rajalin. *Barnboken i Finland förr och nu.* Stockholm: Rabén & Sjögren, 1984--With a summary in English: Children's Books in Finland.

Lochhead, Marion. *The Renaissance of Wonder in Children's Literature.* Edinburgh, Canongate, 1977.

Lundqvist, Ulla. *Tradition och förnyelse. Svensk ungdomsbok från sextiotal till nittiotal.* Stockholm: Rabén & Sjögren, 1994 (Studies Published by the Swedish Institute for Children's Books; 51)--With a summary in English: Traditional Patterns and New Ones. Swedish Books for Young Adults from the Sixties to the Nineties.

Macleod, Anne Scott. *A Moral Tale.* Hamden, Conn.: Archon Books, 1975.

Marshall, Margaret R. *An Introduction to the World of Children's Books.* Aldershot: Hants 1982.

Meigs, Cornelia, et al. *A Critical History of Children's Literature.* New York: Macmillan, 1969.

Miller, Bertha Mahony and Elinor Whitney Field. *Caldecott Medal Books: 1938-1957.* Boston: Horn Book, 1957.

Muir, Percy H. *English Children's Books.* New York: Fredrick A. Praeger, 1969.

Niall, Brenda. Australia *Through the Looking-Glass. Children's Fiction 1830-1980.* Melbourne, Melbourne University Press, 1984.

Nikolajeva, Maria. *The Coming of Age of Children's Literature. Toward a New Aesthetics.* New York: Garland, 1995.

Norton, Donna E. *Through the Eyes of a Child. An Introduction to Children's Literature*. 3rd ed. New York, Macmillan, 1991.

O'Sullivan, Emer. *Friend and Foe. The Image of Germany and the Germans in British Children's Fiction from 1870 to the Present*. TßüßVbingen, 1990

Ørjasæter, Tordis, et al. *Den norske barnelitteraturen gjennom 200 år*. Oslo: Cappelen, 1981.

Pickering, Samuel, F. *John Locke and Children's Books in Eighteenth-Century England*. Knoxville: University of Tennessee Press, 1981.

Saxby, Maurice. *A History of Australian Children's Literature 1841-1941*. Sydney: Wentworth, 1969.

---. *A History of Australian Children's Literature 1941-1970*. Sydney: Wentworth, 1971.

---. *The Proof of the Puddin'. Australian Children's Literature 1970-1990*. Sydney: Ashton Scholastic, 1993.

Schwarcz, Joseph H. *Ways of the Illustrator: Visual Communication in Children's Literature*. Chicago: American Library Association, 1982.

Shavit, Zohar. *Poetics of Children's Literature*. Athens-London: University of Georgia Press, 1986.

Smith, Elva S. *The History of Children's Literature*. Rev. Margaret Hodges and Susan Steinfirst. Chicago: American Library Association, 1988.

Soriano, Marc. *Guide de littérature pour la jeunesse*. Paris: Flammarion, 1975.

Stybe, Vibeke. *Fra Askepot til Anders And. Børnebogen i kulturhistorisk perspektiv*. 2nd ed. Copenhagen: Munksgaard, 1970.

Sutherland, Zena, Dianne L. Monson and May Hill Arbuthnot. *Children and Books*. 6th ed. Glenview-London: Scott, Foresman & Co., 1981.

Svensson, Sonja. *Läsning för folkets barn. Folkskolans Barntidning och dess förlag 1892-1914*. Stockholm: Rabén & Sjögren, 1983 (Studies Published by the Swedish Institute for Children's Books; 16)--With a summary in English: Reading Matter for Working Class Children. 'The Elementary School Child's Nagazine' and Its Publishing House 1892-1914.

Townsend, John Rowe. *Written for Children. An Outline of English-language Children's Literature*. 2nd ed. Harmondsworth: Kestrel, 1983.

Zipes, Jack. *Fairy Tales and the Art of Subversion: The Classical Genre for Children and the Process of Civilisation*. London: Heinemann, 1982.

--- *The Brothers Grimm: From Enchanted Forests to the Modern World.* New York: Rutledge, 1988.

Zweigbergk, Eva von: Barnboken i Sverige 1750-1950. Stockholm: Rabén & Sjögren, 1965.

Index

About the Contributors

DENNIS BUTTS teaches on the M.A. course in children's literature at the University of Reading, England, and is Chairman of the Children's Books History Society. He has written widely on various aspects of nineteenth-century literature and children's books. *Mistress of Our Tears*, a literature and bibliographical study of Barbara Hofland, was published in 1992, and Dennis Butts has also edited a collection of essays *Stories and Society: Children's Literature in its Social Context*. He is Associate Editor of the *Oxford Illustrated History of Children's Literature*.

MARIELLA COLIN is Professor of Italian at the University of Caen, France. She has published a number of articles on Italian children's literature in the nineteenth century.

DAGMAR GRENZ is Professor at Hamburg University, formerly at the University of Cologne. She was Board member of the IRSCL 1985-1989. Her publications include *Mädchenliteratur* (1981), an investigation of girls' fiction, and a number of articles and essays on the German-language children's and youth literature.

KAREN NELSON HOYLE is Professor and Curator of the Children's Literature Research Collections at the University of Minnesota Libraries. She has been Board member of the IRSCL, and served as president of the Children's Literature Association, as chair of the Caldecott Award Committee, and as a member of the Newbery Award Committee. She is the author of *Danish Children's Books Published in English* and *Wanda Gág*.

RIITTA KUIVASMÄKI is Director of the Finnish Institute for Children's Literature and Associate Professor at the Tampere University, Finland. She has been a board member of the IRSCL. She has published books and essays on the history of children's literature in Finland.

MARIA LYPP is Professor of German Literature at the University of Dortmund, Germany. Her research interests include the theory and poetics of children's literature. She is the author of *Simplicity of Children's Literature* (1986), as well as articles in various journals.

RODERICK MCGILLIS is Professor of English at the University of Calgary, Canada. His teaching areas include children's literature, Romantic literature, and nineteenth-century British literature. His recent and forthcoming publications include monographs on George MacDonald, Frances Hodgson Burnett, and on literary theory and children's literature. He has been a board member of the IRSCL.

ISABELLE NIÈRES is Professor of Comparative Literature at the University of Rennes II, France. Her main interests are in children's literature from a social and historical point of view, in adaptation and translation, in the relationships between text and pictures. She has worked on some great authors such as Lewis Carroll, Madame de Ségur, Maurice Sendak, and Jean de Brunhoff.

MARIA NIKOLAJEVA is Assistant Professor in Comparative Literature, Stockholm University. She is the author of *The Magic Code: The Use of Magical Patterns in Fantasy for Children* (1988) and *The Coming of Age of Children's Literature: Toward a new Aesthetics* (1995), editor of several volumes of essays, and has published a large number of articles on children's literature. She was a Fulbright scholar at the University of Massachusetts, Amherst, in 1993. She is the current President of the IRSCL.

EMER O'SULLIVAN is lecturer and researcher at the Institut für Jugendbuchforschung, Johann Wolfgang Goethe University, Frankfurt, Germany. Her research interests include comparative studies of children's literature, and she has published two books about the portrayal of Germany and the Germans in British children's fiction.

JUDITH PLOTZ is Chair and Professor of English at the George Washington University, Washington, D.C. A specialist in nineteenth-century British literature, especially Romanticism and Childhood, she was a Fulbright Lecturer in India 1994-1995. Her recent and forthcoming publications include articles on Kipling, Hartley Coleridge, Frances Hodgson Burnett, and Victorian imperial education.

ZOHAR SHAVIT is Professor of semiotics of culture, with a special emphasis on the child's culture, in Tel Aviv University, School of Cultural Studies. Her field of research covers children's literature, history of Hebrew and

Jewish literatures and cultures. She is the author of *Poetics of Children's Literature* (1986). She has been a board member of the IRSCL.

KARI SKJØNSBERG is senior lecturer at the Norwegian School of Library and Information Science in Oslo. She has written and edited several books on children's literature, the most important being *Kjønnsroller og miljø i barnelitteraturen* (Sex roles and environment in children's literature, 1972). She has written numerous articles and presented papers on children's literature, also in English, French and German.

SONJA SVENSSON is Associate Professor of Literature at Uppsala University, Sweden, and Director of the Swedish Institute for Children's Books in Stockholm since 1983. She was a board member of the IRSCL 1981-1985, and Vice-President 1983-1985. She had published and coedited several books on children's literature and has been lecturing extensively in and outside Sweden since early 1970s. She is also editor of the series "Studies Published by the Swedish Institute for Children's Books."

REINBERT TABBERT is Professor at the College of Higher Education, Reutlingen, Germany. His research interests include reception theory and children's literature. He has published the two volumes of *Kinderbuchanalyse* and edited a collection of essays on Maurice Sendak.

ANNE DE VRIES is Head of the Dutch Center for Children's Literature and lecturer in children's literature at the Department of Dutch Literature, Free University, Amsterdam. His research concerns the history of Dutch children's literature, and responses to children's literature.

TONY WATKINS is Lecturer in English and Director of the M.A. in children's literature program at the University of Reading, England. He is a former Vice-President of the IRSCL and has lectured extensively on children s literature in Europe, North America and Australia. He is Associate Editor for the *Oxford Illustrated History of Children's Literature* and contributor to the *Routledge Encyclopaedia of Children's Literature*.

ISBN 0-313-29614-6

90000>

EAN

9 780313 296147

HARDCOVER BAR CODE